Young, White, and Miserable

WINI BREINES

Young, White, and Miserable

Growing up Female in the Fifties

The University of Chicago Press

Chicago and London

The University of Chicago Press, Chicago 60637
The University of Chicago Press, Ltd., London

16 15 14 13 12 11 10 09 08 07   2 3 4 5 6

ISBN-13: 978-0-226-07261-6 (paper)
ISBN-10: 0-226-07261-4 (paper)

Parts of this book have been previously published. A version of chapter 1 first appeared in the journal *Sociological Inquiry* 56, no. 1 (1986): 66–92, as "The 1950s: Gender and Some Social Science" and is reprinted with permission of the University of Texas Press. Material in chapter 1 was published as "Domineering Mothers in the 1950s: Image and Reality" in *Women's Studies International Forum* 8, no. 6 (1985): 601–8, and is reprinted by permission of Pergamon Press. Chapter 5 first appeared, in altered form, in the journal *Theory and Society* 15, no. 6 (1986): 805–43, as "Alone in the Fifties: Anne Parsons and the Feminine Mystique" and is reprinted with permission.

Library of Congress Cataloging-in-Publication Data

Breines, Wini.
    Young, white, and miserable : growing up female in the fifties / Wini Breines.
        p.   cm.
    Originally published : Boston : Beacon Press, 1992.
    Includes bibliographical references and index.
    1. Teenage girls—United States—Social conditions.   2. United States—
Social conditions—1945–   3. Middle class—United States—History—20th
century.   4. Social history—1945–1960.   I. Title.
HQ798.B66   2001
305.235′0973—dc21   00-046712

For Paul

Contents

Preface

*I*t has taken me a long time to write this book. Its focus has shifted as I've worked, moving from white, middle-class, female adolescents in the 1950s (of which I was one), to gender contradictions, and then to the fault lines of race and gender upon which postwar Americans constructed their culture. These concerns have often seemed the same topic, and in many ways they are. As a sociologist, my interest was to move backward from the social movements of the 1960s, in this case the women's liberation movement, in order to understand how young women who had grown up in the narrowly defined gender environment of the 1950s became feminists. What were the factors that contributed to such a turn of events? What kind of experiences did young, white, middle-class females have? The feminism of the past twenty-five years enables us to see that white, middle-class girls who were taught in the 1950s that their main goals in life were to become wives and mothers only ambivalently internalized these values and sometimes rejected them outright, embracing instead a wider world.

This book is linked to my earlier work on the new left of the

1960s—*The Great Refusal: Community and Organization in the New Left*—which was indirectly concerned with the capacity for rebellion and utopianism that had been nurtured, surprisingly, by the quiescent and prosperous 1950s. The sources and roots of rebellion seemed then, and still do, a relevant subject, particularly in light of the stunned apathy and patriotism of the Reagan and Bush years. Why was it that young, white, middle-class students whose lives were saturated with material goods in the 1950s and 1960s were inspired to action by moral and cultural claims? In this research, too, questions were impersonal and answers lodged in the complex social and cultural events of the postwar period. But my own trajectory from suburban New York (Long Island) cheerleader and aspiring beatnik into the student and women's liberation movements, eventually to academic sociology—itself suggestive of the complex consciousness so characteristic of the postwar period—has informed my queries and hunches. Over time, I have realized that this research has been about how a sector of my generation rejected or at least distanced ourselves from the traditional feminine lives that were resolutely set out for us and that we apparently embraced so enthusiastically. How, in other words, did feminism develop out of the experiences of growing up white, female, and middle-class in the 1950s? How did I become a feminist? This book elucidates the tensions and inconsistencies, the restlessness, and often the misery, of the affluent 1950s. It builds both on autobiography and sociological research out of the conviction that the personal is not only political, as feminists have said, but sociological and historical as well.

Studying resistance to dominant cultural and political values on the part of middle-class young people, in this case women, is a lonely project. I also realize this whenever I write about the new left, since its authenticity as a social movement is often questioned. When historians and social scientists study opposition and resistance, it is typically to the working class and disadvantaged that they turn. Now, too, in the area of culture, a significant amount of academic research is deservedly devoted to those on the margins, the working class or colonialized, ethnic, and third world "others." Scholars interested in social change tend to study those who have little, the exploited and dispossessed people who have the most to gain from collective opposition. In fact, middle-class rebellion in the name of a more equitable and just society has been minimal. When it has flared, moreover, radicals, themselves often from the middle class, have disdained it. The white, middle-class student movement of the 1960s, for example, regularly doubted its own efficacy and proclaimed its own lack of legitimacy. Many student activists attempted to transform themselves into members of the working class. Being middle class and a committed revolutionary, even a radical or socialist, was a contradiction in terms for many in the new left.

I make no claim that middle-class white girls who grew up in the fifties were a revolutionary agency or secret radicals. Rather, my project has been both to study their environment and to discover among them signs of cultural discontent and resistance. The indications were often ambiguous. There were no strikes or protest organizations. Recognition of signs of their subversiveness, if it can be called that, required conviction on my part. Middle-class white girls were engaged in changing the terms of feminine lives in the midst of what seems a most conservative time. I interpret their activity with an eye toward the spaces and strategies that signal resistance, acknowledging, at the same time, only minor opportunities and minor movement. But I believe those small movements away from prescribed roles were of great significance. The most obvious rationale for this is the magnitude of the feminist movement that subsequently developed and that owed much of its force to women's experiences in the 1950s.

I think of this book, then, as a sociological memoir. It is synthetic, bringing together diverse materials from and interpretations of the fifties that, taken together, illuminate white, middle-class girls' growing up in the urban and suburban culture of postwar America and thus the feminism they would generate. I have focused on topics that shed light on the tensions and paradoxes faced by girls born during or near World War II. This has been done with an eye toward apprehending the situations in which they found themselves and how they constructed themselves. I make use of social scientific data and their reinterpretation, archival research, cultural studies, secondary interpretations, autobiographies, letters, fiction, and interviews. There is no specific sample followed, no clearly defined population examined. Rather, I have utilized studies of the families in which girls might have grown up, the movies and magazines and music they watched, read, and listened to, the places in which they lived, in addition to their own testimonies in the form of fiction and autobiography, my own included. The book is not linear; it is more a kaleidoscope than a story moving smoothly from beginning to conclusion.

Before proceeding any further, I should add the obvious fact that eras do not commence and close in neat, round decade numbers; the fifties as a cohering cultural entity is an intellectual construct. It is important to recognize that this cultural entity, if believable, lasted into the 1960s (when girls born in the mid-forties were teenagers). Perhaps John Kennedy's assassination is as accurate a dividing line as any other, but so could be the 1964 murders in the South of young civil rights workers of this generation, the escalation of the war in Vietnam, the Beatles' explosion onto the American scene, or the 1963 publication of Betty Friedan's *The Feminine Mystique*.

Today much of the memory of the 1950s is nostalgic and rosy. Innocent and white (and these descriptives are most definitely linked) teenage girls sipping Cokes at the soda shop after school evoke longing for supposedly simpler and happier times. This book paints a more complicated and painful picture, although the young women's futures were more about exploration and autonomy than might have been expected given the culture in which they were raised. I could not be writing this book if that were not true, since I was one of them. Ellie Langer, a white, middle-class woman who grew up in the 1950s, in an eloquent effort to make sense of her childhood and movement experiences in the 1960s, wrote, "My childhood seems, in retrospect, a 'fifties' childhood: neutral and sentimental, separated from my later life by a geologic fault" ("Notes for the Next Time," *Working Papers*, Fall 1973, p. 51). Much of the evidence I utilize in the chapters that explore girls' experiences in the 1950s (particularly chapters 3 and 4) and the perspective I bring to the work of interpretation and reconstruction is provided by women who share Langer's sense that their earlier lives were marked off from their later lives by a "geologic fault." Our understanding of the postwar period is shaped by our experiences in the 1960s and 1970s, especially the women's liberation movement, which changed much about us and the way we saw the world, including our own pasts. Our memories are imbued with the sense that the 1950s were not a good time for women because we learned to understand our lives as a flight from that time.

While it may feel as if a fault divides us from our childhoods, there are substantial links as well. The fact is that this book on white, middle-class girls growing up in the 1950s is written by a white, middle-class woman who grew up in the 1950s. Continuities are also visible because adolescent discontents and interests found echoes in young adult preoccupations. The youthful women's liberation movement of the late 1960s and 1970s articulated concerns about personal life, sexuality, and fulfillment that were generated in the postwar period. Lives changed in ways that were not predictable but close consideration of historical patterns indicates continuity as well as rupture. The paradoxes to which I refer throughout the book are as much about the internal tensions of postwar culture, from which young women retrieved opportunities and images useful for their own emancipation in spite of the more obvious meanings or "intended" use.

Because one of the motivations of my research has been to understand where the white movements of the 1960s came from, especially the women's liberation movement, I have searched closely for signs of discontent and contradiction. I found them mainly in retrospective accounts and fiction but also in a critical reinterpretation of archival data, social science studies written at the time, and biographical material. Furthermore, while the issue of race was not paramount in my mind in the 1950s, and probably was not for most white, middle-class teenagers then, it is now. The ensuing decades, beginning with the civil rights movement, have taught me how profoundly race has structured life throughout American history, including the postwar period. Thus while race was obscured to me then, it is part of this account since it was incontestably a site of contradiction.

This is an interpretation of the 1950s, then, that employs the strategy of treating as primary sources writings of women who, like me, have looked back on that time from vantage points in the 1970s and 1980s. That this is a book about how I and a distinct group of women from my generation view our gendered past reveals much about what it was like to grow up in the 1950s. This is what I mean by sociological memoir, sociologically inspired yet partial and incomplete, a perspective or invention but not necessarily untrue, in the formulation of James Clifford ("Introduction: Partial Truths," *Writing Culture: The Poetics and Politics of Ethnography* [Berkeley, University of California Press, 1986]). This work and some of its sources are interpretations and artifacts, evidence of the sensibilities of a generation, or segment of it, of white, middle-class girls.

Finally, a word about the title. It is borrowed from the popular "true romance" magazines of the 1950s and is meant to highlight ironically the fact that we associate "young" and "white" with "happy." The incongruity is unsettling. It has a serious meaning as well. Except in the case of Anne Parsons, the subject of chapter 5, I do not dwell on the painfulness of the 1950s for women. But those of us who lived through that time remember it with mixed emotions. Like the undergarments that constricted our bodies—in Marge Piercy's words, "a litany of rubber, metal bands, garters, boning, a rosary of spandex and lycra and nylon, a votive candle of elastic," the "rubber coffins" that were girdles, the breasts squeezed out and up—the culture constricted our minds and spirits. (I quote from "Through the Cracks: Growing Up in the Fifties," *Parti-Colored Blocks for a Quilt* [Ann Arbor: University of Michigan Press, 1982], pp. 120–21.) It also provided middle-class girls with options and possibilities, even confidence. Many of us were feisty and survived to tell our stories. With the help of other voices, I have constructed one. I hope others will tell theirs.

Acknowledgments

Many people helped me as I worked on this book. For serious and sustained intellectual responses throughout the process, I am indebted to Rosalyn Baxandall, Linda Gordon, Elaine Tyler May, Judith Stacey, Barrie Thorne, and Kay Trimberger. I am especially thankful to Ros Baxandall for her thoughts about Beat and bohemian women, facilitation of interviews with some of them, and support and thoughtful insights about women of our generation. Deborah Kaufman and Jeanne Laurel contributed immeasurably by close reading of parts of the manuscript. Charles Lemert's enthusiasm helped me to think about this research as a book and encouraged me when I needed it. I am deeply grateful to Elaine Tyler May, Kay Trimberger, and Gaye Tuchman for the time and effort they devoted to the entire manuscript. I learned an enormous amount from Herman Gray, whose concerns, intellect, and support shaped this work. He and George Lipsitz were untiring in their supply of ideas and bibliographic references about popular culture. Both read sections of the manuscript and patiently helped me to formulate approaches and ideas. I thank them both for their interest. Thanks, too, to Rosalyn Feldberg, Wendy

Luttrell, Susan Ostrander, and Nicole Rafter who aided me at various stages of the writing.

The women I interviewed enthusiastically shared their experiences and thoughts. I want to single out Alix Kates Shulman for help in thinking about Beat and bohemian women. For the work on Anne Parsons, in addition to those already mentioned, I thank Merton Kahne, M.D., Sara Minden, M.D., Malkah Notman, M.D., Nancy Chodorow, and especially Rose Coser, whose time and help were critical. Thanks, too, to Charles Parsons for biographical corrections to the original essay and to Margaret Cerullo from whose idea the original essay grew and whose insights inform the chapter. The research on families was supported in part by funds from the Andrew W. Mellon Foundation given by Radcliffe College for research at the Henry A. Murray Center of Radcliffe College. Antonia Fried, Alyson Cole, and Ferdousi Khanam helped with the research. Of course, none of those mentioned here are in any way responsible for the ultimate outcome; it is I who must take final responsibility.

Northeastern University provided time off from teaching, as well as funds for research and writing. I am grateful for the institutional support, without which the book would have taken even longer, and for the unusually supportive academic environment provided by graduate students and department and women's studies colleagues. Lauren Bryant, my editor at Beacon Press, worked closely with me to improve the manuscript. While completing this book I was a fellow at the Bunting Institute of Radcliffe College, which provided a wonderful intellectual, social, and cultural environment. Our pleasure at the institute turned to grief at the brutal murder of Mary Joe Frug, a sister fellow and feminist. I mourn her and Denise Carty-Bennia, feminist and fighter, who also died this year, too soon. Both women grew up in the 1950s. Their deaths remind us how dangerous women's lives are. Louise Rice and Tess Ewing were always there, good friends and actively involved when I raised issues for their consideration. So were Elizabeth Ewen, Stuart Ewen, Allen Hunter, Lauren Jacoby, and Elaine Scott. My children, Natasha and Raphael, helped me think about the differences between our two generations but mainly made me happy. Finally, I acknowledge Paul Breines, to whom this book is dedicated, who with good humor, enthusiasm even, repeatedly read and edited, and whose suggestions and comments never failed to be thoughtful. But it is his love that has pulled me through the work and just about everything else.

Introduction

Frameworks for the Fifties

As I began to search the fifties for gender tensions, my attention often wandered to other aspects of the time. I became fascinated with the fifties, undoubtedly because those years constituted the historical moment before all hell, that is, the 1960s, broke loose. We know that now. We didn't know it then, which makes the apparent calm all the more curious. But contrary to accepted images, more was going on than met the eye. In Molly Haskell's words, "It was as if the whole period of the fifties was a front, the topsoil that protected the seed of rebellion that was germinating below. The cultural disorientation had begun, but it had yet to be acknowledged."[1] The image of America in the fifties as a facade reappears throughout this book. Themes of pretense and dissimulation run through many of the young women's stories.[2] Their strategies to keep up appearances often literally involved appearance, so that they were keeping up appearances by keeping up appearances. But the girls were not alone. Because the cultural goals of assimilation and homogenization left little room for difference or dissent, discontent percolated. Given the postwar celebration of consensus, developments such as the Beats and the young people they inspired, the spread of rock and roll, the civil rights movement, early student politics, even right-wing anticommunism, cannot help but provoke curiosity. I explore some versions of discontent throughout this book.

Before considering the "other" fifties, and prior to introducing the girls, I want briefly to sketch the outlines of America's transformation after World War II. The historian William Chafe says of postwar America, "Rarely has a society experienced such rapid or dramatic change as that which occurred in America after 1945"; he suggests, despite representations of stability and calm, that the 1950s were "more a time of transition than of stolidity."[3] The period is characterized by shifts from production to consumption, from saving to spending, from city to suburb, from blue- to white-collar employment, and from an adult to a youth culture. Whether it is read as postindustrial, post-capitalist, or postmodern, postwar America is designated by those who study it as a time of significant change. The fifties consolidated central elements of the society we live in today; what seemed remarkable then is commonplace now. Advertising and the mass media, militarism, information technology, automobiles, education, mobility, and style are today recognized as central structuring elements in American society. For those of us born in the 1940s and after, it is often difficult to recognize the magnitude of postwar changes since we take so many for granted.

While some commentators in the fifties were dubious and critical of the changes taking place, for the most part there was a pleased consensus that America was the richest and most successful nation on earth, a nation where all citizens could anticipate living the good life. That good life was defined by a well-equipped house in the suburbs, a new car or two, a good white-collar job for the husband, well-adjusted and successful children taken care of by a full-time wife and mother. Leisure time and consumer goods constituted its centerpieces; abundance was its context. White skin was a criterion for its attainment.

One report, entitled "America's Placid Decade," written at the end of the fifties, expressed it this way,

In one brief 10-year period, America's face was remade. Vast suburban areas sprang up to receive millions of Americans pressing out from the cities. Ribbons of superhighways were laid across the country. A huge expansion of air facilities helped tie the nation into a compact unity. . . . Whole regions changed their complexion. Deserts were turned into boom areas. Power was harnessed on a stupendous scale to ease the burden of work. . . . Nearly 30 million added people were provided for, and on a steadily rising standard of living. A car was put in every garage, two in many. TV sets came into almost every home. There was chicken, packaged and frozen, for every pot, with more to spare. Never had so many people, anywhere, been so well off.[4]

Despite the exaggeration of this assessment, this frenetic activity was made possible by the enormous expansion of the economy that had been shifted into high gear by World War II. Statistics from the postwar period on homes, home appliances, automobiles and televisions purchased, on highways, shopping centers and airplanes built, and on teenage spending on entertainment, cosmetics, and clothes, are remarkable.

To give some sense of the magnitude of the economic growth: the gross national product jumped 250 percent between 1945 and 1960. By 1960 per capita income was 35 percent higher than in 1945, a boom year. Between 1947 and 1960, the average real income for American workers increased by as much as it had in the previous half-century. Short-term credit soared. From 1954 to 1960, installment credit rose from $4 billion to $43 billion. Total outstanding consumer credit rose from $8.3 billion in 1946 to $56.1 billion in 1960. By the end of the decade, 60 percent of all Americans owned their own homes, 75 percent of American families owned a car (between 1945 and 1960 the number of cars increased by 133 percent), 87 percent owned a television set, and 75 percent owned a washing machine. The enormous movement of white families out of the cities to new suburbs was made possible by the G.I. Bill, which made guaranteed low interest loans available to veterans through the Veterans Administration. New highways (more than

40,000 miles of new roadway were authorized by the 1956 Highway Act) and affordable automobiles facilitated the exodus of families to the suburbs. The G.I. Bill fostered the postwar building boom as the demand for homes and home ownership skyrocketed. Fertility skyrocketed too. Families were formed and expanded at fantastic rates. The G.I. Bill also provided educational assistance for veterans by subsidizing college attendance and other training. Millions of returning soldiers went to college.

White-collar career opportunities multiplied as corporations expanded and concentrated. Technology produced new consumer goods and shifted the national economic focus from goods to information (between 1937 and 1958 electronics rose from forty-ninth place among the nation's industries to fifth, with computer technology exemplifying the advances). For millions of working-class people, especially the millions of black people who had migrated from the south to the urban north and west in search of better economic situations, this shift to a service economy was not yet obvious. In the 1950s it would have been hard, for example, to imagine a slackening demand for American cars. But in 1956, for the first time the number of white-collar jobs outnumbered blue-collar, and America officially became a postindustrial or service economy with a new managerial class. For many, including many in the working class, the standard of living spiraled upward. Many Americans were more comfortable and secure than their parents had ever been and than they could have imagined themselves during the Depression; they anticipated more of everything: money, consumer goods, leisure, lessons and education for their children, satisfaction.[5] In short, for many white families it was indeed a good time. The upbeat theme of the postwar period was prosperity. Social analysts, including sociologists and academics, congratulated themselves on a nation capable of almost anything.

It is not surprising, then, that the optimism for which Americans have been notorious was in full flower in the 1950s. William L. O'Neill enthusiastically entitled a book about the period from 1945 to 1960 *American High*.[6] Many 1950s memories exude this certainty and confidence. Backyard barbecues, family television watching, and soda fountains tell of easy times. In spite of the Holocaust, atom bomb, and McCarthyism, Americans, it appears, felt secure and content. For them, Auschwitz and Hiroshima did not presage the end of Western culture's claim to superiority. Americans' concerns focused instead on their personal fortunes. This was a family time that took for granted the democracy, prosperity, and invincibility that allowed many to relish the good life they could now afford.

The students who grew up in the fifties and became 1960s activists shared this self-assurance. Doug McAdam writes that the activism of the white, middle-class babyboomers who participated in the 1964 Mississippi Freedom Summer can in part be attributed to their confidence. The class advantages and the attention they enjoyed helped to produce a "middle- to upper-middle-class youth subculture uniquely optimistic about the future, certain, one might even say cocky, about its own capabilities." He refers to the "self-assurance" and "exaggerated sense of importance and potency shared by the privileged members of America's postwar generation," which he attributes to America's assumption of its role as democracy's policeman, to American know-how and power.[7] A young white woman of this generation writes in her memoir "Storybook Lives: Growing Up Middle Class," "Indeed, I was a special girl who would become a special student who would become a special woman who would marry a special man and have several special children. This was my destiny. Life was going to be comfortable and rewarding. . . . It was assumed that I would go to one of the best colleges and excel in whatever field I chose. I was not destined to be one of those ants on the anthill."[8]

Postwar, middle-class youth imbibed the great American celebration in their milk, orange juice, television programs, Memorial Day parades, and *Life* and *Seventeen* magazines. Indeed they contributed to and were the social and economic stars of the boom. For girls, given the narrowness of acceptable behavior and values, it was a complicated inheritance, but they were as affected by it as were their male counterparts. The youthful social movements of the 1960s, including the civil rights and black power movements, were in part a testament to the sense that good things were a birthright. Women who began to express this expansiveness could not avoid coming up against narrow feminine gender expectations.

But beneath all this confidence, feelings of despair and disorientation thrived. The young, white, female narrator in Alice McDermott's novel *That Night* describes menace stalking the new suburban neighborhoods:

> *They were bedroom communities, incubators, where the neat patterns of the streets, the fences and leveled yards, the stop signs and traffic lights and soothing repetition of similar homes all helped to convey a sense of order and security and snug predictability. And yet it seems to me now that those of us who lived there then lived nevertheless with a vague and persistent notion, a premonition or memory of possible if not impending doom.*[9]

Critics and historians of the fifties have exposed a contrasting underside of postwar American culture consisting of fears and anxiety that mocked the barbecues and hoola hoops.[10] Instead of one familiar and reassuring representation of the fifties, there are two, interdependent and symbiotic. The first, as we have seen, is of a white, affluent, suburbanized society compensating for the deprivations and disruptions of the Depression and World War II.

The alter image is of a people alienated, disoriented, and discontent: "Ours is a time of uneasiness and indifference. . . . Instead of troubles—defined in terms of values and threats—there is often the misery of vague uneasiness; instead of explicit issues there is often merely the beat feeling that all is somehow not right. . . . It is this condition, of uneasiness and indifference, that is the signal feature of our period," wrote C. Wright Mills.[11] In this disorientation narrative, anxiety and dissonance thrive just below the surface of the great American celebration. Juxtapositions of confidence and fear were common. Dale Carter's *The Final Frontier* contrasts the development of the national security state and its engineered passivity with postwar American joviality. Carter and others remark, for example, on the cold war phenomenon of fallout shelters stocked with the latest consumer goods as a marketing device, suggesting that behind cheerful reassurances, images of the grotesque abound.[12]

Indeed, the cold war and the atom bomb bred deep apprehension. Norman Mailer wrote in 1959 that we would probably never be able to understand the "psychic" havoc the concentration camps and atom bomb had created, subjecting us to the "intolerable anxiety" that life and death are causeless. The consequences, in Mailer's words, are brutal: "We might be doomed to die as a cipher in some vast statistical operation in which our teeth would be counted, and our hair would be saved, but our death itself would be unknown, unhonored, and unremarked."[13] The war, the Holocaust, and the dropping of the atom bomb on Japan generated fiction and philosophy notable for its nihilism and alienation, for example, existentialism and the theater of the absurd. The bomb produced a "collapsed sense of temporality," an apocalyptic consciousness that fed the hyperactive consumer market: "No saving, no deferred gratifications, no hanging on a life to come; everything could be more or less bought now, and paid for later."[14]

The bomb haunted young people's imaginations. An English woman who grew up in the 1950s writes, "Born to peace and apparently endless opportunity, we were also born to the stifled groans from Auschwitz, Belsen, Nagasaki and Hiroshima."[15] Attempting to account for this generation's preoccupations, an early student activist remarked, "Even my secretary friends who never participated in political stuff would sometimes wake up screaming, dreaming of atom bombs."[16] Like polio, the bomb flourished as apprehension. Memories of school air raid drills, of hiding under one's desk, dog tags in case of incineration, and fallout shelters populate young people's memories of the 1950s. I remember apparently rational, passionate public discussion about whether one would let a desperate neighbor into one's shelter, of decent husbands and fathers arguing that it would be just to defend their nuclear families with guns, forbidding others to enter, presumably because supplies and/or air were not endless.

Anxiety accumulated around other more personal issues too; sex, gender, and the family were beset with ambiguity. "The nature of family life, particularly in suburbia, was far more complicated and tension-filled than the stereotypes of the fifties would have us believe," notes one historian.[17] The culture was preoccupied with legitimate, meaning marital, sex, while other forms of sexuality were a source of shame, met by ignorance, fear, and punishment. Women remember with dismay and anger the stifling sexual rules. White adolescent girls and young women's lives revolved around the fear of "going all the way" or, worse, of *appearing* to have. The obsession with female virginity until marriage was one version of sexual anxiety. A number of commentators have noticed the parallel, even intertwined, fears and imagery of the atom bomb and sexual chaos. The bikini bathing suit was named for the first hydrogen bomb test site, their powerful effects equated in the naming.[18]

The focus on sexual deviance helped to set new boundaries between normality and abnormality in a climate in which sexual standards were shifting rapidly. Students of postwar campaigns against sexual psychopaths and homosexuals suggest the campaigns were part of an anxious renegotiation process of sexual normalcy. Homosexuality played a large role in popular apprehensions about communists that linked the two as threats to a vulnerable population—children. Condemnation of sexual deviation and concentration on reproduction affirmed the family that, despite its celebration, appeared threatened. William Chafe remarks, "The effort to reinforce traditional norms seemed almost frantic, as though in reality something very different was taking place."[19]

Parents worried about their authority as control over teenagers faded. In this light, it is easy to see how, in the words of one observer, "the 'teenager' [came to replace] the Communist as the appropriate target for public controversy and foreboding." It was a topic that let people "vent their fearful or hostile feelings and declare themselves on the side of order and authority."[20]

Juvenile delinquency, a major 1950s preoccupation, was construed as evidence of social and familial disintegration. Parents worried about how to raise well-adjusted children. It was argued that fathers were too absent or not absent enough; that mothers were too involved in their children's lives, especially their sons', creating homosexuals and sissies; or that because mothers were working, they were not involved enough, producing delinquents. Popular imagery and rhetoric coupled delinquency, homosexuality, and domineering mothers with communism, seeing them as joint dangers to the home and family, the heart of the American way of life.

Whether one argues that cultural anxiety was manufactured by the cold war or was one of its causes, or more likely, both, central to the postwar political story is the cold war campaign against communists outside and within American borders (and against those who were believed to have transgressed borders, like the Rosenbergs, by collaborating with foreign enemies). Literal and figurative boundaries were important in the fifties, a period in which distinctions between "them" (foreigners and deviants) and "us" flourished. The borders of the United States became a central metaphor in the fears of invasion by communists. In popular culture, aliens often circumvented frontiers by invading from the sky. Among those of us who grew up in the fifties, few can forget the world maps in school on which the red flood steadily and ominously spread across the earth, threatening American integrity. All of this was captured in the plethora of science fiction films in which alien pods and blobs invade and destroy everything we cherish. Nora Sayre notes in the era's films the "uncertainty about the nature or location of our enemies: the communist who operates behind the scenes, the delinquents who lurk around the next corner, the prehistoric monsters reactivated by the atom tests of science fiction or the neighbors whose brains are manipulated by Martian technology, seem to be part of a vast mosaic of ambiguous fears. What was threatening was right in our midst—the subversive who belonged to the Parent Teacher Association or the dinosaur that reared up in one's backyard."[21] Andrew Ross suggests that George Kennan's containment thesis seems a more relevant prescription for domestic than for foreign policy. He points out that the policy anticipates "the Red Scare that generated much of the postwar hysteria about aliens, bugs, pods, microbes, germs and other demonologies of the Other that pervaded the culture and politics of the fifties."[22]

The political and sexual repressions, the red scare, and the feminine mystique (the title of Betty Friedan's 1963 bestselling book exposing the relentless cultural pressure on middle-class women to become mothers and housewives and the frustrations that resulted) were often connected in the public mind. Fears of communism and female sexuality melded, leading to a policy of containment for both.[23] Michael Rogin argues that American history is based on a paradoxical duality in which the alien and foreign other, the disowned and negative American self, is split off and demonized as the enemy. He calls attention to the "creation of monsters as a continuing feature of American politics by the inflation, stigmatization, and dehumanization of political foes" and suggests that American identity has been constructed, "against racial, ethnic, class and gender aliens." Countersubversive politics thus splits the world in two and gives unchecked power to the evil other.[24] Rogin suggests that the bedrock of white history (and freedom) is the demonization of peoples of color, aliens, and women, the others who are then self-righteously exploited and destroyed so that white men can protect themselves.[25] In this process, political freedom is curtailed for all. The cold war and the rise of the national security state in which political dissent was transformed into criminal disloyalty thus represented another episode of demonization in American history. Fear and punishment of communists or anyone suspected of disloyalty externalized Americans' uneasiness in the service of pacification.

I want to suggest that postwar culture was a culture of containment, with women and black people its objects. In this perspective, American politics and culture were structured by a defense of masculinity and whiteness; the changes that accompanied the formation of an advanced capitalist society were perceived and experienced as threats from those outside American borders and from those who had been excluded within those borders, women and blacks and homosexuals. In Rogin's terms, these were white men's externalized and disowned subversives. There was good reason, of course, to sense threat to white male hegemony, since the fifties were white men's last time of undisputed dominance. In this scenario, fear produced discourses about gender and race in which women and black people were to be kept separate and contained (despite the 1954 Supreme Court decision outlawing segregation in public schools and the growing participation of white, middle-class women in the labor force). Anxiety over the loss of separate spheres and the integration of the sexes and races was articulated in the celebration of whiteness and traditional domestic femininity. The segregation of women from men and blacks from whites, their containment, took place under cover of an ideological consensus that was constructed as a way of staving off the claims of those who had been excluded. Ironically, the collapse of consensus was underway at the very moment it was being theorized and hailed.

The Girls

What all this leads us to is the puzzling phenomenon that in the recent history of the United States, the 1950s are a paradox. Women continued to enter the labor force, while other indicators—prosperity, expansion of higher education, democratization of the family, and increased emphasis on sexual pleasure for married women—also suggest growing autonomy and equality for women after the war. Yet the 1950s were politically and culturally conservative, particularly regarding gender and family issues, making these difficult years for women. Just as conditions for their emancipation reached fruition, notions of women's place narrowed.[26] For young, white, middle-class women, the 1950s were a time when liberating possibilities were masked by restrictive norms; they grew up and came of age in a time when new lives beckoned while prohibitions against exploring them multiplied. Having begun with questions about the postwar roots of the youthful feminism of the following decades, I suggest that the exaggerated contradictions of the fifties, especially the narrowness of gender norms, meant that girls rebelled and explored. Camouflaged by an apparent and cheerful stability, they were attracted to various forms of difference and to new feminine lives.

The generation of white, middle-class, female teenagers, born during or near the war years, were a vanguard of womens' futures.[27] They would live their lives as middle-class pioneers by working full-time, even after marriage and children, developing careers, and by struggling to articulate an autonomous sexuality. The women's liberation movement of the late 1960s and 1970s confirmed young women's shift away from the traditional and constraining gender values of their mothers, who had come of age during the Depression and war years and had been shaped by anticonsumption and family-centered values. The teens of the fifties and early sixties were a pivotal generation whose early gender and family experiences were conventional. At the same time, they were daughters of the great American transformation of the postwar years. New and liberating options were unfolding for youth. Many girls grew up in abundance, and all of them grew up in a rapidly expanding consumer market and culture. Postwar developments contributed the material out of which girls constructed new definitions of femininity. Among these developments were the creation of a teen market and culture; a dramatic shift away from the authority of parents toward the authority of the peer group, advertising, and experts (culminating a trend begun early in the century); and explicit depiction, discussion, and encouragement of sex or sexiness. Urban and suburban teenage girls were susceptible to cultural messages promising glamour and excitement, at least before marriage, because expanding educational and employment opportunities created possibilities for new lives. College and lifelong participation in the labor force were on the agenda for many girls, in contrast to their mothers, although they often did not recognize this and were, in fact, discouraged from recognizing it.

In this book, I explore the tensions and paradoxes in the dominant definitions of femininity and the ways in which discontent and new forms of empowerment were generated and shaped by these tensions. Many girls knew that they did not want to reproduce their mothers' lives. Some girls managed to construct their own, often secret, strategies for exploration, often identifying themselves as outsiders. Such young women were curious about and tested the borders of respectability. Although marginal, these strategies found their way back into and reshaped the dominant culture. Countercultural influences, rhythm and blues, working-class style and behavior, and the Beats, for example, were used—albeit timidly in most cases—to subvert dominant notions of femininity. Thus the people and cultures that were excluded by white America had a significant underground life in young middle-class imaginations. But the dominant culture contained resistance by identifying the salient issues and structuring the spaces in which girls thought and experimented. One of those issues was race.

While writing this Introduction, I finished reading Joyce Carol Oates's *Because It Is Bitter, and Because It Is My Heart*, a book, from a sociological perspective, about the destructiveness of black/white race relations, of racism, in the 1950s. The life of Iris, its adolescent white heroine, intersects with that of a black male teenager, with whom she falls in love and cannot forget. She is drawn to black people, especially black men. In a way the story is about the forbiddenness of that relationship, the intertwining of racial and sexual tensions, and about the cruel annihilation of hope and possibility black people experience at the hands of whites. But it is also the story of the girl's construction of black people and blackness, and thus of whiteness. At one point she says, "If I was colored . . . I'd know who I was!" Throughout this painful book, Iris is interested in black people, silently sides with them—one of her teachers notes that despite her appearance of goodness and her good grades, she sides with the outlaws—and can find little meaning or feeling in her white life. "*I love you, I would die for you,*" she says of the young man she cannot give up (with whom she has no relationship), "*You are the only real thing in my life.*"[28] She marries well (and up)—a white professional— and will go to graduate school; he, who was smart and talented in high school, enlists in the army because their racist upstate New York town offers him no future, and he will die in Vietnam.

I briefly recount Oates's story here because I read it with mounting excitement, both because it is so compelling and because it is fictionally consistent with much of what I had written about white girls and race in postwar America. I raise questions about race because I believe race is essential for understanding white girls' growing-up years in the 1950s. Before all else, however, is the material reality of black people's experience of racism in postwar America. I begin with this and examine it briefly as a sobering contrast to the second issue, the significance of blackness for white girls. The second topic is what interests me here, although the two are inseparable. I want to make clear that neither this book nor these speculations are about the racial situation in postwar

America or about black girls—as the title of the book is intended to indicate. Other than this introductory discussion, I do not consistently address the issue of race in this work. I have attempted, where possible, to
consider the racial meanings in middle-class white girls' culture, to examine the implications of whiteness in relation to blackness and gender
themes, in other words, not to take race for granted.[29] I have pursued
the notion that white girls' culture was racial, that whiteness was an
issue in postwar America. Black/white relations defined white as well as
black lives, and it is to this murky area that I turn after considering black
people's experience in postwar America.

World War II was a watershed in race relations, and the late forties
saw a continued struggle for racial equality. Despite the rollback of wartime gains and the anticommunist attacks on black organizations like
the NAACP, the civil rights movement developed inexorably during the
fifties.[30] Internationally, third world nations were changing the political
landscape. As in India, African freedom movements succeeded in
achieving independence from European colonizers. The Chinese communist revolution was victorious in 1949. In America, large-scale
migrations of black people out of the South into the cities of the North,
Midwest, and West meant that black people became a more significant
presence for whites who lived or worked in metropolitan areas. The
1954 Supreme Court decision outlawing separate education for black
and white children and the Emmett Till case in which a black boy from
Chicago was murdered for talking to a white woman in the South
galvanized attention to race relations.[31] The fifties were punctuated
with dramatic efforts to integrate Southern buses and schools in which
black people, including and especially children, demanded their rights
in the face of sometimes lethal hostility. Images of Rosa Parks and the
maids and babysitters walking to work rather than taking segregated
buses during the long Montgomery bus boycott, teenage girls integrating Little Rock High School, Autherine Lucy integrating and then being
expelled from the University of Alabama provide a striking contrast to
the private concerns of most suburban, middle-class white women.
Black people in postwar America could not afford to submerge their
awareness of the contradictions built into American society. The dis-

parities between facade, or rhetoric, and actuality were more oppressive for blacks than for whites. They participated only marginally, if at all, in the good life because, simply, they were not included.

The irony was that difference was supposed to be invisible; postwar America described itself as a welcoming melting pot into which everyone could and would be incorporated. Erasing one's difference, assimilating, was a sign of becoming American. But assimilation meant passing for white. Beauty standards were white. So were pluralist theories of democracy and models of the family. Deviants and doubters were outcasts. The America presented by movies, television, magazines, and advertising was white. Black people were practically nonexistent in the dominant mass media. Michelle Wallace, a black woman born in the early fifties, writes, "I ... grew up watching a television on which I rarely saw a black face, reading Archie and Veronica comics, Oz and Nancy Drew stories and *Seventeen* magazine, in which 'race' was unmentionable."[32] The melting pot colored everyone white but thrived on exclusion and racism.

Alice Walker, the child of sharecroppers in rural Georgia, tells of the racism she experienced growing up:

I gazed longingly through the window of the corner drugstore where white youngsters sat on stools in air-conditioned comfort and drank Cokes and nibbled ice-cream cones. Black people could come in and buy, but what they bought they couldn't eat inside. When the first motel was built in Eatonton in the late fifties the general understanding of place was so clear that the owners didn't even bother to put up a "Whites Only" sign. ... I was an exile in my own town and grew to despise its white citizens almost as much as I loved the Georgia countryside. . . .

In those days few blacks spent much time discussing hatred of white people. It was understood that they were—generally—vicious and unfair, like floods, earthquakes, or other natural catastrophes. Your job, if you were black, was to live with that knowledge.[33]

Black women of the fifties generation, who have written autobiographically and fictionally, were mistreated and abused by white people, as were the people around them. For many of them racism was virtually unchecked, especially for those raised in the rural South. But black girls in the North also had their share of discrimination and pain.

Assata Shakur, who grew up in Queens, New York, was often the only black child in her classes. She was treated badly by students and teachers alike. Shakur describes a party (at which she can hardly keep from laughing at how poorly the white kids dance) in which she longed to participate. "But nobody asked me to dance. I don't think it ever occurred to them, and, if it did, they knew better. Dancing with a 'Nigger' was surely good for a week or so of teasing." Finally a boy came over to say that if she paid him, he would dance with her. Shakur says,

My relationship with white kids deteriorated even more. They made it pretty evident that they didn't care too much for me, and i made it clear right back that i didn't care for them. The thing i disliked most about them was their assumptions about me. For one thing, they automatically assumed that i was stupid, and they would really act surprised when i showed i had some brains. One of the biggest fights i had was when this kid in my class couldn't find some pen that his father had given him and accused me of stealing it.

She was so angry she jumped him, and the teachers who had consistently treated her in a racist manner seemed shocked she would do such a thing. School was torture for her.[34]

Black girls' stories are glaring in their contrasts to the carefree representations of white girls in popular magazines, movies, and photographs, of casual teens at the soda shop and school dances, with nothing to worry about but what to wear tomorrow. Like Oates's white heroine, black girls tell stories filled with longing, but their memories are very different from those the white girls recount. The black girls, mainly poor and working class, tell of exclusion, of cruelty, and often of brutal racism. I include them here as a reminder of the reality of black experience in white America of the 1950s. While white, middle-class girls may have been curious about and energized by difference, black girls of this generation faced much more difficult struggles against racism and, frequently, poverty.[35] Nonetheless, their experiences only make sense together, intelligible in relation to one another because racial categories and experience are never constructed in isolation from the other, and white and black were the primary colors of postwar America.

Hazel Carby provoked my thinking about white girls growing up in the 1950s. In *Reconstructing Womanhood*, she writes, "We need more feminist work that interrogates sexual ideologies for their racial specificity and acknowledges whiteness, not just blackness, as a racial categorization. Work that uses race as a central category does not necessarily need to be about black women." Jane Flax, another feminist scholar, argues a similar point: "To the extent that feminist discourse defines its problematic as 'woman,' it, too, ironically privileges the man as unproblematic or exempted from determination by gender relations." Both Flax and Carby suggest that it is critical to examine the "other" component in the oppositions black/white and female/male. By accepting blackness or femaleness as problematic, we falsely simplify the issues by ignoring the interrelationships between them and by defining whiteness and masculinity as standards. We must also interrogate sexual ideology for its racial components and racial ideology for its gender codes.[36]

It has been fruitful to ask what, if anything, racial segregation and the denial of difference or the apparent "invisibility" of race meant for white girls?[37] Part of the answer lies in the rigidity of postwar culture and its punishment of nonconformity. The dominant version of whiteness with which everyone was forced to contend was constricted, a homogenized, suburban, Protestant culture. Suburban domesticity left little room for those who did not fit. Working mothers, homosexuals, and single women were categories of the excluded. So were black people. In the gathering storm that would be the civil rights movement, black people were a threat not only to white people's power but to the exclusionary world of the middle-class suburb.[38] In this context, racial difference was of interest to white teenagers because excluded cultures and behaviors encompassed so much that was off-limits.

Another part of the answer to the question regarding the meaning of whiteness interrogates the question itself. In a review of Gunnar

Myrdal's *An American Dilemma* (1944), a book that shaped postwar academic debates about race in America, the novelist Ralph Ellison said, "In our society it is not unusual for a Negro to experience a sensation that he does not exist in the real world at all. He seems rather to exist in the nightmarish fantasy of the white American mind as a phantom that the white mind seeks increasingly, by means both crude and subtle to lay." Ellison argues that Myrdal's treatment of race in America is guilty of locating the Negro problem, in Myrdal's own words, "in the heart of the white American," thereby denying reality to the African-American. Real democracy, according to Ellison, will mean that the "Negro will be free to define himself for what he is." Ellison's point is that American Negroes are not simply the creation of the white man for they have made a life and created themselves. Theirs is a culture, he argues, from which white Americans have much to learn.[39]

In a more recent version of Ellison's point, Timothy Maliqalim Simone argues that it is of critical importance for whites to be open to African American culture, "to see meaning where before the only meaning obtainable was a deficient version of white processes." This entails "an acceptance of forms of cultural input, value, and solidarity that exceed the white American experience and, for the most part, [are] currently unavailable to it."[40] The import of these perspectives is their implicit criticism of an effort that, in considering the issue of blackness for white people, runs the risk of constructing black people as phantoms of whites' imaginations. Because the meaning of race, for whites as well as blacks, is developed in relationship to the other, exploring the meaning of whiteness as a racial category balances precariously between understanding the meaning of race for white people and exoticizing black people. The "other" race always figures into one's own definitions because racial categories are always constructed on the basis of difference. Trying to make sense of whiteness risks endowing blacks with traits projected onto them by whites—stereotyping them, in other words—and it thereby jeopardizes white people's ability to acknowledge black people's existence and contribution on blacks' own terms. Nevertheless, I want to ask whether black people figured in girls' imaginations in ways that enabled them to escape white middle-class expectations.

Middle-class white girls had little opportunity to know black people. It seems likely that most white teenagers, girls included, were not learning from black culture, considering it from its own perspectives, according it a subjectivity separate from their perceptions. We will see that some white girls used the sensibilities of darkness as a way out of boredom and restlessness. I want to suggest that they were drawn to black music and difference—delinquent and dark boyfriends, working-class, Beat, and bohemian lovers, jazz and rock and roll—because these were inappropriate and forbidden. Such girls longed for something more than their domesticated lives offered, "real life" they often called it. Oates's heroine is so preoccupied with black people that "glancing down at the whiteness of her skin she feels a sensation of vertigo, a physical sickness, as if this whiteness were the outward symptom of her spirit's etoliation, a profound and unspeakable not-thereness."[41] Iris may be an extreme case, but girls like her were curious about people and cultures that were "alive," "real," and "genuine." Otherness was of interest to young white people, and racial difference was part of the "other 1950s" many of them sought. Undoubtedly, by projecting their own needs and desires onto those who were different, white youth often remained as ignorant, and in many cases as racist, as they were when they began to be interested.[42] But was the relationship simply voyeuristic and objectifying?

No. The story is reciprocal, although the whole story is not told here. The attraction of blacks for whites had more to do with whites than blacks since it entailed experiences white girls felt they were missing. But that attraction also took black culture into account; young white people were genuinely interested. A process was underway that led to the social movements and culture of the sixties. Young people and bohemians in the fifties were learning about white culture by appreciating black culture; if they were racist in their objectifications as was, for example, Norman Mailer in "The White Negro" (1957), they were also drawn to it respectfully. George Lipsitz makes the point that working-class and black cultural forms became a model for middle-class youths in the 1950s. The slang, dress, and music of black people, ethnic minorities, and delinquents had a great impact upon middle-class youth, some of whom defected to that culture, many of whom wanted to.[43] Others, too, suggest that the youth culture "had as much to do with interracial affiliations and fantasies of sexual mobility as it had to do with the old containing walls of class divisions and groupings," and that the cultural revolution that can be said to have begun in the fifties was in essence a "kind of 'trickle up' process of cultural diffusion." [44] Subterranean cultures were of passionate interest to some young white people; this was expressed in many different forms, style and music the most obvious. Dick Clark, Pat Boone, and cover records, the segregation of classes and races in urban high schools, the social control exerted by adults who feared mixing and contamination were attempts to create safe and segregated spaces for white, middle-class teenagers. But teenagers resisted. In fact, adults' social control efforts in the high schools, for example, reveal the enthusiasm and curiosity of young white people.[45] As the dominant culture worked overtime to eradicate signs of class and racial difference, indigenous cultural forms thrived among working-class youth and spread to the middle class.

These themes are ubiquitous in the fiction about the period. The teenage heroine of Lynn Lauber's *White Girls*, a novel set in the very early sixties, explores her relationship to black people. For her, the most visible black person in her Midwestern town is the janitor in her school. She remarks that the janitor, Mr. Jefferson, is the "only adult who anyone could order around." He has three children in the school, and she describes the daughter: "Like all blacks in our school, she walked the margins of the halls buffed by her father, expecting nothing from anyone." But Loretta is interested. She likes driving through the black neighborhood. She identifies with black people and is acutely, even guiltily, aware (as were many young middle-class white people) that in her world they appear only in the shape of service workers—janitors, maids, garbagemen. She is warned against them. Describing her attraction to Luther, her secret black boyfriend in high school, Loretta wonders how she can explain how he has "captured her imagination": "Surely part of it was that he was forbidden, always over there—on the other side of the sidewalk, with his laughing, white-toothed friends and their lilting, jeering talk. Who could have resisted him?" She feels comfortable and real (a word white middle-class girls say often in their characterization of what they are missing) with him and his family. Her own family is unhappy and repressed—her mother disappointed and bitter, her father silent and fearful, both of them thrifty and private. Loretta thinks that she has always "been drawn to the elegance of blacks."

[She] thought that they must have been subjugated, like women, because they were so clearly superior. She did not know why or how she had come to think these things, but she thought them anyway, and didn't mind throwing away whatever reputation she had by being with Luther. Already she'd found a note taped on her locker that said "Nigger Lover," and there would probably be worse in the future.[46]

How are we to understand this? It is not irrelevant, in this white girl's perspective, that Luther and Luther's mother are in their own ways also interested in Loretta. It is not simply a one-way process. But if Loretta's account of her relationship to Luther is too complicated to be described simply as racist, it cannot be denied that her appreciation of black people and of Luther is in many ways based on her deprivations. He has been constructed as an alternative to her narrow-minded family and has little voice of his own. White girls' narratives tell of their attraction to inappropriate boys, the wrong class or race, the Elvis's and James Dean's who do not fit the calculus of white middle-class marriage and suburbs.

In the novel *Heartbreak Hotel*, Maggie, the blond homecoming queen, a sorority girl at a small Southern college, disengages from the racist and sexist culture in which she has been brought up, rejecting domesticity and virginity. She falls for a slightly older man, described as hairy and dark, who is committed to racial equality and integration. She sleeps with him when she will not with her fraternity boyfriend, whom she is expected to marry. Maggie eventually finds her way to Greenwich Village, a common ending or fantasy for nonconformist girls. In both *White Girls* and *Heartbreak Hotel*, the white, middle-class heroine gets pregnant by her dark lover. At the turning point in *Heartbreak Hotel* when Maggie consciously breaks from Southern racist norms and—less directly—feminine gender expectations, she sees a black man apprehended by the police: "I had the funniest feeling when I stood there looking at the Negro. I felt like I was looking at myself."[47]

Here the racial component at the heart of the postwar cult of domestic femininity is obvious.[48] Domesticity as women's one true calling kept white women separate, and thus pure. The suburbs and towns in which girls were expected to live their lives were white and feminine; women and children were segregated from men and people of other races (except for the black maids employed by wealthier families). Although she knew nothing about him and he was only an image to her, Maggie identified with the black man because she understood that she was, in her own way, trapped, her options narrowly defined and oppressive. "Throwing away" their reputations, these privileged young women opted for escape from the boundaries that confined their class, sex, and race. That escape involved a longing for a different, more "genuine" life; and in some cases a real effort to listen and learn.[49]

White girls' privilege in a consumer society that encouraged them to dream only narrowly but to spend extravagantly created unintended desires and interests. Perhaps dissatisfaction propelled a sector of both the black and the white middle class toward the borders and an exploration of difference. Perhaps it always has. A desire to escape from the mainstream of both races seems to have taken shape in the 1950s, as it had in the 1920s, as a longing to know a different life, generating a cosmopolitanism on the margins of the dominant culture. Bohemias are filled with middle-class nonconformists, particularly artists. Whether or not they ended up in Greenwich Village, white girls searched in the postwar period for signs and values that spoke to another part of themselves. They were responsive to music and style and people who, in the fifties, were relegated to the margins but who by the sixties were marching toward the center, with young white women in tow.

I want to come back to the theme of paradox in such young women's lives. One woman recollects the problem in this way,

Our childhood had led us to expect a way of life which no longer existed (if indeed it ever had), a life centered around a loving husband and family, held together by shared assumptions and expectations, a happy combination of security and mobility. . . . This middle-class dream, we had to admit, was still deeply a part of us, fertilized by constant pressure from our parents. . . . [We tried] to figure out why our actual experiences didn't fit with what our parents and Susan Hayward had been telling us, why stout-hearted young men didn't come courting, shyly or surely in love, determined to cherish and protect us . . . Wow, we thought, this ain't like Mama said it was gonna be. No one in those romantic movies ever had to go to the VD clinic or get an abortion. Goddam![50]

In the past twenty years, feminist writing about the situation of young white women in the 1950s always circles back to this point, the "geologic fault" between childhood and adult lives. Numerous writers note the contradictions between the messages about women's place and the new possibilities open to this generation. Double messages and conflicting signals crop up repeatedly in the analyses. Mirra Komarovsky, one of the most astute (as well as one of the only) women sociologists studying women in the late forties and fifties, wrote simply, "The old and the new moralities exist side by side dividing the heart against itself."[51] A contemporary writer points out that "the glorification of the housewife, the stress on femininity, the emphasis on romantic relationships, the warnings about careerism, all indicated ambivalence about or opposition to changes in women's activities and life-styles."[52]

I suggest in this book that the young, white, middle-class women who grew up in the midst of these contradictions were "dry tinder for the spark of revolt" and that their revolt surreptitiously began in the quiet fifties.[53] In chapter 1, I consider how social scientists contributed to gender contradictions and ambiguity. Chapter 2 examines the families in which the girls grew up and suggests that the messages learned there, often traditional and narrow, conflicted with the popular culture of the time and with the opportunities young women could anticipate. Chapter 3 is devoted to the sexual and romantic conundrums facing girls and their strategies for constructing feminine selves, and in chapter 4 I look at girls who clearly rebelled. Chapter 5 is a case study of one young academic woman's struggle, a struggle that would have had only indirect impact on girls growing up in the suburbs, but that was nevertheless integral to their cultural milieu. In all of these discussions, the gender contradictions of the postwar period form the context for girls' experiences. In the Conclusion, I address the ways in which the shape of the feminist movement in the late 1960s and 1970s owes much to these ambiguities. Circling the topic and approaching from a variety of directions, I always end with paradox and ambiguity. I am aware that in rapidly changing societies all generations are transitional, but I am convinced nonetheless that white girls' growing-up years in the 1950s were critical. Those years generated the movements of the 1960s that changed far more than our individual lives.

The Experts' Fifties:
Women, Men,
and Male Social Scientists

Some of the occupational and cultural boundaries have broken down
which help men rest assured that they are men.

   David Riesman, "Two Generations" (1967)

I begin this first chapter the way I began my study of the fifties: with the sociology written during and about the postwar period. How did social scientists observe and interpret American society at the time? What can we learn from their work? The work of the social scientists that I consider introduced new ways of understanding what was happening in the postwar period and left a lasting imprint because they helped to shape the terms of discourse about American society, not only in the 1950s but for years to come. For our purposes, what makes these works even more interesting is the fact that they reproduce the ambiguities of gender and family. To read 1950s sociological texts written by professional white men as historical documents is to discover the dramatically mixed messages of the time. Social scientists replicated societal contradictions in their work, and in this way exposed the wider gender context of girls' growing-up years.

The best known social science of the 1950s, however, was concerned not with gender but with American political institutions, specifically with the defense of American democracy against the danger of mass movements such as communism and McCarthyism or, some have argued, against the masses themselves. Except for the radical sociology of C. Wright Mills, the cold war against communism was the salient social science theme of the fifties. Well-known sociologists of the era, men like Seymour Martin Lipset and Daniel Bell, theorized an unideological, prosperous, pluralistic, consensual, and capitalist society based on powerful group interests that kept each other, and the rest of us, integrated and happily in check. Sooner or later everyone—and one must assume black people were included too, although race was practically invisible in these accounts—would be incorporated into middle-class America. Class and racial divisions were evaporating in the face of American prosperity and thriving democratic institutions. According to these writers, things could only get better. One is hard pressed to find awareness that social, political, and cultural conflicts structured by race and gender were germinating and would soon, if they had not already, burst forth. It is instructive, for example, to compare postwar social science writing with Betty Friedan's *The Feminine Mystique*. Friedan also took for granted that white, middle-class problems were universal, but she considered women as a category separate from men, with problems peculiar to their sex. In light of the civil rights and women's liberation movements, the lacunae in the social science of the period are surprising, to say the least.

While political sociologists explored the compelling postwar issues of anticommunism and democracy, those sociologists who did address gender rarely did so from the perspective of women. Consequently gender issues have to be culled from the literature I examine here, which was written at the start, during, or just after the 1950s: David Riesman's *The Lonely Crowd* (which has little about gender but is critical for the story nonetheless); *The Organization Man* by William H. Whyte, Jr.; *Crestwood Heights* by John Seeley, R. Alexander Sim, and E. W. Loosley; *Culture against Man* by Jules Henry; and essays on the family by Talcott Parsons.[1]

The work was located in the new suburbs and expanding corporations and was written by white men about the lives of middle- and upper-middle-class white people. The few black sociologists writing in the postwar period were mostly of an older generation influenced by the Chicago school of sociology, which had flourished in the twenties, thirties, and forties. Both black and white social science did have one thing in common: it ignored women.[2] But although this literature reproduced confusions about gender it also, albeit inadvertently, elucidated contradictions and "strains" (Talcott Parsons's polite term) in the lives of women in the 1950s. Two related paradoxes present themselves. I have already discussed the first, the conflict between forces creating conditions for the emancipation of women and the cultural conservatism of the time. The second, hidden in the literature and traced here, is between the information about gender and the family collected by the social scientists and their inadequate comprehension and theorization of the material. Virtually ignoring the constraints on women, they heralded growing equality between the sexes. They were more sanguine than their own evidence warranted. In this way, their writing heightened and contributed to the first paradox. These narratives were not merely academic. They were duplicated throughout American society in the schools, by family experts, the mass media, and the families in which girls grew up. Academic texts contained more than academic "mistakes." Their contradictions articulate and expose the conservative and liberalizing forces that simultaneously shaped this generation of white, middle-class girls.

The work of the five authors is qualitative and interpretive and thus more interesting and accessible than much social science.[3] The authors are linked by their concern about some of the large social and economic transitions taking place in the 1950s: specialization and bureaucratization at work; growing importance of secondary institutions in the socialization process, especially the peer group, and the concomitant decline of parental influence; the rise of a mass consumer culture able to shape needs, goals, and even personality. Riesman, Seeley, Whyte, Henry, and Parsons all attempted to evaluate the psychological impact of large-scale social change on the white, middle-class personality, more specifically the masculine personality. It was the white, middle-class man who was required to fit into the corporate world of the 1950s, and it was about him that most of this work was written. This literature, then, addressed issues of gender, if at all, from the perspective of work and the changing corporate economy. Its starting point was how changes in the occupational world affected men, and through men, women, children, and the family. The authors unselfconsciously worried about men, although this was not clearly articulated. At the heart of their concerns was the unappealing image, for them, of a new feminized man who had lost his traditional manhood, a demasculinized husband and father unable to hold his own in the face of restless and demanding women.

David Riesman published *The Lonely Crowd* in 1950 with a follow-up book of portraits of Americans, *Faces in the Crowd*, in 1952. *The Lonely Crowd* was an extraordinarily successful book; its central thesis evidently tapped a nerve in its readers. Riesman launched themes that would recur often in American intellectual life. Published as the decade opened, *The Lonely Crowd* provides an apt starting point for this discussion. Riesman suggested that all societies ensure conformity by shaping a "national character," which changes over time. He proposed a modernization scheme containing three kinds of societies, each represented by a typical personality type: tradition-directed, inner-directed, and other-directed. His central thesis was that middle-class American society had shifted from an inner-directed to an other-directed type: from an entrepreneurial, production-oriented society with a typical personality driven by inner ideals and values—the Protestant ethic character described by Max Weber—to a society characterized by economic abundance, bureaucratization, and permissiveness, in which peer groups dictate personal behavior. Economically and socially, consumption had become more important than production. The vital trait in the other-directed personality was the need for approval and direction by others, indicative of the absence of internalized guidelines for behavior. The yearning for approval and the resulting conformity, major 1950s themes, had supplanted commitment to abstract ideals.[4]

A kindred perspective was presented by John Seeley in *Crestwood Heights*. Subtitled *A Study of the Culture of Suburban Life*, it is a community study of a Canadian suburb of Toronto. Seeley suggested that the importance of approval was most obvious in the growing significance for children and teenagers of the peer group, whose judgment and norms were based on advertising and the mass media. Seeley agreed with Reisman that children had become "gifted as consumers," with enormous energy poured into the ever-expanding frontiers of consumption.[5] What counted was the ability to absorb other people's tastes. In this connection, Jules Henry, an anthropologist, painted a nightmarish picture of American teenage life in *Culture against Man*. Its key characteristics, in Henry's view, were obsession with popularity and consumption. Since popularity was based on conformity, teenage conformity, in Henry's account, knew no limit. For Riesman, Seeley, Henry, Whyte, and Parsons, the main child rearing goals were the adaptability and sociability that prepared children for upward mobility and success at work.[6] As the power of the peer group grew, that of the parents declined. There was agreement among the authors that teachers had become powerful agents of socialization and that the schools stressed "life adjustment" and "family living" at the expense of the academic. "Getting along well with others" and flexibility were their real curriculum.[7]

The flexibility and skill at getting along with others demanded by the new corporate environment were in fact becoming desired personality traits for everyone. A mobile, consumer society fosters and requires adaptability, responsiveness to others and things. In *The Organization Man*, Whyte decried the "social ethic" of bureaucratic corporations that encouraged group identification, downplayed individuality and difference, and promoted conformist behavior. The model male employee was constantly worried about what others at work thought of him.[8] The other-directed person, then, had no internalized values, was genial, cooperative, and anxious, and singularly lacking in genuine joy and pleasure in his life.

Although Riesman later denied that his portrait of the other-directed personality had been meant to be so critical, his attempts to point out its positive traits were unconvincing.[9] For all the authors except Parsons, the overall picture was negative. They chronicled changes in which established norms and traditions were being destroyed.[10] They were particularly concerned with conformity and, again, it was male conformity that worried them. We have seen that anxiety about political and social deviance thrived, but so, surprisingly, did anxiety about its twin, the "silent generation," white-collar sheep seeking only security. Riesman, Seeley, Whyte, and Henry all stressed the decline of autonomy in the "new" personality and the costs of social change. They were less concerned and less critical of the gender developments that were simultaneously taking place and that exacted a toll at least as deep.

Gender Themes

We can examine at least three gender and family issues running through the sociological discourse that molded young women's conceptions of femininity in the 1950s. The first was whether feminine and masculine sex roles were converging in modern America? Were sex roles becoming more similar, which implied more equality between females and males?[11] It is probably unnecessary to point out that the literature of the fifties assumed adults were heterosexual and married. There was almost no mention of single adult men or women and certainly nothing about homosexuals. The second and closely connected issue was the changing relationship between husband and wife, defined in the "companionship marriage" ideal, which by the 1950s was accepted as central to the modern nuclear family.[12] The third and final problem, again closely related to the first two, was that of "maternal overinvolvement" in childrearing, spotlighting the relationship between mothers and children. The domineering mother was a powerful image in much literature, some of it popular, of the 1940s and 1950s.[13]

Converging Sex Roles

There was agreement among our five authors that masculine and feminine sex roles were becoming more similar. As babies and small children, boys and girls were increasingly wearing the same kinds of clothes and were taught almost the same things in school; the curriculum throughout the school years emphasized similarities and downplayed differences between boys and girls. Seeley notes about Crestwood Heights that "there appears to be a growing convergence between types of social behavior once ... distinguished as male and female," and Riesman refers to the "growing homogenization of the sexes." Henry suggests that because men are so deprived of emotional and personal gratification in their work lives, they seek close contact with children. He concludes that "increased activity of women in economic life tends to reduce the differences between male and female roles."[14] Parsons suggests that American society is "conspicuous for the extent to which children of both sexes are in many fundamental respects treated alike." Indeed, he argues, "One of the most conspicuous expressions and symbols of underlying equality ... is the lack of sex differentiation in the process of formal education."[15] According to fifties sociologists, the convergence of sex roles was due to the demands of technology. The modern occupational world no longer required the accentuation of sexual differences, and it thus "whittled away patriarchal patterns."[16] Bureaucracy was shaping a new universalistic personality whose main characteristic was adaptability.

The emergence of this other-directed personality was in fact laden with gender implications that the sociologists perceived hesitantly or not at all. In hindsight it becomes clear that the other-directed personality is more "feminine" than "masculine."[17] Being attuned to others, worrying about their opinions and feelings, being adaptable and avoiding conflict—precisely the traits and skills demanded by the corporations and white-collar occupations—are all traditional feminine personality characteristics.

This new personality had little in common with traditional masculinity—the rugged individualist, cowboy, and entrepreneur who is, rather, inner-directed. This fact, not addressed by the sociologists, is key to much of the discomfort and confusion about gender in the 1950s. The sex role "convergence" they noticed was toward the feminine. Barbara Ehrenreich and Dierdre English suggest that *The Lonely Crowd* was really a description of changes underway in American manhood, and that the emerging bureaucratic, other-directed personality appeared to be an "attack on maleness itself." In a separate study devoted to the collapse of the breadwinner ethic, to a "crisis of masculinity" in the postwar period, Ehrenreich argues that the other-directed man was seen as emasculated. She proposes that many men writing in the fifties believed that "conformity destroys not only men's souls, but their very manhood."[18]

There is a good deal of evidence from the popular culture of the time to indicate that middle-class men did feel powerless and worried in the face of new demands and that they were looked upon by others with contempt. Comic strips devoted to family themes, like "Dagwood and Blondie," portrayed married men as henpecked and wives as aggressive and victimizing. Dagwood was small and weak, shorter than his wife, who often towered above him with a rolling pin in her raised hand. Many television shows pictured domesticated "dads," essentially caricatures of patriarchs. Fathers were humble, patient, sad, and focused on their families. Lynn Spigel suggests that not only television images but television watching itself feminized fathers. Spigel notes that in the advice columns in women's magazines and in the magazines' pictorial depictions of families, the woman's traditional passivity was transferred to the man of the house, who came home from work, relaxed, and rejuvenated himself through and around the television while the mother was engaged in household activity.[19]

One of the most important films of the 1950s, *Rebel without a Cause*, shows the father of the troubled teenaged son, James Dean, as a milquetoast in an apron, unable to stand up to his domineering wife. The son's juvenile delinquency is explained as a direct response to his weak father. The images appear in academic texts as well as in popular entertainments: the author of a study of a high school remarks on the adults who scream at the students, "the ill-tempered, belligerent little men and enormous, aggrieved women."[20] Indeed, the theme is pervasive in the rhetoric of the cold war, as John D'Emilio's analysis of the cold war vilification of communists and homosexuals suggests: "Lacking toughness, the effete, overly educated male representatives of the Eastern establishment had lost China and Eastern Europe to the enemy. Weak-willed, pleasure-seeking homosexuals—'half-men'—feminized everything they touched and sapped the masculine vigor that had tamed a continent."[21] Homosexuality was incorporated into the demonology of the McCarthy era by linking communism with immoral and antimasculine behavior.

The deep anxiety about masculinity after the Second World War was closely linked with fears of female strength.[22] Recent scholarship has examined both the empowering wartime experience of women who entered the labor force and survived as wives and mothers alone and the concern on the part of men that women would become too independent, undomestic, and unfeminine. The conservative messages regarding women in the postwar period were part of an effort to ensure that women went home and stayed home after the war, a policy of containment. There was an unprecedented campaign both in government and industry to make sure returning soldiers were given priority over women in jobs and education. Women were encouraged, even forced, to defer to men in the public world and at home: their wartime experiences were to be a thing of the past. The campaign to get women back into the home, to keep them there, emphasized the needs of husbands and children.[23]

In one of its meanings, then, unarticulated but shared by the social scientists, gender convergence suggested an unfamiliar and untraditional masculinity (and, by inference, femininity). Created by the mushrooming bureaucratic order and dramatically juxtaposed to women's wartime experiences and increasing labor force participation, the popular imagery of weak and small "dads" confirmed and encouraged genuine uneasiness about, even disdain for, the middle-class man. Strong females and weak, other-directed males were spectres haunting men and cowing women.

The problem with all this, however, is that masculine and feminine sex roles were not converging. Social scientists stressed only part of the unfolding story, ignoring some of their own observations. In the 1950s, the single acceptable goal for women was to find fulfillment in the family as wives and mothers. The period was characterized by powerful cultural norms that exaggerated traditional femininity, sexual and domestic. Notions of femininity and masculinity were emphatically differentiated, women expected to be domestic and dependent on men, and men to be breadwinners. If it appeared as though girls were being prepared in their early years for futures approximating those of men, they received powerful messages that their lives would be nothing like men's. Girls knew that their scripts diverged dramatically from boys' scripts even if social scientists did not.

While their writing emphasized equality and the growing convergence of cultural gender definitions, a number of the social scientists, observant but uninterested, also noticed an opposing emphasis on traditional femininity. Parsons suggested that the modern nuclear family was becoming more specialized in its functions, with socialization of children and stabilization of the adult personality its most important activities. The woman, a full-time mother, was responsible for these functions, while the father's paid employment enabled him to mediate between the family and the occupational world. Mothers' and fathers' work could not have been more different.

The modern nuclear family was mobile and isolated from extended kin ties. Husband and wife were increasingly dependent on one another; their relationship was the foundation upon which the family rested. In Seeley's dramatic formulation, "The tie between husband and wife indeed becomes preeminently important, providing, as it does the one enduring human relationship in the society."[24] Parsons made clear that this critical marriage relationship required divergent feminine and masculine roles. He argued that contrasting definitions of femininity and masculinity were the cornerstone of the family. In fact, Parsons stated, given developments in the American occupational system, there was a tendency toward increased sex role segregation rather than the reverse in spite of "strong forces . . . leading toward an identical treatment of the sexes."[25] Here is the real confusion about gender that defines the period: boys and girls were formally treated as equals in the midst of a tendency toward increased differentiation of their future roles.

Girls might be treated equally in the early years in the family and school, according to Parsons, but they could only look forward to becoming wives and mothers. Furthermore, he suggested, the most important aspect of the mature role of housewife is that it "shields spouses from competition with each other in the occupational sphere, which, along with attractiveness to women, is above all the most important single focus of feelings of self-respect on the part of the American man."[26] Parsons made explicit the implications for women of the compromise of the modern family with the occupational system: the denial of equal employment opportunity for married women.

What is striking is that Parsons clearly articulated the dilemma facing white, middle-class females in this period—the conflict between gender convergence and the emphasis on traditional femininity. He stated unequivocally that the modern family was based on women's subordination to men. But he did not identify this as a problem for women. None of the authors considered here, talented social observers and analysts, did much more than notice the problem, if they did that.

Seeley noted that girls, like boys, are prepared in school for a career: "In the classroom, the sex of the student is largely irrelevant. The girl who in ten years will be rinsing diapers competes in the trigonometry class with the boy who will be an engineer—and often gets higher marks." But, Seeley says, she understands that future occupation is "considered a more important question for the boy, since it is tacitly assumed that the girl will pursue a career only until she marries." For girls, the "full stamp of cultural approval is given only if she later achieves husband and children."[27]

Margaret Mead summarized the problem: "We end up with the contradictory picture of a society that appears to throw its doors wide open to women, but translates her every step towards success as having been damaging—to her own chances of marriage, and to the men whom she passes on the road." Henry articulated it dramatically. Referring to adolescent girls he said, "In place of their dreams they take husbands."[28] Feeling they have been deceived, the girls develop a high level of anxiety and aggression that, according to Parsons, "undoubtedly underlies the widespread ambivalence among women toward the role of motherhood . . . and the role of being a woman in any other fundamental respect." Neurotic behavior is to be expected given the "strain" built into the adult feminine role, with the "sources of ambivalence . . . so deep" that it is impossible to persuade or force women to accept a role of pure domesticity.[29] This characterization of contemporary femininity is simply astonishing from Talcott Parsons, the champion of a nuclear family predicated on specialized feminine and masculine roles. In effect, Parsons described Friedan's unhappy housewife. This was the family in which many middle-class white girls grew up and that they anticipated for themselves. We will see in chapter 5 that Parsons's insights into the "strains" and "ambivalences" constitutive of the feminine sex role were painfully pertinent to his own daughter's life.

The social scientists remained unshaken in their view of converging sex roles even as they glimpsed alternative developments. Their analyses reflected a contradictory reality and reproduced the exaggerated double bind in which adolescent females were encouraged to achieve in school but expected to forego work or career for marriage. There is no question that there was more similar and equal treatment of girls and boys than ever before. But traditional notions of femininity, understood to be the anchor of the family, were promoted with a vengeance in the postwar period. Although this paradox had enormous consequences for girls and young women, the male observers of society were largely unconcerned and insensitive to its impact.

In his 1956 introduction to *Crestwood Heights*, David Riesman was puzzled by the fact that the authors had discovered two distinct cultures, male and female, with different values. He denied that this was characteristic of most suburbs, where homogenization of the sexes was typical, and suggested instead, without explanation, that it was reminiscent of an older America. Yet in *The Lonely Crowd*, Riesman had offered an important, if fleeting, insight that in part answered his query regarding Crestwood Heights. He suggested that as women became more liberated in ways their mothers would never have dreamed of, men felt uncomfortable. "These uneasinesses caused by the newly liberated are one source of the current attempts to reprivatize women by redefining their role in some comfortable domestic and traditional way." Indeed, he argued, "many middle-class women appear to have turned back, in a futile effort to recapture the older seemingly more secure patterns."[30]

Parsons identified two other feminine coping mechanisms: the glamour pattern and the humanistic or domestic pattern. In the first, women stress specifically feminine forms of attractiveness "in a direction which tends to segregate the elements of sexual interest and attraction from the total personality and in so doing tends to emphasize the segregation of sex roles." According to Parsons, the glamour pattern appears because it offsets masculine occupational status and avoids the taboo on competition between the sexes. In contrast, in the humanistic pattern, which does not offset masculine occupational status, women become good companions who work in the community and stress what the sexes have in common. In Parsons's terms, such women are good (uncompetitive) wives. However, he continues, "too heavy a leaning toward domesticity may threaten the emotional interests of the husband" and thus a "conservative synthesis of these two often conflicting tendencies in the feminine role is one of the most urgent needs of the American family."[31]

These are utterly incompatible scenarios about the feminine role. The fifties were a time in which both the glamour and the humanistic models were exaggerated and mutually exclusive. The idea that being glamorous "offset" or was equal to masculine occupational status is intriguing for a decade that witnessed Marilyn Monroe and an explosion of a graphic female sexiness. Ambitions to movie star attractiveness can be seen to have compensated for more serious life chances. They distracted women from other forms of fulfillment and status. But as we will see, for white, middle-class adolescent girls, it also provided fertile material for imagining feminine selves that diverged significantly from the model their mothers presented. Parsons's "constructive synthesis" was thus nowhere in sight in the 1950s; for the time being gender convergence had been sabotaged by the feminine mystique.

Men and Women in the Family

In their emphasis on the centrality of the family and the husband-wife relationship, the sociologists simultaneously acknowledged, but did not fully explore, marital fragility. Contradictory elements marked the analysis: modern marriage was ideally characterized by companionship, but husbands and wives are far apart in their interests and personalities. In the transformations of the postwar period, the marriage relationship became both more important and more burdened. Often living far from grandparents and other extended family, members of the modern nuclear family had little support or guidance; they had only each other. The social scientists thus portrayed a family under stress. Their complaisance in the face of negative evidence is puzzling.

There were divergent opinions about fathers. Henry was the most extreme in his view that the family served mainly to compensate men for the deprivations of the working world. But this argument was implied by all the authors except Parsons, who saw work as satisfying. The American economic system, according to Henry, generated feelings of competition, inadequacy, hostility, fear, and suspicion. As a result, the family was required to serve enormous therapeutic needs. The father became, in Henry's words, an "imp of fun." Deprived of gratification at work, he turned to his family and discovered it made more sense to relax than to be an authority. Following Riesman, Henry stated that the old superego values of anger and guilt were obsolete. "Dad" wanted to be loved, not feared. He wanted to have a good time and hungered for emotional fulfillment. Dads were needy. Consequently, according to Henry, fathers were permissive with their children and became their "friends." Mothers' and fathers' roles converged as the two parents competed for their children's love. The mother was in a more advantageous position, since she still ran the household, cooked, and took care of the children and was directly needed by them. Fathers *had* to be lovable.[32]

Parsons and Seeley focused on how the occupational demands on the father affected his ability to relate to family members. Seeing the occupational world as one in which status is achieved through competition and individual merit and the family as an institution characterized by loyalty and acceptance, Parsons analyzed the difficulties created for men and women together. The father's interests and energies focused on his specialized occupational role, which separated rather than connected him to his wife. Sharing of interests with persons of the opposite sex became difficult, especially as women were so strongly encouraged to develop their femininity.[33]

Given the pressures on the husband to pursue economic success and the power of the values operative in the white-collar world, the man, Seeley suggested, was not well equipped to meet the new cultural demands on him as husband and father. In addition, he often had an instrumental interest in his family, using it to promote his career; his family's successes and failures reflected on him. Seeley thus concluded that "highly individualistic, success-oriented persons such as those the Crestwood Heights family tends to produce may be eminently suited to the business world but of limited usefulness beyond it."[34] In a damning admission from a champion of the modern occupational system, Parsons, in his understated manner, had this to say about the demands the occupational system made on its employees: "The patterns of behavior institutionalized in the modern occupational system run counter to many of the most deeply-seated of human needs and motivations, such as relatively unconditional loyalty to groups, sentimental attachment to persons as such, the need for security against competitive pressures, and the like."[35] Parsons, Seeley, and Henry thus agreed that the personality demanded of men for success in an advanced capitalist society failed at intimate relationships. Although he was on the surface adaptable and attuned to others—other-directed—his personal relationships were superficial at best.

The marital relationship had been presented as the link that held the family together, the one enduring human relationship in society, based as it was on growing equality and companionship. But at the same time, the factors separating husbands and wives were shown to be substantial indeed. Seeley, in fact, described men and women as possessing "mutually-opposed value systems" and two distinct cultures, making it difficult to achieve emotional unity or a satisfactory sexual relationship.[36]

In this regard, it is fascinating to consider what Parsons had to say about sex between husbands and wives: "A mature woman can love, sexually, only a man who takes his full place in the masculine world, above all its occupational aspect, and who takes responsibility for a family; conversely, a mature man can only love a woman who is really adult, a full wife to him and mother to his children, and an adequate 'person' in her extrafamilial roles."[37] This statement is interesting for a number of reasons. First, it is an ideological proposition committed to maintaining the stability of the nuclear family, an expression of moralistic national family ideology. Appropriate sexual attraction is presented as the instrumental glue that holds Parsons's decorous and specialized family together. (Remember, too, that he has warned that the husband's emotional interest might be "threatened" by his wife's domesticity.) Second, we have seen how the cultural capital of the white-collar man who takes his "full place in the masculine world," was dangerously low. Finally, we shall see that it was precisely the boys and young men who rejected the respectable route who were sexually attractive to many young, white, middle-class girls of the late fifties and sixties.

One of the interesting divisions in Crestwood Heights between women and men was their perspective on the role of mental health professionals in the transition to middle-class and suburban living. Seeley showed how influential the male mental health experts were with the mothers. They embraced, rhetorically at least, the permissiveness the experts advocated for children. Their husbands, however, did not. This created, as Riesman says in his introduction, a "triangle between the male experts and researchers, their female clients, and the latter's husbands." Seeley argued that the wife's childrearing theories seemed nonsensical to the husband and their sources, the male experts, appeared "as inadequate men who have not been able to make the grade in the *really* masculine world."[38] Thus white-collar men whose own masculinity was under suspicion denigrated the experts—one must assume they were primarily psychotherapists—whose gender credibility was even lower than theirs.

In each of the sociological texts, the pattern of analysis parallels the author's discussion of sex role convergence. On both subjects, the evidence diverges in a more conservative (and pessimistic) direction than the interpretations suggest. Signs of gender convergence and companionship in marriage camouflaged their opposites. The sociologists' observations highlight the differences between women and men, their incompatibility, the difficulty of their tasks given their differences, and the very mixed messages that characterized the culture. Women had more options than ever before but were discouraged from acting on them, while men were prevented by occupational demands from realizing the domestic intimacy they needed and were supposed to value.

Maternal Overinvolvement

Unsurprisingly—in light of the baby boom and a family-centered culture—childrearing was a major preoccupation in the postwar period. But the actual experiences of mothers ran counter to society's romanticization of the family and optimism about companionship and equality. Women often found the new childrearing values and goals to be reproachful and burdensome. The psychological relationship mothers established with their children was defined as the key to children's success. However, many women had little experience with parenting that emphasized love and acceptance (rather than, for example, discipline and protection) and felt guilty when they fell short of the new demands. In numerous popular and scholarly books and articles, mothers were blamed for inadequate children. In fact, the discussion was about sons, not children, because it was sons about whom commentators, influenced by Freud and certainly by sexism, worried. Much of the popular literature, like *Generation of Vipers* by Philip Wylie, who coined the term "momism," was explicitly misogynist. Thus, ironically, the most idealized figure of the period, the mother, became a scapegoat. It is one facet of the story of middle-class white women in the 1950s, although all women were affected by and in some measure blamed for the unsettling gender transitions.[39]

It was argued that mothers were tying their sons to their apron strings, making babies of them, even castrating them, by being overprotective. According to Dr. Edward Strecker, a psychiatrist, sons never grow up. He gave as evidence the numbers of men who were rejected by or had to be discharged from the army on grounds of psychic disorders, as well as in the high numbers who attempted to evade the draft. Hard work, productivity, and maturity (i.e., inner-directedness) were no longer key values. Because they lacked other outlets, mothers were too emotionally involved with their sons, imposing on them their own disappointments and frustrations. Strecker and others linked excessive maternal energy to an inadequate sex life with an absent and shirking husband.[40] For Strecker the overprotective mother was also a progressive or permissive mother who dominated her children but veiled her authority. By granting unrestricted freedom and encouraging self-expression, she created dependence on herself and immaturity.

New theories of child development, influenced by Freud and ratified by social scientists, came into vogue in the postwar period. Postwar psychological writers emphasized that exclusive and full-time mothering was essential to the emotional and intellectual development of children; it was the centerpiece of child development. But even this was not enough. Many writers believed that middle-class mothers were destructive: cold, domineering, and rejecting. "Normal mothering is noxious mothering," remarks an observer of the literature.[41] Despite their intentions, mothers created pathology in their children. They were admonished to be full-time mothers, but full-time mothering could not ensure a healthy child. The enormously powerful influence of Freudianism in postwar American culture, which focused on parents' behavior in early childhood for the ultimate outcome of a child's personality, but especially on the mother's critical role in repressing infantile sexuality, placed a heavy burden on mothers. Many observers believed that American mothers did not curb their sons' oedipal drives, thereby creating dependent and immature sons.[42] The problems of children, male children, in the form of dependency and delinquency (and later, dissent) were blamed on mothers.

None of the popular and social scientific writers appear to have questioned whether the onus of "inadequate" children should have fallen on the mother. Nor did they question whether the mother was indeed "overinvolved." They seemed to concur that any irregularity in mothering could lead to disaster in the child, although the child's problems were often unspecified. Parsons, for example, suggested that good maternal care made for a "highly vulnerable situation. Any serious distortion of the mother's emotional attitudes can be seriously disturbing to the child." [43] Despite this, all the authors explicitly or implicitly endorsed full-time motherhood.

The postwar suburbs were repeatedly referred to as a "suburban matriarchy." David Riesman, for example, said in his introduction to Seeley's study that "the evidence goes to show that only the women live in Crestwood Heights, along with the young people and the professionals servicing both, while the men are, so to speak, visiting from the bush—from the 'real world' of Canada's booming economy."[44] Margaret Mead, dissenting, argued that "suburban matriarchy" was inaccurate since American culture was "patrimonal, patrilineal, patrilocal and patriarchal."[45] But the term corresponded to popular conceptions, experiences, and anxieties. It conveyed—ironically, given how extremely dependent they were—the fear that wives and mothers in the suburbs were powerful, perhaps more powerful than their husbands. One clue to the matriarchy theme is that the suburbs were sex homogenous: only women and children inhabited them the better part of each day. If the segregation of adult women from men was what the word "isolated" meant in reference to the suburban family, we have identified one source of the exaggeration of the power of mothers. The apparently frightening vision of unbroken maternal influence on children, especially sons, accounts for the distortion.

This influence was reinforced, the analyses continued, by the husband's immersion in the occupational world. As we have seen, he was often emotionally unavailable to his wife and children, coping instead with his own needs and new work demands. Although postwar values encouraged their active participation in family life, there is evidence that middle-class fathers were not only emotionally unavailable, but physically absent a good deal of the time. Thus while they touted the new participatory family, sociologists also acknowledged the "father absence" that they believed contributed to the domineering maternal behavior that so worried them.[46] Finally, as we have seen, the corporate world required skills that did not fit traditional notions of masculinity.

For all these reasons, the father was both an unavailable and unpromising role model for boys. Expected to be more involved in the family, he was unable and ill-equipped to do so. The combination of omnipresent mothers and dubious fathers begins to make sense of the domineering mother theme. As Barbara Ehrenreich and Dierdre English have written, "Behind the hatred and fear of the mother was a growing sense that men had somehow lost power—that they were no longer 'real men.'"[47] Not insignificant in this equation was the concentration and segregation of women in the suburbs that reproduced wartime patterns: the separation of women from men and uncertain male authority in the family continued to generate men's fears of their own expendability.

Cold war propaganda spread the misogyny of the maternal dominance theme. In propaganda films, subversion was blamed on women who were too independent or who seduced men, sometimes their sons, into being pawns or agents of communism. The threat of subversion thus came not only from without but from within. Motherhood and communism, in this view, cunningly undermined the American family and way of life. In Michael Rogin's words, the mother was used as a "symbol and scapegoat for political and familial worries." In this connection, it is worth pointing out that Kinsey and other sex reformers of the period were accused of being communists; a freer sexuality, even an enlightened attitude, made one vulnerable to charges of subversion. This theme links weak men with homosexuality and a less aggressive and militarist foreign policy. Anxiety about masculinity was used to generate support for cold war policies; weak men and strong mothers implied subversion.[48]

The fear that mothers would incapacitate children was really a fear that they would emasculate their sons, create dependent and weak men whose masculinity was in doubt, and spoil their (and their nation's) chances of success. It was a fear, too, about dependency in personal relationships, especially about dependent men, who in American culture provoke scorn and uneasiness. These anxieties are the underside of the ethic of autonomy and competition, key components of traditional masculinity, which was precisely what seemed to be threatened in this period. In the Freudian idiom then popular, the oedipal power of mothers over sons was exaggerated because of anxiety about diminishing masculine authority and female independence. The mother appears in social science and popular literature as a more powerful figure than she was, and than the sociologists knew she was, given their documentation of the growth of secondary institutions.[49]

The growth of secondary institutions in the socialization process, particularly the peer group, the mass media, and mental health professionals, inevitably raises questions about the autonomy of the family and of parents in raising their children. Emphasis by the social scientists seems to suggest that relative weakness of the mother in shaping her children's personalities. Recent scholarship also supports the idea that in the postwar period a qualitative increase in the strength of secondary institutions entailed the family's weakening hold on children. While the mother's influence in the middle-class family may have increased relative to the father's, the influence of both was diminished.[50] Mothers took on mythic proportions in the 1950s.

The influential social scientific texts considered here were correct in a long historical view that conditions were making gender equality and democratic marriages more possible. But the social scientists' assumptions of progress, shared by the majority of white, middle-class Americans in postwar America, prevented their seeing that the emancipation of women was undercut by the promotion of female domesticity to the exclusion of all else. Their analyses ignored anxiety about masculinity although this anxiety was pervasive. Evidence from their own writing indicates that they, too, disdained the new, other-directed, gray-flanneled "dad." The apparent loss of male power and status and the rejection of cultural norms implied by women's, especially wives' and mothers', increasing participation in the labor force generated a cultural misogyny invisible to many commentators. The anxiety regarding gender transformations was itself a product, at least in part, of attitudes hostile to women's equality and freedom.

In reading for the discrepancies between the social scientists' data and their conclusions, one gets a more complicated and ultimately more accurate portrayal of women's situations than if the authors are taken at their word. The literature helps us to place girls' growing-up years in a gendered context. The authors reproduced the paradoxes that women lived and absorbed. But they did more than that. Their writing contributed to those paradoxes by downplaying, even ignoring, the conservative and anxious forces at work. They reported the progressive news about gender but gave us enough information to see another story emerging: the gender changes and conflicts of the next thirty years.

CHAPTER 2

Family Legacies

By comparison with nonliterate societies the average American standard . . . [with respect to feeding, toileting, dependency, and sex] seems to have been fairly demanding. That is, children were pressed to give up changeworthy behavior comparatively early, and they were required to conform to rather restrictive adult standards. For example, both weaning and toilet training occurred unusually early, and the mature standards demanded with respect to sex behavior were relatively rigorous in their requirement of inhibition and self-control.

Robert Sears, Eleanor Maccoby, and Harry Levin,
Patterns of Child Rearing *(1957)*

What did middle-class white girls learn from their mothers in the 1950s? Is it possible to answer such a broad and general question? Which girls and which mothers?[1] How did the younger women differ from the older generation? In the bulk of this chapter, I consider what it was like for middle-class girls to grow up with fifties mothers in a culture fixated on family life. In the latter part of the discussion, I contrast the younger generation as young adults in the

1970s with the older generation, their "mothers," in the 1950s. Throughout I refer to mothers and daughters who were not literally mothers and daughters but who were the right age for such a relationship. The older women could have been mothers of girls who grew up in the fifties and early sixties. Instead of using quotation marks throughout the text, I remind readers here that I refer to generational, not actual, mothers and daughters, unless I note otherwise. Though I am getting ahead of the story by considering the daughters after their growing-up years, the contrasts between the two adult generations are revealing and useful in comprehending the dramatic gender changes that took place in twenty years of the daughters' lives. Their adult thoughts about their mothers and family training in the fifties clarify the shape of the differences that, we are able to see, were often deliberately chosen. The exercise enables us to recognize the pivotal nature of this generation of white, middle-class women: they grew up learning in their families ways of being in and thinking about the world that were appropriate for earlier circumstances, receiving all the while contrary cues from the larger culture. Most of the teenagers' family training appears anachronistic in light of postwar cultural, economic, and social changes.

The gender contradictions that social scientists overlooked and to which they contributed were lived daily by 1950s mothers and the next generation of women. In this and the next two chapters, women's perceptions, adjustments, and solutions become more apparent when juxtaposed with social scientific analyses of family and gender. Fulfillment through family roles and family "togetherness" were national ideals even as they were being undermined by opportunities in the world outside the family. Girls were socialized in families by mothers whose values and behavior were traditional regarding gender and discipline. Girls' responses to domesticity were not uniform but neither were the responses of the older women, who often communicated a sense of anger and self-sacrifice to their generational daughters. We have seen that social scientific evidence was not reassuring regarding women's status and situation. The gap between the mothers' ideology and their experience is, in fact, a motif in the younger women's stories;

the older women's lives could not be unambivalently embraced by the younger. Both generations of women struggled to find a way to feel at home in the midst of profound social transformations. This is one of the reasons, according to Elaine Tyler May, that the mothers stayed home.[2] Home was a safer place to be, given the disruptions of the Depression, World War II, and the cold war.

Home, especially in the suburbs, meant a white, heterosexual, nuclear family–based society. The suburbs were segregated, racially and sexually. In gender terms, home meant women with their children, safe, domestic, and dependent on their husbands. Racial and gender codes reinforced one another; suburban womanhood was idealized as true womanhood. The feminine mystique was as white as the suburbs, a code to ensure white women's segregation from and dependence on men and their differentiation from black women.

It is not irrelevant that the foundation for casual suburban life was white and middle-class status. Much of the ease of the suburbs was based on the labor, including domestic, of the black working class. Memoirs, fiction, and recollections by white middle-class people who grew up in towns and suburbs often include black maids, nannies, janitors, and garbagemen who played significant parts in their caretaking or imaginations. The suburbs' dependent relationship with the cities, based on racial and class segregation, was hidden or poorly understood, although some young people became aware of, were uncomfortable about, and eventually rebelled against that relationship.

Thus, despite the safety of domesticity, older women's experiences were not reassuring, sometimes not even helpful, to younger women. Some young women simply did not want to be safe. In the twenty years between the 1950s and the 1970s, attitudes about appropriate gender behavior and behavior itself changed dramatically. The contrasts in values and behavior between these two generations of women suggest ways in which broad social shifts are articulated in individual lives. The family mediated and contributed to those changes; young, white, middle-class women growing up in the fifties were shaped by that family, the gender and racial ideology constitutive of it, and their mothers' experiences in it.

Scholars agree that family and reproductive behavior in the postwar period were aberrant, a "last-gasp orgy of modern nuclear family domesticity." This domesticity was sentimentalized and yearned for at the time and has been ever since.[3] Demographic patterns in the 1950s do not conform to long-term historical trends; they constitute deviant blips on the charts. Nostalgic memories of family stability and tranquility do have a basis in fact, though they were shortlived facts: "Rates of divorce, single-parent families, and illegitimacy were half what they are today; birthrates were twice as high; and many more young adults married at young ages."[4] Americans formed more families at a younger age and had more children earlier and in closer succession than they had ever before or have since: "In 1945 an incredible 31 percent of white women thought the ideal number of children was four, but a decade later the total had leaped to a more incredible 41 percent."[5] The family and the baby boom were the demographic and cultural news of the postwar period.

At the close of the 1950s, 70 percent of all women were married by the age of twenty-four; the average age of marriage in 1955 was twenty-two years for men and twenty years for women. Since the early nineteenth century birthrates had been declining, but this was reversed in the 1950s: "The fertility rate rose 50% from 1940 to 1957—producing a population growth rate approaching that of India. The birthrate for third children doubled and for fourth children tripled. Nearly one-third of all American women had their first children before they reached their twentieth birthday." Almost one-half of all women married while they were still teenagers. Two out of three white women in college dropped out before they graduated. A declining proportion of college women prepared for professions or pursued advanced degrees.[6] This family system, described by Talcott Parsons, was based on clear and strict gender definitions and segregation; woman's place was in the home and her husband's responsibility was breadwinning. Getting married and becoming a mother were the only genuinely valued activities for women, to which women's behavior conformed. To remain single or pursue a profession, as we will see later in the case of Anne Parsons, was to be considered deviant and marginalized. Given the abnormally high marriage rates, singleness was at an all-time low in the twentieth century. This was the domestic culture and family configuration in which girls like me came of age.[7]

Mothers in the 1950s

In 1957 and again in 1976, a large representative sample of Americans were surveyed about their mental health and attitudes toward their lives. Both surveys were published as books, the first as *Americans View Their Mental Health* and the second as *The Inner American*.[8] Both books provide a great deal of information on the fifties and the seventies and are useful for documenting the two periods and the contrasts between them. They are a good way to chart the changes between the mothers and daughters.

The authors of the 1957 survey stated that Americans looked to the home for their greatest happiness and satisfaction. Indeed, every survey, every possible indication of Americans' cultural inclinations and behavior, confirms this. The family and the home were the expected sites of fulfillment for all Americans; there simply were no others. The historian Warren Susman suggests that throughout American history there has been an "effort to connect our consciousness, civilization, and demography to the American home and the American Dream."[9] This effort reached its culmination in the period after World War II. With the economic boom, low-interest housing loans, and a remarkable explosion of house- and highway-building in the suburbs, the "suburban ideal" that symbolized fulfillment of the American dream could be realized. A character in W. D. Wetherall's novel, *The Man Who Loved Levittown*, swoons, "I'll never forget those years. The fifties. The early sixties. We were all going the same direction . . . thanks to Big Bill Levitt we all had a chance. You talk about dreams. Hell, we had ours. We had ours like nobody before or since ever had theirs. SEVEN THOUSAND BUCKS! ONE HUNDRED DOLLARS DOWN! We were cowboys out there. We were the pioneers."[10]

By 1960 as many Americans lived in the suburbs as lived in the central cities.[11] Clifford Clark suggests that postwar suburbs, especially the ranch houses that were energetically promoted as family space, enabled middle-class people to imagine they could create the ideal American family: "For generations who had grown up with the ever-present legacy of Depression frugality, the new home stressed the pleasures of consumption—the emphasis on relaxation, children, and enjoyment."[12] Every major institution in the United States promoted the home, togetherness, and the family. One sign of this was the family focus that proliferated in advertising: "family-size carton, family room, family car, family film, family restaurant, family vacation."[13]

The 1957 mental health survey noted that despite the conviction that happiness was to be found in the family, the family was often a source of deep unhappiness: "Upon closer questioning, it appears that for women the home is also a great source of distress, more so than for men; they are unhappier in marriage, more aware of problems with it. This holds true in their roles as parents as well as spouses; they feel more inadequate as parents and have more problems with their children." The survey continued, "The greater distress of women is replicated in other parts of the study," with women in general more negative about life. The authors remarked on the importance of parenthood: "In the same way that marriage becomes a status one has to achieve in order to enjoy the trademark of a full-fledged adult, to be a parent is also a necessary status for the truly responsible adult." They noted that parenthood was more important for women, and that childless people were "viewed with compassion . . . as people who have missed the full richness of adult experiences."[14] A study of marriage at the end of the decade found that "marriages which [were] childless by choice [were] practically nonexistent."[15]

We know from the reception of *The Feminine Mystique*—its impact documented in memoirs, fiction, letters to Friedan, and academic studies—that many white upper-middle and middle-class housewives did not feel they had discovered perfection in their well-equipped single-family houses. We know, too, of feminine difficulties with a single-minded domestic focus from careful consideration of postwar social science. There is evidence of sacrifice from many quarters, some of which will be discussed below. At the same time, there is evidence that wives and mothers were convinced that despite their discontent, they had made correct choices. These two facts are important in understanding young women's experiences in the fifties family. The older generation's commitment to domesticity was not at issue, but for the women who grew up in such families, their mothers' happiness was.

Middle-class women preferred to be housewives than to participate in the labor force, although increasing numbers of them did both. One survey found that only 60 percent of wives experienced self-esteem in their jobs, especially among younger women.[16] This preference for home was not a real choice since women's career opportunities were limited in every way. Women "chose" to find satisfaction in childrearing and homemaking, as wives to men who could adequately provide for them and their children. For women in the 1950s, there was probably nothing less desirable than being on one's own. A study of wives identified as mentally ill in the fifties suggests that being a housewife provided the only legitimate social and economic space for women:

Those madwives whose fantasies led them to contemplate separation, or who looked back with nostalgia to their premarriage days . . . , were held in place ideologically by the metaphor of old maid, just as they were held in place economically by personal indigence. Whenever the women contemplated being alone, they tempered perception of the benefits of release from an unsatisfactory marriage with the pariah status of the old maid.[17]

The fear, pity, and disdain for "old maids" were noteworthy. Repeated use of the term suggests its symbolic value in reinforcing women's commitment to family. That "old maid" came up often in surveys about women's roles (and popular culture) suggests its centrality as a condition for women to avoid at all costs. Attitudes of young single women interviewed in a 1955 survey were summarized in the following manner: "A particularly acute form of sanctioning of the home occurred in a . . . common phrase, old maid . . . An old maid was a person who had failed so seriously in her understanding or execution of a woman's role that she hadn't even established the marriage prerequisite to having a home. Old maids were not figures of horror so much, nor of abhorrence, as they were objects of somewhat condescending pity."[18] The "old maid" stood as a warning against finding oneself a woman alone and excluded. (Remember the card game, in which the goal was to avoid getting the Old Maid card?)

In Elaine Tyler May's study of families in the 1950s, based on a twenty-year survey of white, middle-class couples, the women's prevailing sentiment was that motherhood was the best job a woman could have and children were their main achievement and reward in life. They referred often to the material and status benefits associated with the roles of wife and mother, recognizing the social rewards. The single most common response to the question of what they had sacrificed to marriage was "nothing," although many more husbands than wives answered in that way. Womens' answers to the question of what they had gained from marriage were framed, not in terms of happiness but rather in terms of family, children, companionship, and security. Twice as many husbands as wives answered in terms of happiness and fulfillment when asked what they had gained through marriage.[19]

Children were more important to women than husbands. A strikingly unromantic notion of marriage characterized women's attitudes. May points out that in her data, and in other studies done at the time, the women were "much more likely to express their desire for children than their eagerness for marriage (a much higher proportion associated pleasure, love, and joy with having children than with getting married). They also gave more reasons for having children than for getting married."[20] Authors of another study of married couples in the 1950s remark, "Despite the prominence of love as a basis for marriage, the wives in this study rank the husband's expression of love and affection next to least valuable of five aspects of marriage. Only 10% of the city and farm wives list love first of all and nearly half omit it completely from their three choices."[21] In yet another survey, single women aged eighteen to twenty-four questioned in 1955 about their family attitudes emphasized children almost to the exclusion of marriage, and "love" as a justification for anything appeared rarely. These women, like the women in May's study, believed that family life was "natural," but it was childbearing, not marriage, that they linked to fulfillment (although it is doubtful there was a difference in their minds, since marriage was equated with children). In a typical statement one said, "I think children bring a lot of life and happiness into a home and marriage. I really think children are the foundation of a marriage. More or less the living proof of the marriage you have."[22] John Modell puts it succinctly: "To be a mother was very much more vivid, important, thought-about, and valued at the height of the baby boom than to be a wife."[23]

Elaine Tyler May argues that heterosexual sexual tensions in the 1950s—articulated as fears of sexual chaos and translated into rigid taboos against female "promiscuity"—were dealt with through renewed adherence to traditional gender norms and, more specifically, by submerging tensions in the celebration of marriage and children. Marriage and, particularly, motherhood were ways of avoiding the sexual impasse in which the conditions for a more autonomous female sexuality were in place but were obscured by the double standard: "Through children, men and women could set aside the difficulties of their sexual relationships and celebrate the procreative results."[24] Although the postwar period was one that encouraged and acclaimed marital sex, evidence of unhappy sexual relationships was not hard to find. Marital sex and simultaneous orgasm were promoted as ways to stabilize the family, and attention to marital sex in marriage and sex manuals thrived. Experts prescribed sex in marriage; the effusive encouragement of marital sex contrasted sharply with the obsessive warnings about premarital sex and threatening admonitions to females to remain virgins.[25]

Marriage was the one site where women were given permission to express sexual desire that included intercourse. Thus pressure on wives and husbands, in a period characterized by extensive media and professional attention to sex, was intense. Sex was considered essential for a good marriage, and sexual failure a source of marital failure. But sexual ignorance was common. All the ingredients for self-consciousness and tension were present. May reports that 84 percent of the wives in her study said their sexual relations were "pleasant," while only 66 percent experienced orgasm regularly. One third of the wives said they rarely or never achieved orgasm. Nearly one in five enjoyed sex in spite of their lack of orgasms, saying they found satisfaction in the closeness and affection. These findings are echoed in other evidence, probably more a sign of accommodation than ignorance. May reports that both partners believed it was more important to please one's spouse than to please oneself and that providing sexual pleasure for one's mate was required in a happy marriage. May concludes that the women made the best of the situation, "keeping relationships intact and defining them as successful were apparently more important than actually achieving the promise of conjugal bliss. Many couples simply learned to live with sexual incompatibility or frustration."[26] Their attitudes toward sex were consistent with the valuing of children and family over love and with their emphasis on companionship as a central ingredient for a good marriage.[27]

The painful theme of difficult sexual relationships comes through strongly in the letters two women, born in 1930, wrote to each other for over a decade beginning in 1953.[28] Pat writes about the early years of her marriage, "Months and months of nightly attempts, . . . with perhaps half a dozen successes (out of which came my first two pregnancies, unbelievably!). I cried in the bathroom as I used to when I was an unhappy child, holding my breath till I nearly fainted, hoping I'd die, from the rage and frustration and shame and impossibility of it all . . . never once in our nearly three years of marriage have we discussed this problem." She continues that her pain was so great because she "couldn't *do* this for him" (p. 69). It was only when she was twenty-nine, after years of marriage, in an affair with another man, that she experienced an orgasm. Her friend, Joyce, writes in 1962 about how ghastly her sexual relationship with her husband has been, how she cannot escape the conclusion that she must be "frigid" although she knows she is not really and that it is not her fault. In return comes the reply from Pat, "What can I tell you? You are quite right that a man who knows anything at all of women and/or biology knows whether she has had an orgasm. You cannot pretend the real thing, they say, but I've gotten away with it for years, just to get the whole thing over and done with.

Maybe I'm frigid too" (p. 259). Acknowledging her sexual deprivation (and incidentally revealing why pregnancy was confirming), Joyce, pregnant with her third child, says, "I feel like a dried fruit in my marriage. . . . And indeed, this is about how my body behaves sexually. The only sense I have of being in a warm, fleshly, woman's body is the sweet awakening the baby's movements create inside, truly inside me" (p. 278).

Central to the letters are the womens attempts to force themselves to accept their unhappy marriages and their desperation at their failure to do so. Pat writes in 1956 about her infant son, "But am I horrible and unmaternal when I whisper quietly to you alone that he is not my whole life? . . . Have you ever felt anything conscious of this sort? Do all mothers feel it and are just ashamed to admit it, or am I unnatural and different?" (p. 75). For her, marital and maternal doubts were inseparable. Pat and Joyce consistently encouraged each other to accept their lot in life and be grateful despite their feelings: "I *must* stop aching for things I can't have and be satisfied with what I do have" (p. 83); "I suppose I really ought to have one more baby" (p. 204). The "challenge," they responsibly admonish each other, is to " . . . stick to it all in all its occasionally boring routine" (p. 108). Thus Pat reflects,

If I am to go on here, in this life, which after all . . . I did choose consciously, knowing I didn't love P., then how much more must I do it properly, and be a GOOD HOUSEWIFE AND MOTHER? *. . . You may eventually destroy the most important thread in the fabric of a* marriage, *. . . that of respect for the Head of the Family. Nothing is so important as that. I'm afraid I must say what I believe to be of utmost importance in marriage, and that is for you to be there when the husband wants you, keeping a pretty, pleasant, quiet, gracious, well-ordered home without rush or absences, or working so obviously all hours to get it and keep it that way. (pp. 205–6)*

Throughout their prolonged misery, these two women heroically attempted to make the best of their marriages and thwarted aspirations. These were college-educated women whose marriages were admittedly unsuccessful and who undoubtedly had higher expectations than many women. Despite the extremity of their perceptions, their forbearance and efforts to shape themselves into accepting and self-sacrificing wives were characteristic of mothers of the postwar period. As the adolescent heroine of *White Girls* states, "Across the valley of cold mashed potatoes, the picked chest of turkey, my eye would be pulled back to what it was always pulled back to, the disappointment on my mother's face."[29]

The poignancy of their lives, of the lives of all the women who suffered from what Friedan called the "problem with no name," was that they wanted more, not that their situations were so deprived. In fact, it was just the opposite. They wanted more because they were privileged women alive in an expanding capitalist society that promised work and education for women, a time in which traditional patterns were giving way to a more integrated and equal gender system. But unlike the women who came after them, they were not young or free enough to take advantage of new possibilities, although they sensed and wanted them. Their lives were evidence of the "strains" Talcott Parsons saw in the feminine sex role. These two women were too young to be the mothers of adolescents in the 1950s, but they became mothers in the 1950s and reveal, as do the rebels and the victims, the underside of the domestic celebration that girl children could not fail to recognize.

In short, mothers and young single women anticipating marriage valued above all the home, the ability of children to bind a couple together, the sacrifice and fulfillment of parenthood, companionship rather than pleasure or love as the basis of marriage. They were committed to being wives and, even more, to being parents. While many were unhappy, most believed that they had sacrificed little or that what they had sacrificed was minor compared to what they had gained. Many women were dissatisfied and hurt but zealous in their need to see their marriages as successful. Despite their ambivalences, they believed it was their job to keep their husbands happy. They were accommodating. Thus the 1950s "problem" of appearances again presents itself, since the appearance of a happy marriage was more important than happiness—another, unintended, lesson for the girls in these families.[30]

It is worth pausing here to consider the sense of self-denial, even martyrdom, that characterized these mothers and mothers-to-be. We see women, similar to those presented in *The Feminine Mystique*, who were invested in being wives and mothers but who, when questioned more closely, articulated anxiety and dissatisfaction. The author of a study of letters from white, middle-class women written to Dr. Spock about his childrearing manual, *Baby and Child Care*, remarks that the letters reveal that the Spockian mothers, "trying so intently to lead lives of balance and good cheer, experience difficulty acknowledging aberrations—a husbandless home, a struggle making ends meet, and emotional trouble in pursuing model mothercraft." Implicit in Spock's advice was the lesson to "whistle a happy tune on the darkest of nights, even when it is inappropriate."[31] Arguing about the differences between them, Vivian Gornick's mother states that in contrast to Vivian's, her generation lived with "order, quiet, dignity," they lived "decent lives." Her daughter replies, "That's a crock. They didn't lead decent lives, they lived hidden lives. You're not going to tell me people were happier then, are you?"[32] As we have seen, the older women's commitment to "balance and good cheer" mirrors the fear of singleness embodied in the pity of the old maid. Even more significant, the culture of the time condemned the selfish woman. A woman who chose career over home or childlessness over children, or from the perspective of the dominant culture, her own pleasure over her husband's, was defined as selfish, and selfishness in women was deeply disapproved.[33] Women believed that family responsibility was good and good for them. They believed in self-denial in the interest of family security, even as the society around them exploded in an orgy of possibility and abundance. Children prevented selfishness because they required sacrifice and responsibility, values still operative for the older generation. In Riesman's terms, the mothers of the girls who grew up in the fifties were inner-directed. "Marriage is not complete without children. It's a selfish life without children. You indulge yourself too much," said one young, single woman in 1955.[34] Ironically, despite the older women's commitment to children, to us, their daughters, their commitment to domesticity and their denial of their own discontent were ambiguous legacies.

Childrearing

It is useful to view childrearing attitudes in the context of findings of the 1957 mental health study *Americans View Their Mental Health.* As we have seen, the authors found that the home and marriage were greater sources of distress for women than for men; their roles as parents and spouses were more problematic for women than they were for men. Women felt more inadequate as parents. At a time when children were considered women's only legitimate achievement, women expressed more negativity about parenthood than did men. In one way, of course, this is not surprising; there was more pressure on women because of the enormous ideological and literal space in their lives devoted to family. They had few alternative sources of satisfaction. Like other observers, the survey authors suggested that postwar child-rearing norms created difficult tasks for mothers. Those norms stressed interpersonal warmth and tolerance as the new criteria by which to judge one's parenting success. They contrasted dramatically with earlier, more practical and concrete goals of providing for and protecting children. In an age that measured successful parenting emotionally, as a "good relationship" with one's child, feelings of inadequacy and doubt were expressed by mothers.[35] At the same time and contributing to those feelings, we have seen, mothers were blamed for children's real and imagined problems.

The common impression of postwar, white, middle-class family life is of relaxed, tolerant, and equitable relations between the generations and marriage partners, facilitated in part by the ease and openness of the suburbs. Dr. Spock's childrearing advice was "easy-going," "balanced," "breezy," and "cheerful."[36] Social scientists contributed to the optimistic, democratic picture of the family despite evidence of gender inequality, strained relations between husbands and wives, and mother-blaming. But contrary to postwar advice and popular imagery of family life, many 1950s mothers, born during the 1910s and 1920s, engaged in controlling and rigid childrearing practices: "Parents want their children to be obedient, to behave courteously, to be independent, to feel close to the family group, and to be religious," summarized a childrearing study of the period.[37] "As the eldest child in a well-

educated middle-class family living on the North Shore of Massachusetts . . . , I endured at least as much regulation of my language as of
my dress and behavior," recalls a woman who grew up in the 1950s. She
continues, "[Even] quite ordinary words (stinker, for example), were
off-limits in my household."[38] These rules suggest the propriety, even
prudishness, with which many middle-class girls were brought up.
Liberalization of childrearing values and practices in the middle-class
family developed less evenly than optimistic postwar analysts and family experts implied. On reflection it is not surprising, given the historical
experiences of their mothers, that many middle-class white girls were
raised in families that were traditional, even strict, about manners, toilet
training, sex education, educational aspirations for girls, and gendered
behavior. The mothers, often of working-class and immigrant background, with vivid experiences of the Depression and war, worried
about scarcity and security. They were themselves only learning to be
participants in middle-class suburban consumer culture, apprentices in
the liberal permissiveness so acclaimed in postwar America. Finally, it is
also worth pointing out that as a child shaped by the consumer culture
of the fifties and changed by the sixties, it is not surprising that I would
consider the childrearing of my parents' generation narrow and restrictive, despite the fact that for the most part the researchers themselves
did not.

In the following pages, I rely mainly on a detailed study of
childrearing practices of mothers of five year olds in 1951 and 1952. The
report was published as *Patterns of Child Rearing* in 1957 by Robert
Sears, Eleanor E. Maccoby, and Harry Levin.[39] Using Sears and other
childrearing studies, I argue that the trends toward restrictiveness are
indisputable. Most middle-class mothers were not unambiguously permissive. This does not mean that they were as restrictive as earlier
generations. Historically children's needs have become more central in
childrearing, and this was especially noticeable in the postwar period.
Thus, for example, demand feedings rather than imposed timetables
were more widespread in the fifties than in earlier times. Nevertheless,
mothers' strict childrearing is striking if for no other reason than its contrast to representations of the casual postwar suburban lifestyle.

Most (80 percent) of the Sears families had mothers at home full time and fathers at work in the paid labor force.[40] Almost all the women did all the childrearing and housework. Some of the women stated that their husbands were helpful, although in concrete terms the men did little. One respondent's comment was typical: "He's a man who just thinks he's to work, and the house is for the wife and the children are for the wife to take care of." Others noted that their husbands would only mind the children when they were asleep at night.[41] In *Crestwood Heights*, the study of suburban family life considered in chapter 1, the authors found that the husbands might "pitch in" in emergencies, like the husband who washed dishes and did laundry when his wife was pregnant.[42] A strict sexual division of labor was typical. Citing Glen Elder's study of the influence of the Depression on the family configurations of the 1950s, Elaine Tyler May explains that "the adults of the 1950s would thus [have been] eager to establish secure families with traditional gender roles that had been so seriously threatened during their childhoods in the 1930s."[43] Mothers who had worked before their babies were born were asked how they felt about leaving work. The vast majority were glad to give up work: "I would rather stay home and take care of my family than work," and "I was glad. I didn't really care much about working anyway."[44] These statements conform to the typical, middle-class family configuration of the 1950s. Most white, middle-class girls had mothers at home full-time.

One of the striking aspects of the Sears study is how unrelaxed the mothers were regarding sex-specific behavior and sex and toilet training. An emphasis on traditional sex roles is consistent with the generational experiences of women whose youth or young adulthood was shaped by the Depression. Although the authors found less evidence of sex differentiation than they expected, they noted that many of the mothers "disliked the notion of doing things differently," and they concluded that the mothers' answers were more egalitarian than their beliefs and behavior. The researchers suggested that many mothers did not recognize their own efforts to produce sex-appropriate behavior, that when mothers did acknowledge differences in their treatment of sons and daughters, "they tended to interpret such differences as natural reactions to innate differences between boys and girls." The

Sears authors concluded that "very few of the mothers felt that boys and girls were exactly alike at this age [five years] or that they should be treated alike."[45]

Since the fifties were a time when, according to social scientists and childrearing experts, boys and girls were being treated more equally than in previous generations, the mothers' explicit concern with masculinity and femininity is noteworthy. Although their answers to queries do not indicate that most mothers in the Sears study perceived and stressed wide differences between boys and girls, 63 percent of the mothers were scored a combination of moderate to high in sex-role expectations.[46] When the authors considered the mothers' behavior and not simply their attitudes, they remarked that there were "surprisingly few" dimensions in which girls and boys were treated differently. However, like other postwar social scientists, the Sears researchers downplayed signs of difference in sex-role socialization. They did in fact find differences, the most salient being in permission to act aggressively. Boys were permitted more aggression in relation to neighborhood children and especially toward parents than were girls. The other significant differences were in sex-typed chores and in expectations for school achievement. Among mothers who were strongly inclined to differentiate sex roles, higher demands were made upon girls than boys for table manners, being neat and orderly, and instant obedience. These mothers were more strict with daughters than with sons, expecting girls to be clearly feminine.[47]

The mothers' responses suggest strong assumptions about differences between and expectations for boys and girls. Mothers consistently expressed concern that boys should not be sissies and girls should be ladylike. Many stated that boys should not be babies, should not cry, should fight back if attacked by other boys but should not treat girls roughly. References to daughters as "ladies" or "ladylike" were coupled with a vigorous emphasis on good table manners, especially for girls. Thus one mother said, "I tried to talk to her and tell her she is a little lady and that she is old enough now and that she isn't a baby like Johnnie and that she should have manners and people won't think she is very nice if they see her eating that way." Referring to her husband's relationship with their daughter, another mother said, "He gets a kick out of her little feminine ways, and he wants her to be perfect." A third mother said, "I think there should be a certain mark of daintiness about them. . . . I think girls, little girls, are easier to manage—the boy played a lot rougher and wrestled and of course she didn't do anything like that." A fourth said about her daughter, "Well, she likes the idea of being a girl because she is going to be a mother some day—and she is going to wear nylon stockings—and she loves clothes and she loves colors and she takes an awful lot of pride in her dresses."[48]

Daniel Miller and Guy Swanson, the authors of another study of childrearing in the 1950s in which mothers assigned chores to adolescent children by sex, concluded that despite parents' stated expectations, "it is still true . . . that, in every case, a majority of mothers try to preserve the differences between the sexes. The boy or girl whose performance of these five activities [shoveling walks, washing the car, dusting furniture, fixing light cords, making beds] does not follow the traditional patterns can still expect censure in many homes."[49] The significance of these findings lies not so much in mothers' traditional gender expectations, but in the fact that girls' family experiences did not prepare them for social and economic developments that were more determinative of their futures. The disjunctions between their family training and changing social conditions were sharp.

The age of weaning is of interest. Breastfeeding was undertaken by a minority, and of short duration. Of the 39 percent who breastfed, 31 percent nursed for less than five months, 24 percent for less than three. Only 3 percent nursed for seven months or more. The authors argue here, too, for a correlation between discomfort about sex and avoidance of breastfeeding. Considering another indicator, we find that the mothers in the Sears survey were early toilet trainers. Seventy-seven percent of them began toilet training by the time their babies were fourteen months old; almost 50 percent began before babies were nine months old. Nearly half of the mothers used moderate to severe pressure to train their children at these ages. The authors found a connection between beginning training before five months and the mother's high degree of sex anxiety (a measure of tolerance with respect to modesty, masturbation, and social sex play), expressed in prohibitions and restrictiveness about sexual play and exploration. The stricter prohibition regarding sexual activity in children "was stronger among the mothers of girls than among those of boys." Thus early and pressured toilet training was not unusual.[50] The authors of the Crestwood Heights study state, "Despite the prevalent view that too early and too severe toilet training may be traumatic for the child, many a Crestwood mother, given the setting of her immaculate home, is virtually compelled to focus attention upon this training." Carpets and nice furnishings, they continue, are "incompatible with permissiveness in toilet training."[51] The authors point to the discrepancy between experts' advice and mothers' behavior. Corroborating the Sears study, Miller and Swanson's study of six hundred mothers in Detroit discovered similar early patterns.[52]

In what the Sears researchers call "modesty training," 44 percent of the mothers were on the restrictive end of the scale (with criteria that included keeping the child clothed at all times or believing that nudity was "not nice"), 16 percent moderately permissive, and 36 percent quite or entirely permissive. The moderate pressure, permitting a child to remain unclothed briefly on the way to the bathroom, seems by contemporary standards restrictive. In hindsight, postwar childrearing was prudish, at least by measures used by these social scientists, which also give us some sense of the standards and concerns of both researchers and mothers. Regarding masturbation, 18 percent of the mothers were considered quite permissive (would worry if too frequent, but a certain amount to be expected) or entirely permissive. The remaining 77 percent were almost evenly divided between moderately permissive (don't want to make too much of an issue, but important not to let it become a habit), slightly permissive, or not at all permissive categories. The Sears authors conclude that the mothers "were not very permissive toward masturbation. They thought it undesirable. When they noticed it, they attempted to stop it."[53]

Mothers told their children they would hurt themselves if they touched themselves: "We just don't touch our body—that would make it very sore." Some mothers believed that children touched themselves because they were dirty or that they would become dirty by touching themselves. There was thus an emphasis on keeping childrens' genitals very clean, especially the girls'. Mothers often stated that their girls were just naturally modest or clean, thereby confusing symbolic and material issues. The conclusions of the Sears authors regarding 1950s mothers' "demanding" childrearing is quoted in the epigraph to this chapter. They suggest that in the case of sex behavior, mothers' major method of control was its avoidance; particularly avoiding labels for sexual matters. "Many families got along without any names for the genital area" and many tried either to ignore their children's sex play or associated it with dirtiness or with going to the toilet. The Sears researchers point out that mislabeling and misinformation were also common and that telling a child not to touch herself because her genitals were "dirty" or she might "hurt herself" did not create healthy associations about sex.[54]

It is important to put these family behaviors in context. The media increasingly utilized sex to sell products. Sex was openly portrayed in movies and magazines, even encouraged within bounds. The Kinsey reports on sexuality were bestsellers. American dating culture revolved around necking and petting, and sexual norms were set by the peer group; young people had ample opportunity to be alone together and experiment sexually. The music embraced by girls and the movie and rock-and-roll stars they adored communicated strong sexual messages. In light of all this, the discrepancy between what girls learned about sex in their families and in the popular culture was large indeed.

In Alice McDermott's fictional account of growing up in the suburbs in the 1950s and early 1960s, the female narrator reports her mother's attempts to explain how a young neighbor, Sheryl, had gotten pregnant: "After a botched, embarrassed and only sporadically explicit attempt to explain what Sheryl had done, she told me, 'Let's say the stork missed our house and landed on hers.'" Of her mother and her mother's friend, she says, "They were of the generation who spelled the words they couldn't speak and followed strict rules regarding what could be discussed in mixed company."[55] Loretta, the adolescent protagonist in the novel *White Girls*, tells of a pamphlet her mother gave her: It showed the "profile of a woman's body with black arrows pointing to certain parts. 'You're going to be wearing a bra soon,' she told me as I looked at it. 'But don't ever say breasts, especially to boys. Call them bumps.' 'Bumps?' 'But don't even say that. There's no reason for you to talk about them.'" When she got her period, her mother gave her a Tampax, a diagram, pushed her into the bathroom, and "then shut me in, and herself out." Loretta says, "The body—it was a feared thing in my family, tended to only in the strictest of privacy. My mother covered her small breasts, as if wounded, the few times I barged in on her when she wasn't wearing a bra; the first and only time I glimpsed my father naked, he slammed the bathroom door."[56] The avoiding and mislabeling noticed by the Sears authors is quite clear in these fictionalized accounts. Attempting to explain the mothers' concerns for modesty and restrictiveness regarding sexual matters, the Sears authors stated, "It is important to remember, too, that many, if not most, of the current generation of mothers have deep inhibitions and some anxieties about sex themselves. Considering the kinds of sex training they report, we may expect their daughters to be not unlike them."[57]

Their observation is another example of the gender paradoxes to which social scientists contributed. The general tone of the Sears report was optimistic regarding the progressive cast of childrearing attitudes in the fifties. In a pattern with which we are familiar, the sanguinity of the authors' generalizations conflict with their findings and their occasionally more sober conclusions. Richard Flacks's account of the origins of the rebellious sixties generation in the social, political, and cultural transformations of the 1950s underscores the contradictions in the middle-class family:

One source of such strain is the difference between the comparatively strict atmosphere in which most middle-class parents were raised and the atmosphere they try to create in their own homes. Another is that many parents continue to be emotionally committed to the traditional virtues of cleanliness, obedience, emotional control, and the like. Undoubtedly, then, many mothers and fathers are quite inconsistent with respect to discipline and demands.[58]

Finally, educational aspirations give us some clue to the hopes mothers had for their children. The Sears authors note, "It is no surprise that boys were expected to go farther in school than girls. Their mothers usually had planned to send them to college, while the girls' mothers were more likely to expect that, unless they were gifted, their girls would finish high school." Other postwar researchers confirm this: middle-class families stressed achievement and autonomy in their sons more consistently than in their daughters.[59] Mothers of girls consistently said they didn't expect their daughters to be geniuses and that it would be up to the daughter if she wanted to go to college. "Oh, well I hope she does well—but I hope she does to her ability—but I think an all around development is more important than scholastic grades," said one mother. Another mother stated, "I don't expect any genius—but I hope she will be an average student, anyway, or better than average."[60] Some girls, we shall see below, recall their resentment of brothers who were given advantages or encouraged scholastically, while others who did well in school recollect their discomfort. Nevertheless, school achievement and ambitions often provided an escape from the dominant domestic expectations for girls.

One of the striking themes of the fifties mothers is how academically unambitious they seemed for their children, or rather, how much they wanted their children to be "normal" and "average." Many stated that they were not "pushy" about educational achievement but wanted their children to get along well with others. The desire for normal children, defined as cooperative, congenial, and well-adjusted children, was characteristic of 1950s childrearing goals. As we have seen, conformity and adaptability were personality traits valued by the new large-scale bureaucracies that employed more and more adults.[61] In *The Organization Man*, William H. Whyte, Jr., asked parents what they wanted their children to learn in school, and they replied: "How to be citizens and how to get along with other people."[62] In contrast to women in the 1970s, these mothers did not seem particularly concerned that their children be special or outstanding, in spite of their greater educational aspirations for boys. In fact, unlike the next generation, they did not appear to think of themselves as remarkable. The younger generation, on the other hand, wanted their children to be individuals, to "be themselves," just as they searched twenty years later to express their own individuality.

Childrearing advice and values reflect large social currents. A number of analyses of 1940s and 1950s childrearing manuals, particularly Dr. Benjamin Spock's *Baby and Child Care*, suggest that the advice explicitly fostered parent-child relationships geared to producing appropriate personalities for a bureaucratic, consumer society. The Detroit childrearing study by Miller and Swanson itself embraced these values and behavior patterns. Miller and Swanson analyzed the childrearing differences they found according to a dual system that defined entrepreneurial families (mothers who emphasized self-denial and self-control, or inner-direction), which they considered outdated and dysfunctional in postwar America, and bureaucratic families (in which mothers encouraged cooperation, confidence, spontaneous expression, and relaxation in their children, or other-direction). The new child was free to enjoy "his" feelings and the present, as opposed to controlling his behavior and saving for the future.[63]

Using Miller and Swanson's terms, despite postwar childrearing advice, the majority of mothers born in the 1910s and 1920s were more "entrepreneurial" than "bureaucratic." The point, perhaps, is that many white, middle-class mothers in the 1950s were not yet Spockian permissive parents. Shaped by the deprivations of the Depression and the war, often by poverty or by immigrant family experiences, they did not easily or unambivalently adopt new values and behavior. They valued traditional family patterns and followed a traditional feminine course. Their daughters grew up in this environment. But those daughters who became mothers in the next decades—influenced by postwar abundance, consumerism, media sexuality, and education and career opportunities—were more able and willing to embrace permissive childrearing standards than were their actual or figurative mothers.

The 1970s:
The Younger Generation Twenty Years Later

In the following pages, I focus on changes that the daughters of fifties mothers experienced and spearheaded. In comparing them with
their mothers, it becomes obvious that many of the differences between
the generations were sharp, and most were articulated in terms of personal fulfillment and autonomy. We see that to a large extent the
daughters defined their later selves in reaction to their mothers' lives
and family training, and in this way we learn about the daughters' early
lives (or, just as revealingly, their representations of those lives) in the
fifties. Data about the younger generation suggest that the most
dramatic change between the fifties and the seventies was the decrease
in salience of parenthood for women. This was evident in the declining
numbers of women who did not have children early and in their relationships to work and family.[64] Furthermore, this generation's goals for
their children and themselves were very different than their mothers'
had been. Images of their mothers' lives motivated many young women
to construct different lives; many did not want to replicate their
mothers' situations.[65] Unlike their mothers, the young women in the
seventies wanted for themselves what they wanted for their own
children: to find fulfillment as individuals. I utilize a number of sources
for this portrait of the younger generation. One of the most interesting
is David McClelland's interviews of the daughters of some of the
mothers in the Sears study. Letters written to Betty Friedan about *The
Feminine Mystique* and Diane Franklin's study of women who participated in the women's liberation movement also tell us much about
women who as adolescents were discontent, many of whom later
became feminists and who attribute their political development to
growing-up experiences in the fifties. The portrait is corroborated by
surveys and secondary work about family and life-cycle changes in
American society since the Second World War.[66]

In the space of twenty years, enormous changes took place in
Americans' attitudes toward marriage, children, male-female relationships, and self. John Modell remarks that features of marriage that had

in the fifties evoked positive reactions—learning to get along with another person, doing things for one's partner, assuming new responsibilities—no longer generated a sense of satisfaction in the seventies. The loss of freedom that comes with marriage was remarked on much more frequently. Modell states that marriage and parenthood, which had been assumed by many to be "natural" twenty years before, by the 1970s were evaluated more critically: marriage was undertaken more carefully, terminated far more commonly, and parenthood was entered into more reluctantly. The basis for marriage had changed in people's minds, "Between the mid-1950s and the mid-1970s, Americans rated the importance in a marriage of understanding, love, and companionship increasingly high relative to the importance of children to the marriage." Modell refers to the "privileging of private feelings as the basis for marriage" and "heightened expectations and desires for intimacy between husband and wife."[67] In one generation attitudes shifted dramatically, and women born in the 1940s were the pioneers.

In *The Inner American*, the 1976 follow-up to the 1957 mental health study with which we began the consideration of mothers, the authors observed about the 1950s, "It was apparently not possible in the normative climate of that time for a parent to say s/he was dissatisfied or unhappy with her/his experience of parenthood." Twenty years later, however, children of 1950s mothers who were parents were more open to seeing the negative features of parenthood because they were no longer so invested in the role. Younger people in particular were more negative about parenting and this was especially true for women. In 1976 there was a stronger sense of the difficulties of being a parent and a less negative moral judgment about the choice not to have children. Childlessness was not viewed with pity. The spectre of the old maid had diminished. "In general, the parent role seems only moderately relevant for most people's social selves," the authors summarized.[68]

Compared to the older generation, a significant number of women in their twenties and thirties had not had children at the time they were interviewed in the 1970s. Many of the women, married and unmarried, said they chose not to have children, although in fact most eventually would have children but fewer and later than had their "mothers."[69]

"That's why I don't have children yet. I'm not ready to give up my career," said one. A married woman who could not have children said, "If I adopted, I would like to have an older child, who would be in school or day care. I like my job, and I would be bored with an infant. It just couldn't give me the stimulation I want." Another said, "I don't want a child; I don't want the responsibility." It was precisely responsibility, we may recall, that the older generation believed was good for them.[70] Of the unmarried, childless women in the McClelland study, many lived independent and sometimes chaotic lives, with job or career and geographic changes common. It is apparent that for these women, unlike their mothers, family and children were options, "marriage and parenthood by choice."[71] Controversy abounds about the fertility behavior of this and future cohorts, but as Kathleen Gerson summarizes, girls born during and after the war and into the fifties are responsible for the "decline in the birthrate, and the increasing proportion of childless women in the later stage of their reproductive lives. The personal decisions of young adult women, most of whom came of age in the 1970s, underlie these rapid social changes."[72] Happiness for the younger generation was dependent, they believed, on making correct choices, choices their mothers either did not have, did not want, or did not feel they could make.

As we have seen, despite women's growing participation in the labor force after World War II, most white, middle-class wives did not work outside the home in the 1950s, and few worked, especially full-time, when they became mothers. It is of interest that in a time when mothers were bitterly castigated for leaving children to enter the labor force and blamed for juvenile delinquency and other youth ills, a postwar study of employed mothers found that the evidence did not support the proposition that neglected and maladjusted children were the result. The study found, in fact, that daughters of mothers employed part-time had better relationships with their parents, were more autonomous, energetic, and aspiring than girls whose mothers did not work at all or who worked full-time. These mothers, the study suggested, provided girls with an unusual model of independence and responsibility. It found, too, that middle-class mothers who worked full-time produced self-reliant daughters.[73]

Many in the younger generation of middle-class women said that if mothers of small children wanted to or had to work, they should. Having been raised in families in which fathers did almost no housework or childcare, it is noteworthy, too, that many believed fathers should take care of children, particularly if mothers worked. Many recognized that full-time middle-class mothers were often unhappy, frustrated, or bored. They said such things as, "I don't think I could go through the infancy stage again—I felt it was a great imposition on my time," or that housework was boring and repetitive, "It wears on you."[74] In contrast to the older women, the younger refer to motherhood as one part of their identities, one definition among many, a choice evaluated according to its liabilities and rewards. The liabilities were almost always couched in terms of restrictions on personal fulfillment.

Education

The greater educational attainment of the younger generation is of course a critical factor in these changed attitudes and in marriage and childbearing patterns.[75] The cultural lag in which the young women grew up, the gaps between family, school, and culture, are apparent in their educational experiences. Despite greater educational opportunities and achievement, many 1950s daughters were encouraged neither to excel in school nor to prepare for careers. This was obvious in the greater numbers of Sears parents who had higher aspirations for sons' college attendance. Even if it was assumed that girls would go to college, they were often discouraged from serious educational pursuits and careers in the name of marriage and family. It is not uncommon for girls who grew up in the 1950s to talk of the stigma of being "too smart." A letter from an eighteen year old to Friedan said, "Every time someone would say to me, 'Oh but you're such a brain,' I would simply wince and quietly try to wish myself out of existence." Anne Parsons, whose story chapter 5 relates, also referred to her unhappiness at "being called a brain."[76] Another woman who grew up in the fifties remembers,

The boys in my class regarded me as an intellectual and showed unanimous disinterest in my company. When I was in eighth grade I lived in trepidation lest I be cited as class bookworm, and defended myself against that threat by going steady with what surely must have been the dumbest boy in our set. He was no fonder of me than I was of him; we needed each other because you had to be part of a couple in order to get invited to parties.[77]

In the next chapter, we will consider the dating and going steady regimen, but for now it is enough to point out how this young woman disguised her intelligence by forcing her social life into "normal" shapes. Since intellectualism and popularity in teen culture were mutually exclusive, smart girls could achieve social acceptance only by disguising their book interests. They had to appear "average" in order to be popular. In this we see, once more, the appearances that were so much of the fifties experience. But as we shall see in chapter 4, being a "brain" or smart in school also created an impetus toward nonconformity for some young women, releasing them from narrow definitions of femininity.

The ambivalence expressed by many girls about academic accomplishments was exacerbated when brothers who did not do as well in school received more support. Indeed, many women of the younger generation look back with some bitterness at how they were discouraged by parents, guidance counselors, and teachers, sometimes contrasting it with the encouragement and opportunities available to their brothers. This is a clear example of a fifties paradox: young women who would spend many years in the labor force were being socialized to consider marriage as their only future. One said, "It's considered more important for a boy to get an education and be able to do things. What little money my parents had went for my brother's education. They didn't put me through school." Another remarked, "When I was a teenager, I was told that women shouldn't become doctors because they'll get married, have children, and abandon their practice." A third complained, "I was in a family of three brothers. Even today, when I go home, nobody's interested in my opinions. Professionally, less channels were open to me. When I was in graduate school, they told me the first places have to go to men because they're the ones who have to make the living."[78]

Many, if not most, of the daughters were raised with traditional domestic expectations about their futures, futures that would often turn out to be untraditional. As this generation grew to adulthood, the rules changed, or perhaps they changed the rules. One indicator of this was the number who married and had children relatively early and later returned to school to prepare for the careers from which they had been discouraged. Others did not marry early and lived on their own, but they endured constant pressure from their families to "settle down." Because the daughters defined happiness in different terms than their mothers' had, crises were often precipitated by their doubts regarding traditional feminine expectations.[79]

One woman who wrote to Friedan described her sister, who had dropped out of college in order to marry: "Her plans are, however, a complete contradiction of her thoughts [because she intends to return to college and get her degree]."[80] Such contradictory behavior was not surprising, was perhaps even characteristic of a generation that was living through transitions from one kind of women's life to another. Even middle-class girls who went to college and prepared for marriage or careers often took typing and stenography, as a pragmatic back-up, one supposes. Girls who grew up in the 1950s pursued a number of lives that combined the traditional and the new simultaneously. The mother of a Radcliffe undergraduate, whose husband was a chemist, had high aspirations for her daughter but undercut them by saying, "You don't want to be a lady chemist . . . They're all like men." Another time she said, "Well you know, frankly I just think it's better if you just have babies and give up all these crazy ideas of being . . . of doing everything else, cause it takes up your time and that's what a woman's for."[81] An Englishwoman remembers, "Our mothers were torn between vicarious pleasure at what we might enjoy and achieve and a fear (born of their own experience) that the bubble might once again burst, that their educated daughters might find themselves discarded." For her mother the conflict was never resolved. While ambitious for and encouraging of her daughter, her mother also undermined her confidence: " 'Who'll ever marry you?' [she would say] as I lost my temper, shouted too much or behaved in some other 'hoydenish' way, or [she] would warn, 'You'll never have children.' . . . Marriage and children were still, it was perfectly clear, the only safe goal."[82] The ambivalence of their elders toward younger women's achievements and the younger women's own internalization of traditional goals created guilt, confusion, and a lack of career planning. "Many of the daughters seemed to be trapped between two ideologies—'traditional mother' and 'modern woman.' They wanted to be both, but their attempts at reconciling these ideologies often seemed awkward and tentative," remarks Lucy Fischer in her study of mothers who reared children in the fifties and their adult daughters.[83]

Members of the younger generation who were mothers in the 1970s wanted their own children to be individuals who understood, valued, expressed, and fulfilled themselves. Their mothers had believed it more important to teach children what was right and to guide them in getting along in the world.[84] One 1970s mother stated her goals for her daughter as follows: "I hope my daughter grows up to have a rewarding life—because being traditional isn't fulfilling for women."[85] When we turn to the women who were the actual daughters of the mothers interviewed in the Sears study, we see their differences clearly. Thus one of the Sears daughters interviewed by McClelland said that she wants her own daughter "to be able to go out and do it, whatever [she wants] to do." The imprint of feminism is clear here, but the same kind of goals were expressed in the McClelland interviews by mothers of both boys and girls, suggesting a new emphasis on individual choice and personal realization: "Morals have opened up. Before it was right or wrong. Now they don't know which is which. They must decide for themselves." A mother speaking of her son said, "It's also important for him to see me as a fallible person. I saw my parents on a pedestal. I don't want him to see me like that. I don't want him to see me as a policewoman. We talk and I tell him that I did something wrong when I do." She added, "He has alot to say and I don't want to squelch it. I felt very squelched as a child." Some of these Sears daughters pointed out the differences between how they were raised and how they were raising their own children. Speaking of her parents, one said, "They emphasized things like proper bedtime. That makes better children, but not better people." Another stated that her mother put more emphasis on how her children behaved in front of other people than she did with her own kids, and a significant number of mothers who were Sears daughters said they were too sheltered growing up in the 1950s: "My upbringing did not prepare me for the world," said one, and another echoed, "My parents didn't let me do enough on my own."[86] Without belaboring the obvious, the transformation in attitudes in one generation was dramatic.

Mothers as Models to Avoid

One source of the changes in the daughters' values was their feelings about their own families of origin and particularly about their mothers' marriages and happiness. In *Habits of the Heart*, a study of contemporary American culture, Robert Bellah observes ambivalence about their parents' relationships in those influenced by the 1960s:

> *Those influenced by the therapeutic attitude often express extreme ambivalence about ideals of obligations and self-sacrifice, particularly when they consider their own parents' marriages. They long for the unquestioning commitment their parents seemed to have, yet they are repelled by what they take to be the lack of communication, the repression of difficulties, and, indeed, the resigned fatalism such commitment seems to imply. These respondents both envy their parents and vow never to be like them.*[87]

When asked how their parents' marriages influenced their own, most young women stated that they wanted their marriages to be different and used their mothers as negative models.[88] One of the Sears daughters maintained that she did not want to marry at all: "[My mother] tried to protect my father's ego more than she should have. . . . My parents haven't talked to each other for thirty years."[89] Betty Friedan's young correspondents also worried about becoming like their mothers. As one wrote, "She has stayed at home for twenty-three years and raised four children. . . . The emptiness of her life appalls me; her helplessness and dependence on my father frightens me." Another survey respondent stated, "I feel deathly afraid of devoting all my time and energy to being a wife and mother and then being nothing in middle age, because that's what happened to my mother in her marriage."[90]

Lucy Rose Fischer begins a chapter of her book about the relationships between mothers and their adult daughters with the following statement: "When I was growing up, I thought my mother's life was a waste of time. What she was most interested in, it seemed to me, was playing bridge. . . . When I decided that I never wanted to be a bridge player, it was clear to me, even then, what I meant—I did not want my life to be anything like my mother's life!" Fischer found that despite similarities in the mothers' and daughters' lives, most of the daughters wanted to be different from their mothers. Although her cohort was a bit younger than ours—she interviewed mothers who raised children in the 1950s and girls born between 1948 and 1958—she also concludes that "most daughters either view themselves as different from their mothers and/or want to be different."[91] This theme is pervasive in the coming of age novels of the 1950s. A character in *Hot Flashes* remarks, "None of us wanted to do any of the things our mothers did—nor anything the way they did it—during the postwar years." Lynn Lauber's heroine in *White Girls* portrays her mother as discontented, frustrated, and controlling. Loretta says that she understands her father's "wanting to escape the terrible monotony of our living room, the clack of my mother's knitting needles, those low, oppressive, predictable nights. I could understand how he might have tired of the way my mother never spoke except to complain." At one point Loretta and her mother are in a public restroom together, the girl at the mirror: "I moved off as soon as she advanced close enough to brush her teeth, not liking to see us together, trapped, afraid of resemblance."[92] Fischer suggests that daughters rejected both lives viewed as dull or stagnant and the selfless

or, in some cases, martyrish family role their mothers enacted, particularly in relation to their fathers.[93]

We find an interesting contrast when we compare these white,
middle-class daughters to black women of the same generation. While
the white women often had negative perceptions of their mothers' lives
and rejected them as models, the black women were much more likely
to celebrate their mothers and claim a link with them. In fact, some of
the white mothers' traits were not dissimilar to common descriptions of
self-sacrificing black mothers, represented as strong, forbearing, capable, practical. Thus Annie Dillard writes of the upper-middle-class
WASP women of her fifties childhood: "They coped. They sighed, they
permitted themselves a remark or two, they lived essentially alone.
They reared their children with their own two hands, and did all their
own cooking and driving. They had no taste for waste and idleness." But
there were significant class and race differences. Black mothers were
often the pillars of their families, and their strictness, repressiveness
even, could be seen as strengths because of the burdens of racism and
poverty. The written record suggests that the white daughters were less
able to be empathic or experience solidarity with their mothers than
were black daughters. What was commendable for one group of women
was a source of tension and ambivalence for the other.[94]

But the daughters' rejection of their mothers' lives was far from
complete. Saying her mother had lived for her children, a woman who
had graduated from college in 1964 wrote to Friedan, "Now I resent (a
little) her not having a full-time profession through my younger
years. . . . Yet I know a family whose mother worked full-time when the
children were small. The children still resent this fact."[95] Ironically,
many women of this generation found themselves repeating—or thinking about repeating—the patterns that so discouraged them. One
young woman wrote to Friedan, "You caught my college graduate
mother's goals for me, my refusal to elect the honors program I was offered, my decision to trade a senior year [at Pembroke] for a quick start
in the baby business." Another who was due to graduate from college in
a few months confessed to Friedan, "Despite the fact that I was lucky

enough to be born to a woman who did not let herself be taken in by the mystique, I found that often my fantasized plans for next year and later were no more challenging, were no broader than they were 'supposed' to be. That is, in my low moments I too considered making a career choice of wifehood and motherhood." And another noted, "I would be the *ideal* wife—unaggressive and feminine, subordinate . . . you know, a nice ball of fluff for a rock of a man."[96]

These are testimonials to the power in the 1950s of the idea that women's happiness and destiny could be found only in the family. Indeed, for some girls the cultural glorification of domesticity competed with, and overpowered, their mothers' aspirations for them for education and satisfying occupations. Working mothers inspired resentment. A girl from a politically left family remembers how desperately she wanted her mother to be "normal," not to work or be politically active. She wanted her mother to be home and to bake cookies like other mothers.[97] The heroine of *Sinking Stealing*, one more example from a by now familiar genre, remarks, "There was no way for a first grader to grasp that the chilly, ungenerous atmosphere at home wasn't really a matter of being deprived of the birthright suggested by the images of blonde, beaming mothers featured in the pre-primers from which we would soon learn to read."[98] The blond imagery is not irrelevant, for the ideal to which everyone aspired, especially those who could not meet the standard, was a suburban, white full-time mother. Assata Shakur, a black woman, had the same feelings:

"Why didn't my mother have freshly baked cookies ready when i came home from school? Why didn't we live in a house with a backyard and a front yard instead of an ole apartment? I remember looking at my mother as she cleaned the house in her raggedy housecoat with her hair in curlers. "How disgusting," i would think. Why didn't she clean the house in high heels and shirtwaist dresses like they did on television?[99]

Thus, paradoxically, mothers who worked or had aspirations for their daughters were often resented and blamed by them. The younger generation learned this from a culture that questioned mothers' femininity by accusing them of dominating their husbands and ruining their children with too much or too little attention. As a young teenager when my younger sister was in second grade I, too, recall being outraged when my mother went to work part-time and was not available every lunch hour. In the suburbs it was assumed that mothers would be there when their children came home for lunch. I was convinced that my mother was a bad mother because although she left a sandwich for my sister, she herself was not home.

Beginning with David Riesman's *The Lonely Crowd*, social and cultural commentators remarked on the changing nature of the American personality and American values in the postwar period. By the 1980s a large literature had appeared that documented the evolution of these changes in the shape of a culture in which the individual and individualism had run amuck.[100] This literature chronicled the celebration of individual happiness and achievement along with the dissolution of any meaning and behavior that encompassed more than the individual. Experts, corporations, the state, and mass culture provided the goals and instruments that hastened the collapse of the family, community, and of morality itself. Christopher Lasch's books, particularly *The Culture of Narcissism*, and Robert Bellah's *Habits of the Heart* followed in the tradition of Riesman's wide-ranging critique and analysis of American society. In their view, we moved from a society of shallow conformists obsessed with fitting in and getting along with others to a society in which community was nonexistent: "In the absence of any objectifiable criteria of right and wrong, good or evil, the self and its feelings become our only moral guide."[101] Internal controls were relaxed in the service of limitless consumption, and a self was spawned that required constant gratification. Over a period of twenty or thirty years, in other words, other-directedness had ushered in the me-generation. The fears articulated in the immediate postwar period had come to pass: secondary institutions undermined the family, self-gratification was the norm, and a larger moral or political meaning in social life had been lost.

In this perspective, the changes between the mothers and daughters of the 1950s mirror the changes in the culture at large. The mothers were shaped by an older culture for whom notions of scarcity, propriety, sacrifice, and family were strong. In Riesmans' terms they were inner-directed; in Miller and Swansons's terms they were entrepreneurial. But we, the younger generation, while heirs to those values, were defined just as forcefully by an increasingly prosperous society that valued individual gratification. Furthermore, our race, class, and generational legacies gave us high expectations for ourselves, in spite of the sexism to which we were subjected. We shared these high expectations with the men of our race, class, and generation. One way to formulate the changes between the older and younger women, then, is to say that we became individualists to an extent impossible earlier. We came of age in the postwar period amid unprecedented wealth, when the corporations were targeting our parents in order to get "a generation that was small in number but high in per capita income to consume more than they needed in their houses, their appliances, their cars and all aspects of personal and family life."[102] Women, in other words, were able to join men in a culture based on individual desire at the expense of traditional institutions, including family and community.

But there is more to it than that, more than the negative picture drawn by the cultural critics. The social movements of the 1960s, specifically the women's liberation movement, intervened between our mothers and ourselves. Our pursuit of fulfillment and happiness was not simply selfish, narcissistic, or regressive. The movements were primarily about freedom, democracy, equality, and participation. They were also about diversity. Economic and cultural changes created the conditions that seemed to make it possible for women to participate equally in society. Freer from family and economic constraints than had been women before us, we were freer to expand and explore. Born of the contradictions between a conservative family and gender culture and new opportunities for work and education, the women's liberation movement embodied the grievances of white, middle-class girls, their hopes for equality and freedom. It codified the enormous advances women were making under cover of the old culture and challenged that culture in which their mothers were so deeply implicated.

Our lives were structured by lifelong tensions between the old and the new—between the double standard that created guilt and conflict about our bodies and a freer sexuality; between the sense of obligation to family and notions of entitlement and individual fulfillment. Many of us came to reject not only our mothers' family-centeredness, but their narrow childrearing practices and conventional expectations.[103] We rejected as models the families in which we had grown up, but as we struggled to work out new ways of living we continued to be shaped by and measure ourselves against those families that taught us about a world in which we no longer lived.

Sexual Puzzles

When I was about nineteen, pureness was the great issue. Instead of the world being divided up into Catholics and Protestants or Republicans and Democrats or white men and black men or even men and women, I saw the world divided into people who had slept with somebody and people who hadn't, and this seemed the only really significant difference between one person and another.

I thought a spectacular change would come over me the day I crossed the boundary line.

Sylvia Plath, The Bell Jar *(1963)*

The truth was, I feared sperm almost as much as I feared Communists.

Lisa Alther, Kinflicks *(1975)*

When I think of my adolescence, I remember with dread the importance assigned to clothes and boys and popularity, undoubtedly a signal that I was not a wholehearted participant in teen culture. I was a successful participant, however, an interesting doublemindedness that was characteristic, I believe, of many girls' lives. I read the movie magazines and saw the movies and listened to the music with pleasure. I pasted Rock Hudson's picture on my wall and joined movie star fan clubs.

Rock Hudson's name evokes a great sense of irony in those of us who were young in the 1950s. Hudson, one of the most popular movie stars of the time, appeared in films as the quintessential American heterosexual man, the boy next door. He was, however, during his whole career, a closeted homosexual, a fact that came to light only when he died of AIDS. The significance of this is not to be found in the daydreams of girls like me who imagined romantic trysts (platonic, I am sure, or at least not "going too far"), but in how Hudson's life symbolizes the postwar era of conformity and intolerance. He too was a casualty of the 1950s, even if his death lacked the drama of Marilyn Monroe's or Sylvia Plath's or the other suicides associated with that time. Hudson's personal tragedy illuminates the underside of the celebration that defined all those not heterosexual or in families as deviants and outsiders. It illuminates, too, the duplicity so characteristic of the fifties. Rock Hudson was in the closet; it is tempting to see that as a metaphor for many Americans, especially young people, who were in the closet and on the verge of coming out. Everyone was keeping up appearances, fearful of revealing who they believed they "really" were. That millions of girls swooned over Hudson in movie magazines as the perfect mate while his sexuality was a secret is a sobering if fitting image for the culture of postwar sexual life.

But these observations are today's, not yesterday's. So I, like so many girls, read movie magazines and imagined myself discovered by one of the handsome, antiseptic white men who smiled from their pages. I spent a lot of time turning myself out, browsing in Woolworth's for lipstick and barretts, working on my hair. I listened to the Hit Parade and watched sentimental situation comedies like "I Remember Mama," "Father Knows Best," and "My Little Margie." I was not a discriminating consumer, but I was probably typical of my peers.

When I think back, I shudder over the narrowness of permissible behavior, both within my family and among my peers. Yet I wasn't obviously unhappy, and I found ways to explore what I thought of as real life even within the confines of my white, middle-class world: I listened to rock and roll, and even to rhythm and blues played by Alan Freed on the radio. Even at their tamest, the music, movie stars, and magazines—to say nothing of the Beats—kept me interested and occupied. If I wasn't unhappy, I was certainly restless—"young and restless," as the so-called bad girls were described in teen films and magazines. I wasn't a "bad" girl, although there was no way that a "good" girl growing up in the fifties could not have been curious about badness. We will see how the images and sounds of both popular and subversive culture fed that restlessness and curiosity in so many girls of my generation, enabling us to imagine different lives for ourselves.[1]

The social and economic transformations that weakened young people's links to the family generated spaces and ambiguities that young middle-class women could explore. In conjunction with new employment and education opportunities generated by advanced capitalism, a consumerism that celebrated youth and emphasized sexuality and appearances translated into a growing openness about and opportunities for sex. Despite their family lessons, girls were quietly receptive to the new messages.

Sex was commercialized, glorified in movies, advertising, and movie magazines. Teenage girls were encouraged to become consumers through the promotion of sex and glamor.[2] The music teens adopted and consumed, rock and roll, although sanitized for white audiences, was charged with sexual meaning. In fact, the permissible boundaries for the sexual activity of the young had been widening for decades. Sexual exploration controlled by the peer group was central to the youth culture that developed early in the twentieth century. Sexual discourse had become a way of articulating, seeing, and encountering oneself: a source of identity for youth as a group but also, by the 1950s, for the individual young person.[3] For modern adolescents, constructing a sexual identity was a means to construct a personal identity. In young lives no longer circumscribed by the family but shaped by a society that promoted sex through its mass media, sex was a culturally recognized activity, even sanctioned within limits. Sex was available for public viewing, no longer private and hidden. Magazine articles, polls, books, and experts such as sociologists, marriage counselors, and therapists provided a national frame of reference against which to measure oneself.[4]

But the growing significance of sexuality in the youth culture and the sexualization of popular culture unfolded amid prudish families and narrow, even cruel, sexual norms. Thus girls were encouraged to pursue the sexual cues that assailed them but were threatened with the loss of respectability (and acceptable futures) if they did so. One sociologist remarked, "It seems that half the time of our adolescent girls is spent trying to meet their new responsibilities to be sexy, glamorous and attractive, while the other half is spent meeting their old responsibility to be virtuous by holding off the advances which testify to their success."[5] We have seen how nonmarital female sexuality was linked to political threats such as the spread of communism and the subversion of democracy. Fears of the power of both communism and female sexuality to undermine the family resulted in a policy of containment for both. Finally, embedded in the sexual codes prescribing feminine chastity were racial codes prescribing segregation of white women from black men and women. "Virginal" was compounded by racial meanings; it was the white girl who was expected to be a virgin. Testing gender boundaries implied testing racial boundaries as well.

Sexual puritanism is a central ingredient of American cultural history. But it is in the contrast to postwar expansiveness, particularly with regard to consumerism and leisure, that sexually repressive policies, a "reinvigorated purity movement," were especially noteworthy.[6] The sexual codes confronting teenage girls were puzzles, not because girls could avoid being aware, for example, that they should remain virgins until marriage. It was impossible not to know that given the virtual cultural obsession with virginity. Girls were bombarded with advice about how not to "go all the way," the only sexual activity that counted, or that was counted by sexologists and sociologists. The sexual rules were puzzles, rather, because of their conflicting images and messages regarding sexual freedom. In short, white, middle-class girls growing up in this period were in the midst of a deeply contradictory culture.

The social and cultural incoherence implied by gender equality and its denial suggests the critical juncture occupied by these girls in the historical development of sexual freedom for women. They balanced precariously on the edge between two cultures. In Raymond Williams's terms, this generation was inventing an emergent culture, one in which "new meanings and values, new practices, new relationships and kinds of relationships [were] continually being created" in contrast to a residual culture "effectively formed in the past, but . . . still active in the cultural process." The values of their parents exerted a powerful influence on young women as they struggled to form new discourses and practices.[7]

Girls experimented within these contradictions and in the process subverted the codes they were expected to live by. The situation was full of possibilities whose legacy would be not only sexual confusion, anger, and discontent, but the youthful women's liberation movement with its focus on intimacy and fulfillment and a culture finally forced to respond to women's sexual concerns. Sex was the site of contestation for good reason: it was the weak link that the culture of domesticity attempted to disguise. Sexual freedom was on the agenda for young educated women, many of whom would, sooner or later, be on their own. Girls were both victims and agents, recipients and manipulators of inviting images and punishing advice, their growth stifled at the same time that they themselves appropriated new concepts and potentials for their own ends.[8] Postwar girls' sexual conundrums and strategies, then, were historically significant, more than simply personal stories of growing up. Collectively, their experiences represent a source of young women's subsequent rebellion. For girls of the fifties generation who were positioned between the world of their mothers and the world of women's equality and autonomy, the sexual story encoded in American culture was simultaneously punitive and permissive. Social and cultural shifts were reflected in the provision to white, middle-class girls of the time, space, and money with which to explore. At the same time, sexual discourses calculated to retard the construction of new feminine identities thrived.

"Going All the Way"

The impression left by personal and fictional accounts from the fifties is that more sexual intercourse was happening than most social
scientists, other than Kinsey, acknowledged and than most girls admitted. "Everybody was doing it. . . . But it was the Big Lie that nobody
was," says a respondent in Benita Eisler's study of young adulthood in
the fifties. Eisler herself remarks, "Of all the secrets of coming of age in
the fifties, sex was the darkest and dirtiest. As sexual beings, people
became underground men and women. For some, leading a double life
was no metaphor."[9] As we shall see in chapter 4, the inscription of darkness into the fifties secret of sex linked sexual fears to black people
and rhythm and blues. Darkness and sex, sometimes in the shape of
rock and roll, threatened white girls' purity. Referring to teenage girls'
sexual ignorance, Sara Davidson corroborates Eisler: "My girlfriends,
alas, were as benighted as me. It was characteristic of the fifties that no
one really talked about those bubbly and confusing feelings, questions,
emotions. We kept up appearances; we swept what was messy under
the carpet."[10]

That approximately 50 percent of the females in the 1953 Kinsey
sample said they engaged in premarital intercourse came as a shock to
most observers of the American scene. Nominally, females were virgins
until they married. All seven hundred and fifty-seven pages of *Marjorie
Morningstar*, one of the best-selling novels of the fifties, were about
Marjorie's endless struggle to retain her virginity. She unhappily loses
the struggle in the last pages, a fictional confirmation, perhaps, of Kinsey's 50 percent and, in her unhappiness, a reaffirmation of the wisdom
of the virginity norm.

Also contrary to accepted values, many of the autobiographies and
novels about women's experience in the 1950s reveal experimentation
with sexual intercourse. But unlike Marjorie Morningstar, the heroines
are not remorseful. Angry would be the more appropriate description.
Fiction such as Alix Kates Shulman's *Memoirs of an Ex-Prom Queen*,
Marge Piercy's *Braided Lives*, Lisa Alther's *Kinflicks*, Kate Stimpson's

Class Notes, Philip Roth's "Goodbye, Columbus," and Sylvia Plath's *The Bell Jar*—all but the last two written retrospectively and all based on the authors' experiences of growing up or being a young adult in the fifties—depict the heroines engaging in sexual intercourse and usually denying and hiding it. This discrepancy confirms the oft-noted divergence between conservative sexual values and more liberal sexual behavior, a discrepancy that was especially sharp in this period. The active sex lives chronicled in the Kinsey reports in particular were responsible for forcing attention to the gap between what people said about sex and how they behaved.[11] Such dissimulation reveals much about the fifties; the older generation of women, too, committed themselves to appearances. Dissemblance, even hypocrisy, were coping strategies for girls engaged in experimentation and rulebreaking. The numerous references to a "double life" and "keeping up appearances" reveal much about how life was lived by young women in this period.

Although feminine sexual disappointment and anger do not distinguish this generation or epoch from earlier ones, exaggerated expectations do.[12] Many of the fictional and autobiographical accounts describing the intercourse that girls and young women had postponed express bitter disappointment. In the novel *The Bell Jar*, first published in 1963, Esther's experience of the sex she had been relentlessly warned against left her unimpressed and hemorrhaging: "I lay rapt and naked, on Irwin's blanket, waiting for the miraculous change to make itself felt. But all I felt was a sharp, startling bad pain. 'It hurts,' I said. 'Is it supposed to hurt?'" Irwin gets up and showers while Esther bleeds more and more profusely. She leaves his apartment, still hemorrhaging, and ends up in a hospital emergency room.[13] In Caryl Rivers's novel of the 1950s, *Virgins*, the heroine's best friend's first intercourse consists of her boyfriend's clumsy efforts to penetrate her and when he does, she feels "this little tearing sensation inside—like a Band-Aid being ripped off" and she begins to bleed. She too ends up in the hospital.[14]

Lisa Alther's description of intercourse in her novel of high school is less physically traumatic, but she can't believe that she has spent two years building up to it: "'You mean that's *it?*' I asked with dismay. It hadn't been unpleasant, except for the first pain, but I couldn't exactly view it as the culmination of my womanhood. Frankly, rupturing my maidenhead had been just about as meaningful as the breaking of a paper Saniband on a motel toilet."[15] After her first intercourse, the heroine of *Class Notes* reflects, "She was no longer a virgin, but after the romantic tales, the hints, the jokes, her mother's warning, it came to this. Big Deal."[16]

The movie star Cher describes her first intercourse in terms not un-like that of the fictional heroines:

When I was fourteen, my girlfriends were all telling me how much fun sex was, that I could get away with it and that boys would respect me— as long as I didn't go all the way. But I thought stopping short was ridic-ulous. I wanted to find out what it was all about so I just did it, all at once, with the little Italian guy next door I was madly in love with. When we'd finished, I said, "Is this it?" He said, "Yeah," and I said, "Well, you can go home."[17]

In *Minor Characters*, Joyce Johnson also describes her first experience of sex as a letdown: "He shuddered against me and cried out a little and it was over. Lying there, I was troubled by an entirely new question: Was this all there was?"[18]

Such questions, asked repeatedly—Was this all there was? You mean, that's *it*?—echo the housewives who asked, "Is this all?" in Betty Friedan's description of the "problem that had no name," the lack of fulfillment from which middle-class housewives suffered in the 1950s. In both cases, reality fell far short of the extravagant hopes of fulfillment fostered by postwar culture. For brides as much as for single women, disappointment was proportionate to the fixation, the waiting, and the glorified expectations created by the narrow focus on intercourse and its fantastic romanticization in movies and magazines. "Going all the way," an apparently perfect and effortless experience despite the lack of prep-aration and sex education, could never have measured up to all the en-ergy and thought expended in avoiding it.

Writing of her youth in the 1950s, Joyce Johnson links the meaning of sex to rebelliousness:

Real life was sexual . . . Or, rather, it often seemed to take the form of sex. This was the area of ultimate adventure, when you would dare or not dare. It was much less a question of desire. Sex was like a forbidden castle whose name could not even be spoken around the house, so feared was its power. Only with the utmost vigilance could you avoid being sucked into its magnetic field. The alternative was to break into the castle and take the power for yourself.[19]

While "going all the way" was mystified and dangerous and could be disappointing, in Johnson's formulation sexual exploration also meant a rejection of the passivity so admired in girls and of the dominant feminine norms that defined women as "bad" if they crossed the line. It signified rebellion. For some girls boundary testing took place on sexual turf. Their hunger for "real life" was palpable in a cultural millieu that stressed conformity and material comfort. Sexual experimentation led toward more liberating constructions of femininity.

Teenage Culture/Girl Culture

We have seen how affluence and the development of the mass media, particularly advertising, created enthusiastic consumers out of those many Americans who could afford to participate. An extravagant consumer society was in the process of consolidating itself. The abundance encouraged visions of perfect, painless futures.[20] Girls who grew up in the fifties inherited this "fervor of optimism," a sense of limitless possibilities: "It was in that moment in the fifties, when I felt set up, set up to want, to want to be different, special, when I was chosen to be one of the children of the post-war boom," says Valerie Walkerdine, an Englishwoman, in "Dreams from an Ordinary Childhood."[21] In the explosion of postwar consumerism, teenagers were a new and enormously lucrative market targeted by the movie, music, and consumer goods industries. In 1959 *Life* magazine estimated teenagers' discretionary income in the range of $10 billion, most of it going to the entertainment industry. Three-quarters of the American movie audience was teenagers.[22]

The story of the postwar recognition of teenagers as a major consumer market has been told elsewhere, a part of the larger, also familiar, story of American postwar prosperity and cultural homogenization. Products, conventions, entertainment, and images with teenagers in mind mushroomed. Only in the United States had the idea of the "teenager" become commonplace and had they been accepted as a group separate from adults. The "teenager" was the most revolutionary invention since the automobile, a study of youth culture argued: "In the years just prior to World War II, there were no teenagers, no teenage magazines, teenage music, or teenage culture. The word itself had not even been invented."[23] The youth of the 1950s, born during the war years, before the baby boom, were the first who could be called teenagers. They were linked by national and generational, rather than local or class, bonds. "Teenagers had a new economic and symbolic power and from it, cultural and political power eventually followed."[24] A national culture that shaped teenage life and against which those who rejected or were excluded from dominant conventions defined themselves, successfully established itself in the postwar period. The conventions of middle-class youth were articulated as if they were everyone's. This hegemonic white culture had pretensions to classlessness that worked more often than it did not. Black and white teenagers of all classes participated, if differentially, and were able to function as a group not only in market terms but self-referentially as well. The ideas, artifacts, and images of national teen culture were disseminated widely. Thomas Doherty argues that "what lent 1950s teenagers a sense of group identity both peculiarly intense and historically new was that their generational status, their social position *as teenagers*, was carefully nurtured and vigorously reinforced by the adult institutions around them." Marketplace, media, home, and school all acknowledged and fostered teens as a separate group. But it was the prominence of young people as consumers and the impact of popular culture that created and spread, in Jon Savage's words, a "new peer culture that existed on the edges of adult society."[25]

I want to mention here an ongoing academic discussion about the capacity of local expressions of difference, of race, class, gender, and ethnicity to invent practices that resist dominant values and to create alternative subcultures and meanings. Some argue against emphasizing the importance of a national postwar youth culture, citing the power of working-class, black, and ethnic groups to subvert and revitalize established social norms. Others prefer to focus on the local and particular, arguing that class, race, and ethnicity defined young people much more powerfully than did a single, national youth culture, but they make no claims about the oppositional nature of this local culture. Still others suggest that the interaction between the dominant culture and working-class or ethnic experiences created spaces for resistance and were the site of subversive and original constructions.[26] But analysts have largely accepted the evidence of growing commercialization, bureaucratization, and centralization in postwar American institutions, and those who study youth note the powerful postwar teenage or youth culture. Conformity, for example, was of great concern to critics precisely because they did assume the homogenization of American culture in the postwar period. I want to make clear that it is my assumption that a national, middle-class, popular culture was a central event out of which girls constructed their feminine selves and to which they contributed.[27] More important, I do not believe this culture precluded resistance or creativity. Girls invented and imagined uses for commercial popular culture that, while not obviously emancipatory or subversive, were effective in their movement toward new definitions of femininity.

James Gilbert argues that "the emergence of young people as independent consumers gave a foundation to youth culture that appeared, especially during the 1950s, to threaten the stability of the family." Consumerized youth culture "severely challenged family ideology" because it was to peers teenagers listened, not parents.[28] This culture aimed at the peer group wooed the young away from the family by creating, as Jon Savage puts it, "an acute sense of *difference* from the adult world." Popular teen culture became a decisive fact of American life. In pursuit of teen pocketbooks, advertisers and the media sought to win teenagers' hearts and minds, and in the process created a generational consciousness structured by sexual and racial meanings: "The advertisers and the mass media flatter and cajole. They seek to create desires in order to satisfy, rather than, as the parent, teacher, or minister must often do, to discipline, restrict, or deny them. The advertiser is, thus, on the side of the teen-ager."[29]

Advertisers were especially interested in teenage girls. In particular, the fashion, grooming, and entertainment industries focused their appeals on girls' appearances. In 1958 young women, "in the commercial teenage vanguard" for years, spent twenty-six cents out of every dollar on beauty products and cosmetics, evident in the advertisements of magazines like *Seventeen* and its competitors. Young women spent $20 million annually on lipstick, $25 million on deodorants, and $9 million on home permanents.[30] Even "health" or, more revealingly, "hygiene" classes in high school featured "good grooming." Emphasis on character was a thing of the past, transferred to a surface image. In no uncertain terms, femininity was achieved through the construction of an image. "Appearance was everything." The most important ingredient, according to the media, was sex appeal. In 1952 the cosmetic industry was selling over $1 billion worth of beauty products yearly. Beauty parlors expanded by 38 percent between 1954 and 1958; bra and girdle sales increased enormously as women struggled to approximate the Hollywood "sweater girl" shape.[31]

Advertising, movies, movie and teen magazines, and music exerted a powerful impact on teenage girls. The ideal female image was unattainable by the vast majority of women, who were made miserable as a result. The image was impossible to escape. Being middle-class and white were the indispensable building blocks, but a certain kind of body, complexion, hair, and face were required too. It helped to be fair in all ways: skin, hair, eyes, and disposition. It was a white Anglo-Saxon Protestant version of beauty that millions of girls of immigrant background, to say nothing of women of color, could never hope to emulate. The lighter the skin and hair, the straighter the hair, the more attractive one was considered. No girl, white or black, could mistake that ideal. In the early fifties, the advertisements in the most popular movie magazine, *Photoplay*, were mostly of young blond women selling beauty products.[32] They couldn't have been whiter. Who can forget the Breck girls, pure, pale, blonds selling "mild" shampoo? (It never occurred to me to even try it; there was no way that weak shampoo could help my wild, coarse dark hair!) The 1950s were the last white decade, a time in which whiteness and traditional femininity were celebrated, their heyday before threatening hordes of young women and blacks pushed open the gates. Marge Piercy writes that these years "represented the last gasp of WASP history as history: the history of the affluent white male Western European and latterly American presence in the world given to us as the history of humankind; Western European culture of the better-off sold as Culture."[33]

Thus to become American was to become white. Although many white, middle-class youth never even interacted with black people in their segregated towns and suburbs, the whiteness of the culture and images suggests a distancing from "otherness" that made white teen's enthusiasm for rock and roll and white girls' interest in unsavory boys, including movie and rock stars, all the more threatening. William Graebner explores the self-conscious efforts of urban school and youth authorities to contain black and working-class youth culture and prevent its contamination of white, middle-class students. Public school authorities attempted to create a uniform teen culture that delegitimized ethnic, class, and racial difference. Graebner argues that adults went to great lengths in their cultural segregation of middle-class youth, undoubtedly with more concern about girls than boys, from the more aggressive and open expression of sexuality in working-class subcultures.[34] It is not coincidental that the civil rights movement, particularly the movement to end segregation, was underway and in the news. Hegemonic cultural representations were a defense of whiteness and domesticity, part of a desperate attempt to maintain racial and gender segregation. Beauty standards that excluded large numbers of women suggest the racial codes beneath the construction of gender.

In many cases the "otherness" was white teenagers' own, the recent immigrant history and bodies many brought to the suburbs. From Eastern and Southern Europe, suburban American assimilation took the form, for many girls, of aspiring to WASP beauty standards. Nose jobs were common among middle-class female adolescents of

immigrant background: upturned, pert noses enabled girls to approximate white beauty standards. "I used to sit in class pushing my nose up,
trying not to have a Jewish nose . . . wishing I had blue eyes, wishing I
had straight hair," recalls a young woman interviewed by Benita Eisler.
In the novel *Useful Gifts*, two working-class Jewish sisters discuss how
beautiful Elizabeth Taylor's nose is. The younger girl tells how her older
sister hates her nose; she wears her hair in a pompadour in order to
draw attention away from it: "She grabbed her nose between her fingers
and started twisting it. 'Stop,' I said. 'Don't!' 'I can't stand their laughing
at me. I want to kill myself. What would *you* do with a nose like this?'"
The younger sister does not understand her despair. "A wild look came
into her eyes. 'LOOK AT IT!' she yelled. Then she banged the mirror
down and came over to the bed. She shook my shoulders. 'See how it's
hooked?' She grabbed my fingers and pressed it hard over the bones of
her nose. 'Then why don't you get it done?'" The younger sister "plays
Hollywood" with her friend: "'Close your eyes and make a wish,' [I
said,] closing my own eyes to wish I'd be as pretty as Doris Day when I
grew up."[35] Another teenager remembers she wanted Marilyn Monroe's
blond hair and dyed her hair to get it. "It is blond hair that—Hollywood
still agrees—all gentlemen prefer, even those with soft beards and barely cracked voices. For Appearances, it is standard equipment."[36] It was
crucial to have hair that could go into a ponytail, blue eyes, turned up
nose, fair skin. Eisler also recounts how an informant who was tall for
her age desperately wanted to be like Debbie Reynolds: "She was little,
cute, and feminine. I wasn't any of those things. So I felt like a failure. I
wore her shade of bright red lipstick but it didn't help."[37]

White beauty standards have always been used to evaluate black
women's attractiveness and the 1950s were no different. The valuing
of domesticity and whiteness for women infected not only the leading
white but the leading black magazines of the postwar period. Idleness,
childishness, and whiteness in women were prized.[38] Like the parent
culture, teen culture encouraged black and white girls into similar
feminine patterns. While racial, class, and ethnic differences were obviously significant, a national teen culture influenced all girls. Mary

Wilson of the Motown group the Supremes, for example, remembers how important an image James Dean was for her and her friends and how they attempted to dress and look like him. She adored a number of white singing groups and imitated them. Other black women recall wanting to look like Debbie Reynolds or Doris Day and other white, mainstream movie stars. One woman who grew up in Louisiana recollects, "A white girl worked at the corner store and she was friend-ly and would play. Talked with us and traded comic books, *True Con-fessions* and what have you, until white folks were around. One day I paid her and I touched her hand. And she said, 'Oh, get that nigger off of me.'"[39] The racist betrayal apparent in the white girl's reaction is un-speakable; racism was part of the black girl's everyday experience. But also part of that experience was the sharing of comics and romance magazines with white girls. The mass media created common spaces that made it possible for girls to share an often oppressive popular cul-ture. Black and white girls alike suffered from white images of beauty.

Historically, writing by black women has been filled with thoughts about skin color. Women of this generation were no excep-tion. In her autobiography, Ann Moody proudly describes being the black homecoming queen in eighth grade and surprising white people in her Southern town because she looked so beautiful. Alice Walker writes about a "very, very black girl":

She was beautiful. However, the word "beautiful" itself was never used to describe black women in those days. They might be called "handsome" in a pinch.... "Beautiful" was for white women and black women who [looked] like [them]. Medium browns like me might evoke "good-looking" or "fine." A necessary act of liberation within myself was to acknowledge the beauty of black black women, but I was always aware that I was swimming against the tide.

Assata Shakur writes,

I hated for my grandmother to comb my hair. And she hated to comb it. My hair has always been thick and long and nappy and it would give my grandmother hell. She has straight hair, so she was impatient with mine.... When she combed my hair she always remembered something I had done wrong the day before or earlier that day and popped me in the head with the comb. She would always tell me during these sessions, "Now, when you grow up, I want you to marry some man with 'good hair' so your children will have good hair. You hear me?"

Assata made fun of her sister's full lips and recalls a girl in her school whose mother made her wear a clothespin on her nose to make it thin. Girls routinely bleached their skin and straightened their hair. Mass mediated versions of beauty permeated America; no one was immune. Black women who were considered too strong, loud, and assertive were ridiculed, demeaned, or masculinized in mainstream media as were the black men the media represented as cowardly, childlike, and emotional, not really men.[40]

In general the postwar media worked to glorify women's place in the home, as wives and mothers, and to exaggerate femaleness, especially female bodies, a peculiarly contradictory project. Even clothes exaggerated women's specifically female features. Lacking any functionalism whatsoever, they were restrictive and impractical: hourglass shapes of large breasts, small waists compressed by cinch belts, skirts made huge by enormous crinolines, and high-heeled and pointed-toe shoes.[41]

Breasts are worth considering here. The masculine fetishization of breasts could not fail to register as one more puzzling piece of postwar popular culture. The crude anatomical focus clashed with body phobias and asexual dreams of romance, but nonetheless, big breasts were important in the 1950s, an unusual comment about a culture. Glamorous movie stars had big breasts prominently displayed. Girls studied large white breasts on movie screens throughout America. Marjorie Rosen refers to the decade's obsession with breasts as "mammary madness," noting that 4,500,000 falsies were sold in 1948.[42] In his study of female sexuality Kinsey says, "American males are said to be more interested than most European males in female breasts. There is evidence of greater interest in female buttocks in most European countries." A spoof on American culture written in 1957 by anthropologist Horace

Miner includes the following observation: "General dissatisfaction with breast shape is symbolized in the fact that the ideal form is virtually outside the range of human variation. A few women afflicted with almost inhuman hypermammary development are so idolized that they make a handsome living by simply going from village to village and permitting the natives to stare at them."[43]

Some observers of postwar America perceive an oral fixation: So many products, like chrome on cars and cars themselves and Coca-Cola and cigarettes, imitated "shapes that look as though they are to be put into the mouth and sucked . . . the Fifties contribution looks like a celebration of the great American breast."[44] Others, like Beth Bailey, suggest that by dating women with big breasts, men showed they could afford expense and command abundance. In line with this, she argues, "just as countless sources told men that they could evaluate women on the size of their breasts, others told women to evaluate men on the thickness of their wallets."[45] Still other commentators link the two great national obsessions, sex and communism: "Since mid-century was a big era for bosoms, there was more print devoted to touching, feeling, and handling bosoms than to any other subject of the day, including the Communist menace."[46]

Although much of this is humorous in retrospect, girls remember misery, physical discomfort, and painful self-consciousness about breasts. Marge Piercy recalls "high conical breasts" and bras that raised "rigid" breasts "till their padded peaks brushed the chin." A woman in Susan Brownmiller's study of femininity recounts the fear of being too buxom, like her mother, but when she got to college in the fifties—that "inflated mammary era"—she wore her "small breasts unnaturally high and pointed in a push-up bra with foam-rubber padding."[47] Girls who grew up in the fifties remember padded bras (and padding bras) and the fear of being found out—by girls and boys. There were an amazing number of bra advertisements in movie magazines, even one for an "inflation bra." The quantification of measurements in inches—breasts, waist, hips—was the standard way to identify desirable women. Beauty contests used measurements as proof of beauty. Numbers revealed everything.

The fetishization of breasts was a gross parody of women, neither sexual nor romantic, even more bizarre in light of prudishness about sexual intercourse and of dreamy romantic representations of heterosexual relations. Commentaries about the 1950s remark repeatedly on the absence of adult images of sex, for example, in the widespread use of twin beds in movies and television and the plethora of infantile sexual obsessions (including breasts). This meant that most young people were sexually frustrated and usually ignorant. "The entire country seemed fixated on sex: young women beckoned suggestively from billboards, movies, magazines; young men were in a state of near constant arousal, but there was no outlet," writes Sara Davidson. Molly Haskell, echoing other film critics, writes of fifties movies, "They were all *about* sex, but *without* sex. The fabulous fifties were a box of Cracker Jacks without a prize; or with the prize distorted into a forty-inch bust, forty-year-old virgin." Practically middle-aged professional virgins like Doris Day were idolized, their age and sexual experience erased. Mark Burns and Louis DiBonis, in their study of postwar household and consumer artifacts, remark on their unadultlike nature. "Color added to the general agitation: cars were colored, food was colored, the utensils and the crockery were colored. Everything was zippy. The Eisenhower years were a kind of childhood for all Americans. To that extent, looking around the Fifties kitchen, we have more than a passing sense of something toylike, childlike—a kind of grown-up nursery." They continue, "Love was a euphemism, too—the ideal was dream-like pleasure. We were so innocent still; none of us, not even adults, especially adults, wanted to grow up."[48] "Childlike" in their delight in the new, "daydreaming" through life, "asexual" and "orally fixated," peculiarly innocent, clean, and deodorized, Americans were described as infantile, interested in fun, not really grown-ups. Benita Eisler says, "Nobody talked about sex in the fifties. Nobody talked about anything." Douglas Miller and Marion Nowak sum up the weirdness in the midst of which girls were growing up: "In that decade, America was a culture daydreaming of a false world, with Mr. Clean, Doris Day, General Ike, and universal luxury, without stress, Negroes or genitalia. We were daydreaming, and rock was one of the sources that woke us up."[49]

Appearances

The variety of images of women in the movies narrowed as Hollywood focused on women as either sex objects or wives. Commentators agree that strong, independent, single, and sexual women disappeared from or were "bad" in fifties films. Passion and ambition were portrayed as neurotic and unattractive.[50] Whether the stars were wholesome and pretty (like Debbie Reynolds, Doris Day, Natalie Wood, and Audrey Hepburn) or blond, buxom, and sexual (like Marilyn Monroe), they were powerless and inhibited, unable to explore life or love. "Sex and brains, head and heart, both in the same body were evidently too hot to handle," writes Peter Biskind. Writing of Monroe, Molly Haskell suggests that wholesome stars "materialized in conscious or unconscious opposition to her and the type she represented," that "if she hadn't existed we would have had to invent her, and we did, in a way. She was the fifties' fiction, the lie that a woman had no sexual needs, that she is there to cater to, or enhance, a man's needs." This dichotomy between the "good girl" and the "bad girl" structured social life for young women in the fifties.[51] Movies, magazines, and teen advice columns all echoed the same message: if you broke the sexual rules you were "bad." Movies desexualized the good, marriageable women (Talcott Parson's humanistic or domestic woman) and pitted them against the sexy, bad women (in Parson's schema, the feminine identity that offset masculine occupational success).[52]

Indeed, movie stars were the apotheosis of glamor and sexiness. Larger than life on the screen and on the page, they created an image millions of girls desired. Girls imitated and dreamed of becoming movie stars. In her autobiography Caryl Rivers recalls, "The women we saw on the screen on Saturdays at the Silver were goddesses. There is no other word for them. They stood at the very pinnacle of mid-century's altar of success. For a woman, no other triumph could equal Being a Movie Star. Nothing could compare—not writing a bestselling novel or winning the Nobel Prize." As Benita Eisler says, "We saw ourselves in terms of the movies. . . . That's where we learned what men and women were supposed to be."[53] Thus a young woman in David Wallechinsky's

Class Reunion '65 relates her first experience with sexual intercourse: "I did all the things I thought you were supposed to do. I put on a pile of romantic records; I poured some wine. Then I leaned back on the couch and tried to be seductive. I squirmed and wiggled and pouted and thrust my chest forward and rotated my hips. All this stuff I had seen in the movies." Predictably, it didn't work because the young man was a virgin and as unknowledgeable and terrified as she.[54] Sylvia Fraser looks at photos of herself from a time when she was in deep emotional trouble. She was always smiling: "These pictures are of me but they are not. They are of the 'glamour girl' I glued together out of tinselly bits cut from movie magazines—Marilyn Monroe's sultry eyes, Rita Hayworth's mouth, Lana Turner's sweater. Like the fairytale princess I once fancied myself to be, this glamour girl was an alter ego I created to hide my shadow-twin."[55]

The female movie star was a fantasized goal, and daydreaming was central to the process. "Thank God for daydreams. I could always escape by mooning away about my fabulous future as a movie star," writes Mary Wilson. The extent of daydreaming about being seen and discovered and the effort to approximate a glamorous look were gargantuan. An adolescent in Benita Eisler's *Private Lives* tells how Madison Avenue defined her ideal. Trying on lipstick at a local drugstore at fourteen, she saw her: "I was hooked. Revlon's 'Fire and Ice' girl became my fantasy self. She was everything I wanted to be . . . (Hours of practice proved that the look didn't work if you were nearsighted and astigmatic.)" Caryl Rivers recalls trying to achieve "The Look" featured in movie magazines: "So I pumiced and I brushed and I sprayed and I bleached and I rinsed and I polished and I trimmed and I squirted and I slathered and I rubbed. And I discovered a terrifying fact. If I did all the things the magazines told me to do I would spend my entire life in the bathroom."[56]

Rivers's reference to the bathroom is worth a digression. Americans spent a lot of time in the bathroom. "The fifties also saw a big increase in the agitation over how we smelt," writes Benita Eisler. Underarms, mouths, and vaginas were potentially bad odor sites. Americans fled into the bathroom to work on these problems, and in the words of Mark

Burns and Louis DiBonis, "what better place to perform these daily acts of contrition that make one 'socially acceptable' than in these palaces of gleaming chrome and glossy two-tone pastel tilework?" Bathrooms became known as throne rooms, "creating a 'cute' euphemism for the toilet, so typical of the period. No Bodily Functions Please." Eisler remembers, "Given a new license to go public with once unmentionable personal concerns, manufacturers and advertisers seized upon the most profound terror of the period in ads warning of the social perils of 'halitosis,' sweat, and menstrual odors. Marriage manuals ... hectored readers with reminders that good sex began with scrubbing and bathing."[57] The effort to control the body (hair, smells, pimples, breasts) was a central project of fifties culture. Recall, too, that a salient childrearing theme was mothers' concern with cleanliness and modesty. Adolescents could not miss the antiseptic messages. Controlling the body was one way to contain postwar fears of sexual chaos and contamination. That sexual and body anxieties were manipulated in order to sell more products contributed to the story of why grandiose expectations of sexuality failed to materialize. Advertisers underscored the disgusting nature of bodies while sex was portrayed as clean and neat; unsurprisingly, the sexual resolutions were often not happy.

"Modern courtship patterns placed premiums on superficial qualities—appearance, athletic prowess, sex appeal. ... Rather than shared interests, goals, and needs, the Technicolor concept of rainbows and happy endings prevailed. ... Hollywood had inundated the public with romantic notions," writes Marjorie Rosen of 1950s movies.[58] Girls were encouraged in a romanticism that had little to do with the realities of sex and sexual negotiation. Marge Piercy remarks that "a generation of women [were] raised to impale themselves on knives or pound themselves mushy on rock, while fantasizing to order about womanly fulfillment, surrender, and the big bang orgasm."[59] The dream of a single, true love won through appearances, of romance as the key to women's fortune, requires an indefinitely suspended emotional life prior to the appearance of Prince Charming. Movies, white teenage music, and romance and movie magazines bombarded girls with themes of love and romance.[60] Everything was for love, for him, for a perfect future together. No amount of material success could compete with the happiness of true love. Stories and films that depicted love's dissolution would start the process over again without a hint of cynicism on the part of the writers.

Exaggerated media romance fantasies reinforced the feminine passivity valued in the rest of the culture. Emphasis on female attractiveness strengthened traditional feminine behavior; females were to be chosen by males on the basis of their media-defined sexual allure. Creating an image, the notion of being seen, of imagining HIM or others watching you, was encouraged by the media on a massive scale and an important ingredient in the experience of being a girl in the fifties. The relentless concentration on girls' appearances, and transformations, as the condition for their success in life—"I was a hopeless fatty! Now I'm a model," spoofs Caryl Rivers—meant that girls constructed themselves with being seen and chosen in mind: "She had entered the world of boys and men, and there didn't seem to be a moment, from when she rose each morning, her skull a complex arrangement of split curls and spike rollers, that appealing wasn't on her mind. In fact she left her hair up for two days and nights before we went for Bobby Vee's autograph," reports Loretta in Lynn Lauber's *White Girls*.[61] Being seen was a critical element in the movie star fantasy, the commodification of one's look became the basis of success. Even the postwar dating system in which dates were commodities that validated the individual's worth was based on display, on being seen, since unseen, one's value could not be measured. High schools became an important place to be seen, perhaps one of the main attractions of attending school.[62]

In American society, the mass consumption of the goods that advertising sells teaches that style and exteriors, appearances, count for a good deal. Some argue they count for everything. Theorists of postmodernity believe this is the characteristic feature of our time, and many, like Frederic Jameson, date its clear configuration from World War II.[63] Owning the correct products, approximating the "in" style, is the means through which people build identity, belong, and create status; they represent themselves through consumption. Surfaces determine one's fate. The individual learns to measure herself through the eyes of others. Image is the most important element in social life. No matter what attributes she has or achieves, she learns to focus on what she lacks, how far she has to go to create the desired look. In this culture, what your body or wardrobe is missing is always more important than what is there.[64]

For women especially, "self-image ... is enmeshed with judgements about desirability. And because desirability has been elevated to being the crucial reason for sexual relations, it sometimes appears to women that the whole possibility of being loved and comforted hangs on how their appearance will be received," writes Rosalind Coward.[65] Being seen is linked, as are romance and fantasy, to the more enduring and unchanging aspects of the feminine sex role. John Berger points out that historically in Western culture "a woman must continually watch herself. . . . From earliest childhood she has been taught and persuaded to survey herself."[66] Thus although image and being seen have always been central to feminine identity, white, middle-class girls in the 1950s learned to construct and imagine themselves almost exclusively through consumer goods and images in the media. The importance of being seen, while not limited to consumer society, is linked to it in ways that highlight postwar transformations and the strategic position of adolescent girls and young women. For this generation, the weakening hold of the family magnified the contradictions created by passive romance fantasies of being discovered (the way movie stars were by Hollywood) and chosen. Love and romance permeated girl culture and competed with ambitions for education and work, with their mothers as models to emulate, and with the dating etiquette that required pragmatic expertise to negotiate. Dreams of (white) princes rescuing their beautiful selves on white horses occupied much psychic space as girls "prepared" for adulthood.

In their excellent 1955–56 study of 2,005 girls from eleven to eighteen years of age and 1,045 boys from fourteen to eighteen years of age, psychologists Elizabeth Douvan and Joseph Adelson suggest that because girls could not plan their futures as boys could—since their future and self-definition depended on the men they would marry—there was a lack of reality evident in the girls' imaginations of their futures.

Numerous letters written by young women to Betty Friedan complained that the future after the age of twenty-one was difficult to imagine: "One night at dinner [in college] three of my friends and I were talking about our futures. None of the four of us had any plans for marriage after college—just to get a job and 'hope for the best'—a husband, of course. Suddenly the enormity of the vague, insecure future without a husband to take care of us, scared us all. One girl started to cry; the thought shook us for the rest of the evening." Another letter to Friedan suggested that fear about the future impelled her into sex: "And to top it off, my boyfriend and I nearly went too far (as they say) supported by *my* anxious feelings that he was all there was to hang on to, and the only future."[67] Since most young women prepared for little other than marriage, these laments, and the situation that gave rise to them, are poignant, even painful. That they recognized their plight for what it was—dependency on finding a husband without a courtship system that guaranteed success and no preparation for meaningful work— reveals their doubled position. Their awareness shows they were caught between two worlds, a vanguard of postwar gender transformations.

Marriage, the only sanctioned goal for girls in the 1950s, does not lend itself to rational planning, as does a career. Girls were explicitly discouraged from planning; their activity revolved around their gendered identity, particularly their appearance. Analysts of youth culture point out that even there girls' activities reproduce the more passive feminine roles, particularly the preparation for courtship and marriage advocated in the parent culture.[68] Douvan and Adelson were struck by the vagueness of the girls' occupational plans, the recurrent lack of coherent plans of any sort, and the general lack of interest in jobs that required commitment. Confirming their observations, a teacher in a small Catholic women's college wrote to Friedan: "I am overwhelmed by the explanatory value of your theory. We have witnessed hundreds of girls aimlessly, begrudgingly, dutifully, doing papers, taking exams, etc. Few of them ever really see any particular future in it."[69] But in the opinion of Douvan and Adelson, fantasy was the only route open to girls, and "given the world as it [was], they [were] more realistic, fundamentally, to be 'unrealistic.'" Popularity and attractiveness predominated in girls' imaginations because, simply, they were the keys to their futures.[70] From this perspective, the entire culture colluded in keeping girls passively focused on appearances, daydreaming of movie stars and romance, longing to be seen and chosen, waiting to become wives and mothers.

But the sexual messages were ambiguous. Images and desires generated by the media could not be controlled and often blatantly contradicted stated values of chastity and lifelong monogamy. Consumer capitalism breeds its own contradictions, incoherence even, by breeding fantasies that can not be attained or contained. Recognizing this, Benita Eisler recalls the double-message movie plot: "Hollywood saw to it that our fantasy selves led straight from that walk into the sunset to settling down as home-loving, God-fearing, hard-working Americans." Even while sexual images were used to attract viewers, movie magazine readers, and consumers, the resolution always took place in marriage, the moral of the story for young women in the 1950s. "In Hollywood as in life, marriage-as-goal is what fifties womanhood was all about."[71] Sexiness never led to sex or pleasure or happiness before marriage. Heavy-handed sexual moralism was intricately spliced with stories of romantically glamorous lives.

But the contradictions worked both ways. The movie magazines, whose circulations skyrocketed in the fifties, were ambiguous. "Out of the staid fifties' abyss these glossy pictures were offering a secret alliance, presenting glamorous alternatives and striking imaginative chords," writes Marjorie Rosen.[72] Sensational photographs of female stars told a different, far more compelling, story than the text, which focused on their down-to-earth, even domestic lives. Ambivalence was blatent in the gorgeous photos of stars alongside scandalized stories about sexual exploits and downfalls or life at home with baby. "Pronounce sex backwards and you come up with EXCESS," says Sheila Graham in a *Photoplay* article entitled, "Is Hollywood Carrying Sex Too Far?" She continued, "And that's exactly the state of affairs in Hollywood, which is going all out in a hysterical effort to sensationalize— only here we call it glamorize—the female of the film species." Graham describes the "pageant of sex on celluloid and off—the like of which hasn't been since the decline and fall of the early motion picture empire." Marilyn Monroe is identified as the "spearhead" of this trend. "Look at the billboards! They scream of Hollywood's new attitude and latitude. Bustlines getting bigger and more revealing, and lower."[73] Hedda Hopper tells the stars "Behave Yourselves!" because they lose their fans by acting immorally. She reports that a woman has written her who will not let her daughter go to the movies: "How can I teach my child one set of morals at home, then let her see certain movie stars, glamorized and successful, flaunt that moral code in the face of the world—and get away with it? To impressionable youngsters it must seem that misdeeds pay off handsomely."[74] A prominent theme in *Photoplay* stories was the immorality of stars who were too exhibitionist, loud, and unladylike, stars who went wrong and who made poor parents, who lost their men, used sex but did not understand what true love was, ultimately paying with unhappiness. But alongside these stories were lush color photos of the glamorous lives of the very same stars who were excoriated.[75]

Jane Gaines's insight about 1940s "fan mags" is true for their 1950s counterparts: "Fan magazines allow the reader to assume two sexual identities—one the safe position of judging the star's scandalous life, the other the dangerous position of admitting vicarious desires."[76] Analyses of fan and romance magazines note that their ambiguities create possibilities for multiple interpretations. The sense that the reader was really better off in her unfulfilled life than were the heroines and stars, who only appeared happy, powerful, and sexual, vied with images that implied a different story. The didactic moralism of movie magazine stories and advice columns and movies themselves competed with the glamor and sexuality that held out the possibility, and likelihood, of a break with the family. It was the latter that girls found compelling. "Double texts" regarding women were common, most visible in the divergence between words and pictures. Using Kathy Peiss's study of early twentieth-century working-class women, it can be said that these texts called for a "doubled vision, to see that women's embrace of style, fashion, romance and mixed-sex fun could be a source of autonomy and pleasure as well as a cause of their continuing oppression."[77] Gaines argues a similar point for young women in the 1940s: "There are parallels between women's use of cosmetics to challenge existing order—parental or social—and the fan actively resisting and transforming what she was supposed to absorb passively."[78] This doubleness infused postwar middle-class life. The puritanical didacticism of American sexual culture competed with abundance, consumerism, media representations, and optimism. Passivity and agency coexisted in the most unlikely places. Girls were encouraged to think of their "work" as improving their appearances but were provided language and images with which to construct themselves as sexual and active. Double texts permeated not only movie magazines but the entire gendered culture. But before celebrating white, middle-class girls' resourcefulness, we turn now to the dating codes they lived by and out of which it was more difficult to see a liberatory path. Coincident with their daydreams of romance and beauty, perhaps intimately linked, feminine adolescent behavior was rigidly regulated.

The Double Standard

The media not only bombarded girls with romantic images, it coached them in practical matters. Teen and movie magazines and advice columns were teaching their young female readers how to get along with many people without getting emotionally close to any of them, a reasonable definition of popularity (and other-directedness). Theirs was a culture founded on "patterned, social, intellectual, and physical competence. . . . The socially successful girl was the one who acted *as if* she was sexually mature, but who [did] not allow herself to feel the emotions which she appeared to be acting out," writes Charles Brown in his study of teen magazines.[79] The conflicting nature of the advice given to teens was similar to that given by Dr. Spock to insecure parents during the same period. While Spock reassured parents who were confused by evolving childrearing norms and the barrage of advice directed at them by admonishing them to trust their own instincts, he simultaneously undermined their authority by upholding peer, in contrast to, parental standards.[80] While much of the advice in teenage advice columns and books upheld peer-group norms, it contradictorily told teenage girls to trust their own impulses. They were repeatedly admonished to "be yourself, like yourself, accept yourself" and popularity would naturally follow.[81] Teen and childrearing advice had in common the conflicting encouragement to be oneself and guidance in other-directedness.[82] Clearly hypocritical, since what really mattered was popularity and acceptance, for parents by their children and children by other children, this bifurcated advice revealed a deep ambivalence in postwar values. As the society shifted from scarcity to abundance, from a producer-driven to a consumer-driven economy, from accumulation to spending, one's "own" inclinations, if they could be said to exist at all, would not do as a guide for behavior. The noisier that advice, the more obvious it became that the most important message was its opposite, to fit in.

For girls who lived through it, just hearing the word "popularity" is enough to generate a cold sweat. Caryl Rivers says simply, "Popular. It was a big word at mid-century," and Benita Eisler remarks, "What was an immortal soul, compared with popularity's incandescent aura? Breathed there an adolescent in the America of the fifties who did not know its every permutation and calibration?"[83] Social analysts refer to popularity as an obsession of teenage culture, particularly among girls. In his study of a high school in the 1950s, Jules Henry states, "By the time she is twelve, an American girl is preoccupied with proving, by becoming 'popular' with boys, that she is female, and in this task she is alternately cheered and goaded by her family . . . Much of the time when girls talk about 'popularity' they mean 'sought after by boys.'" Jessie Bernard notes that the numerous magazines aimed at teenage girls reveal "the major positive—fun and popularity—and negative—overweight or underweight and adolescent acne—values of its readers. How to be attractive in order to be popular in order to have fun is the major burden of their contents."[84]

Girls' popularity was based on attractiveness and "good clothes" and a certain kind of poise more characteristic of middle-class than lower-class girls. In general, criteria for success were superficial, generated by consumer culture and mediated through the peer group. They were also white. We have seen how paragons of beauty—or even more accurately, "prettiness" or "cuteness," the latter a common fifties category (another sign of childishness)—were fair and wholesome. They represented qualities possessed by only a minority of girls and achievable by others only through sustained effort to restrain dark and unruly physical or emotional traits. Being middle-class was also important. Clothes, money, and coming from the right neighborhood weighed heavily.[85]

Douvan and Adelson remark on the more repressed sexuality of the teenage girl, in contrast to the boy, and suggest that popularity depended on negotiating heterosexual social life successfully. This required of the girl the ability to charm and please without giving too much of herself: "Feminine sexuality, consciously inhibited from active and direct expression, seeks more subtle, limited and covert expression. The search for popularity, the effort to charm, all the many and varied interpersonal ties which serve as setting for the girls' practice in winning and maintaining love—these engagements filter and express a good deal of the girls' erotic need." Barbara Ehrenreich puts it less elegantly: "The pedagogical burden of high school was a four-year lesson in how to use sex instrumentally: doling out just enough to be popular with boys and never enough to lose the esteem of the 'right kind of kids.'"[86] Girls in the 1950s were taught to use sex as a power lever, which made it difficult for sex to relate directly to erotic or affectionate feelings. This undoubtedly contributed to sexual disappointment, since, as Nora Johnson wrote in a 1959 article on sex and the college girl, "at the first feeling of lust her mind begins working at a furious rate. Should she or shouldn't she?"[87] The absence of female passion was a much noted phenomenon in the fifties in numerous references to and jokes about female frigidity. Older women, their generational "mothers," worried about and were accused of frigidity. The younger woman, after all the negotiations and deals, Johnson says, was expected "to shed her clothes and hop into bed with impassioned abandon." She was expected, in Ira Reiss's words, to be unaware "what strange companions love and propriety are," a feat not easily accomplished.[88] Young women were required to chart a treacherous path between the demands of popularity and sexuality, which, because of the double standard, required being "crafty, cool, and careful." Strategy, not imagination, and certainly not fantasy, was what counted.[89] Complex rules and conventions were the underside of media glamor, a way to check, even squelch, young feminine sexuality. Teenage sexual etiquette, dating and going steady, channeled female sexuality into a routinized sexual system that controlled and punished female spontaneity and ensured that young women followed the prescribed steps to marriage.

A complicated dating system enforced the premarital sexual taboo. Unsurprisingly, the obsession with virginity appeared when it was too late to enforce, which accounts for the suspicious energy with which it was promulgated. Too many factors conspired to make it an impossible, even obsolete, norm. The oral contraceptive delivered the death blow in the early 1960s (although it was not available to single women until later). While this seems obvious in retrospect, the unhappiness, even terror, that punitive categories elicited are central to this generation's story. The preoccupation with virginity, or sexual intercourse, articulated an extreme double standard; punishment that followed from its violation was visited only on females. It is worth mentioning that marriage counselors and teen advisors believed that females were less sexual than males, a belief with a venerable history and one that suggests that the double standard did not represent real deprivation for girls. They warned girls that males had animalistic urges. Needless to say, these advisors recommended chastity before marriage and a long courtship, which, they argued, seemed to have the effect of diffusing and sublimating sexual expression in the male.[90]

The fear of being known as a "bad girl" loomed as terrible punishment for girls who were not careful and served to control and create distinctions between them. A woman remembers her terror in the sixth grade: "Lessons, lectures, what one must do. You must be careful with your reputation. . . . I feel eyes on me, expectant. They are waiting to see what kind of girl you will turn into once your period starts. Good girl or bad?" Vivian Gornick describes her difficult relationship with her mother: "Compounding our struggle, stimulating our anguish, swelling our confusion was sex. . . . Safeguarding my virginity was a major occupation. Every boy I brought into the house made my mother anxious."[91] Others remember the gossip, particularly by the girls, that could bring a girl down. The male hero of *Going All the Way* muses about girls and sex and is worth quoting at length:

The ones who made out with guys and weren't in the right clubs and came from big, poor families usually got the reputation of being sluts. But you take a girl like DeeDee, she was always in the in group, and in the top clubs and sororities, and she wouldn't do it with a guy unless she was going steady or pinned or chained to him, and that made it all right, that wasn't being whorish or anything, even though if you counted up, she had gone steady and been pinned and chained to a hell of a lot of guys, ever since she'd been a freshman in high school. But getting laid by all those guys didn't count against her. Also, it didn't count against her to do it with a guy she used to go steady with or be pinned to or chained to. . . . All in all, if you figured it out, DeeDee Armbrewster had probably fucked a pretty fair number of guys between the ages of fourteen and twenty-one, but there wasn't a guy or girl in town who would have thought her a slut.[92]

In other words, coming from the middle class and being popular exempted some girls from censure. Barbara Raskin writes in *Hot Flashes*, "It was not that Prettygirls were actually prettier than we were; but rather that they always looked like Nicegirls who Didn't (But Who Really Did.)" In Michael Anania's novel about the fifties, an apparently chaste cute couple ("two really swell personalities") engage in oral sex, which others in their high school discover. Portraying students' reactions, Anania suggests how "going all the way" calls forth "secret longing and late, anonymous telephone calls that went to girls who were said to have *done it*, the standard *it*, the ones who *came across* and *put out*." The fear of being found out, of being judged promiscuous, was deep and internalized by many girls. "Our list of sexual pejoratives was suitably long—boy crazy, fast, cheap, hard rock, man-hungry, pushover, pickup, round heeler, makeout artist," Sylvia Fraser recalls.[93] Another major factor was the fear of pregnancy.

I mention only in passing, despite its importance, the terror of pregnancy, shared by all girls who considered or engaged in sexual intercourse. It mediated girls' appropriation of the pleasure-seeking ethos of sexualized consumerism and diminished their pleasure of heterosexual sex. The point, again, is not that this fear was unique to white, middle-class adolescents in the postwar years, but that the juxtaposition of sexual opportunities and encouragement with ignorance, condemnation, humiliation, and the unavailability of birth control is unusual. The contrasts consistently distinguish this time. Girls' recollections are often of real panic they might get pregnant, one of the deciding reasons they did not engage in intercourse. If they did, their fear often prevented them from enjoying sex. Middle-class white girls were whisked out of school and sight if they became pregnant, their babies put up for adoption, a disgrace to their families. Others married early. Sylvia Fraser puts it this way when her friend finds herself pregnant: "Lulu is pregnant. Lulu is over. She is no more." Stories abound of looking for a doctor to perform an abortion, of ignorance about and the impossibility of obtaining birth control, of the disappearance or forced marriage of pregnant high school girls. Unmarried women could only with luck and perseverance obtain birth control and then usually only in cities. Mothers were in general nervous and conventional, instructing daughters to be ladylike and chaste, and offering them little sex education.[94]

Going Steady

The postwar dating system was based on careful negotiation of heterosexual social life and feminine restraint. A peer-controlled system of dating had been evolving since the 1920s. Historians of courtship agree that this system seems to have been perfected as a means of mate selection in the post–World War II years: "Going steady became the linchpin of the whole system of developing adolescent heterosexual relationships in the 1950s." By the 1930s going steady was common, although its meaning continued to evolve so that by the postwar period dating and going steady had lowered the marriage age and brought "dating and marriage into closer articulation."[95] One girl recalls, "Even though we had just kissed each other goodnight, it seemed very normal that we were just going to go through the process of getting pinned and engaged and we were going to get married."[96] There was a direct progression from dating and going steady to marriage; going steady in fact predicted prompt marriage. The dating system was one of the factors that led to earlier marriage after the war.[97]

"What I wouldn't give to be going steady with anyone just to get out of the rat race," says one teenage girl. Of girls who go steady, she says, "Half of them admit its just for the social security. Going steady doesn't have to mean you're madly in love. . . . It just means you like one boy better than the rest."[98] Going steady was a way to play it safe not only sexually, but as John Modell suggests, a "youth-controlled, ritually solemnized sequence of stages of commitment, ideally eventuating in marriage" created order out of the independence and space postwar youth had inherited.[99] The shift from the 1920s' and 1930s' ideal of many and varied dates to the postwar ideal of going steady as symbols of popularity had its sources in a need for security that paralleled the adult celebration of domesticity. "The 'home' found a junior counterpart in the steady couple," Modell remarks, and Beth Bailey points out that teenagers reproduced married life.[100] By the first year of high school, millions of American teenagers were launched on a lifetime of serial monogamy. One girl remembers, "You latched onto a boyfriend and started to go steady in ninth grade. It was the security thing."[101]

In general, there are two explanations for the dramatic drop in the marriage age. The first is the widening gap between the world of youth and of adults that meant an unfamiliar, even frightening, independence for young people; going steady and early marriage were coping strategies. The second is that early marriage was encouraged as a solution to the conflicting sexual messages young people received. Studies of teenage sexual practices during this period suggest that going steady increased because imitating marriage gave girls permission to engage in sexual activity without risking a bad reputation. Marriage solved girls' dilemmas; there was more intercourse at an earlier age but the partners were married. In *Heartbreak Hotel* the heroine's boyfriend tries to persuade her to get married because her unwillingness to pet or have intercourse has made him sexually frustrated: "We'd have a place, an apartment, the old man would pay for it and for us to finish school. And we'd be—together all the time. We are going to after graduation anyway, you knew that. I just don't think I can wait any longer." Again, Dan Wakefield's male hero wittily captures the point: "It seemed like unless you were married and had your own place, you had to be a combination acrobat, woodsman, and stud to ever make out. Which is why some kids got married, so they could fuck when they wanted without getting thorns in their ass or find themselves putting on a show for a bunch of bushwhackers."[102]

It was the girl's work to control the sexual interaction in order to maintain her reputation.[103] Media and schools gave female adolescents expert instruction in techniques of deflecting, graciously of course, advances (for example, change the subject if a boy is forward). Movie magazines combined the infatuation with stars with practical advice to young people, often using the stars as models to live by or as founts of wisdom.[104] How "far will she go" was the question on both sexes' minds. Douvan and Adelson were direct in their appraisal: "The dating system, as we find it in the middle class, forces its participants to be their own executioners of impulse," and is based on the girl's prior socialization against sensuality.[105]

Plath's Esther says that the only real difference between young people in the fifties was whether they had slept with someone. But necking was a different story. In Caryl Rivers's words, "Going all the way was perilous, bad for the reputation and probably sinful. Necking was another story. Everybody necked. It was considered quite respectable." Jane Lazarre describes herself at fourteen "making out" in the same room with another couple similarly occupied. She wonders if they are "going all the way" and if it would sound different? "If I listen carefully enough will I be able to sense the moment when that infamous border, that mythical line, is crossed? Will I hear a new sort of sigh? One that I have never heard before?"[106]

Almost all studies of sexual behavior propose that although petting became more widespread in the postwar period, the dramatic sexual changes had come at the turn of the century when premarital intercourse increased and in the 1920s and 1930s when petting significantly increased.[107] What seems to best characterize youth practices in the postwar period was the widespread acceptance of necking and petting within the context of a dating system. Beth Bailey suggests that the significance of necking and petting "lay in their naming, in their rise to conventionality, and in their symbolic importance to youth. Sex was accepted by youth, male and female. Necking and petting were public conventions, expected elements in any romantic relationship between a boy and a girl." Kinsey's 1940s and 1950s studies of male and female sexuality indicated that although nearly 50 percent of the female sample said they had engaged in premarital intercourse with one partner, much of it in the year or two preceding marriage, this was a gradual increase from earlier decades of the twentieth century. It was only in the 1960s and later that premarital intercourse increased dramatically for females. Kinsey, too, found widespread petting, which he considered a middle-class convention devised to delay gratification.[108]

Commentators point out that the taboo was on intercourse and not precoital sexual activity. This meant that many girls could engage in considerable sexual behavior without violating the taboo. Extensive petting led observers to refer to girls as "technical virgins." Going steady achieved what was difficult to achieve in dating, the association of sex with affection, critical from girls' point of view because of the double standard. The goal-oriented fixation of the media and social scientists and experts on intercourse as the only meaningful, the essential, sexual activity, to say nothing of their assumption of heterosexuality, is noteworthy. Practices leading up to penetration were of little interest to researchers. In their view, necking, petting, touching, and oral sex did not "count." Using this definition, young women could engage in a wide variety of sexual practices without jeopardizing their virginity. Clearly these categories and definitions mystified intercourse.

Thus although the social scientific surveys indicate little evidence of a dramatic increase in sexual intercourse among teenagers in the postwar period, adults believed there was such an increase. Petting, dating, and going steady—peer-organized practices—fueled fears about teenage sex and female sexuality. Going steady, in particular, frightened parents because it seemed to invite sexual intimacy. Throughout the twentieth century, sex had been a developing part of the discourse by and about youth and youth culture and adults had tried to control and defuse it. Their efforts were especially frenetic in this period because teenage culture was too much a part of consumer society, youth too separate, and daughters potentially too independent for control to be successfully reinstated. Despite survey findings that the turn of the century and the twenties had been the critical periods of change in sexual behavior in the twentieth century, something *was* happening in the postwar period. The salience of sex in girls' lives increased. Peer relations and popular culture's encouragement of girls to consider themselves sexual beings did not fall on deaf ears. Adults intuitively understood this, social science survey findings to the contrary.

Although boys wanted to pursue sex further than did girls, boys condemned girls who gave too much of themselves sexually and in general had more conservative sexual values than girls. Boys did not set limits on sexual interactions but disapproved of girls who behaved as boys wanted them to. Boys' condemnation of girls who "went all the way" often prevented girls from pursuing sex as far as they would have liked.[109] In an autobiographical essay, Jane Lazarre describes petting with a boy who then calls her a whore, saying that if any boy had done with his sister what he had done with her, he'd kill him.[110] A large 1950s college student survey found that "the degree of physical activity actually experienced or considered permissible is among males *inversely* related and among females *directly* related to the intensity of familiarity and affection in the male-female relation." Being in love meant a decrease among males and an increase among females in the incidence of premarital intercourse and in the acceptance of this behavior, especially just prior to marriage, when most premarital intercourse took place. Distinct and distant male and female cultures existed; girls felt justified and less guilty when they were more emotionally involved and boys preferred to have intercourse with someone they did not care for or would not marry because other girls were "too good."[111]

A sexual struggle was underway in which what was considered appropriate and what was attained were constantly negotiated. The metaphor of sex as a struggle or contest is especially instructive for the fifties: "Bodies became battlegrounds, shooting ranges, scorecards. Behaviors besides satisfaction itself grew in importance. Conquest, titillation, deception, and manipulation were regarded as pleasurable in themselves," write Douglas Miller and Marion Nowak. In his analysis of twentieth-century masculinity, Joe Dubbart concurs: "As there was a cold war in politics, there was a psychic war between the sexes."[112] The level of intimacy females considered permissible and felt guilty about if they went beyond was always less than the level males wanted to reach. Margaret Mead says of petting among the young in American society, "The first rule of petting is the need for keeping complete control of just how far the physical behavior is to go; one sweeping impulse, one acted out desire for complete possession or complete surrender, and the game is lost." Mead continues, "The boy is expected to ask for as much as possible, the girl to yield as little as possible."[113] The hero of one of Russell Banks's stories makes this experience graphic: He wants to get even "with all those Catholic schoolgirls who'd said, 'Stop,' and I stopped, all those passionate plunges frozen in agonizing positions in midair over car seats, sofas, daybeds, carpeted living room floors, beach blankets and hammocks, all those semen-stained throw pillows on the asbestos tile floors of pine-paneled basement dens."[114]

As would be expected, in boys' representations of sex, boys were active and girls passive. More interesting for our purposes was the fear that sex might elude the male's control if it were not sanitized, idealized, and negotiated, all of which kept girls in check. This fear is critical to the gender narrative of the fifties. Anania's male narrator says, "Like the Bomb, whose power bent back on us in nightmare, sex threatened to take more than it gave. Sex was something you did to a girl, an act through which she was defeated; the fear was always that she would do something to you in the process."[115] Here, too, is the analogy of the frightening power of the atom or hydrogen bomb with female sexuality. Russell Banks's hero says about the young woman whom he plans to marry until he discovers she is not a virgin, "The absence of [her] virginity meant that I could no longer idealize her, could not deal with her as an abstraction. It removed her, and therefore me, from ritualized sex, which was the only kind of sex that did not terrify me."[116] Ideology about female virginity structured young men's sex lives too. There is no way that young men could be immune to the adult fears of uncontrolled female sexuality and sexual chaos that were such important cultural themes in the fifties. We have seen how anxiety regarding personal and political uncertainties generated ideologies of containment. In this context, ambivalence about mutual heterosexual sex and comfort in ritualized sex, central to which was male activity and control and female passivity and inexperience, is unsurprising.[117]

It has been impressed upon the heroine of *The Bell Jar* that she has to "save" herself for her husband, and her boyfriend has given the impression he approves and is doing the same. When Buddy confesses he is in fact not a virgin, Esther realizes that he has all along been pretending innocence. She says that it isn't the idea of Buddy sleeping with someone that bothers her so much: "What I couln't stand was Buddy's pretending I was so sexy and he was so pure, when all the time he'd been having an affair with that tarty waitress and must have felt like laughing in my face." Although her mother sends her articles defending chastity until marriage, Esther muses, "I couldn't stand the idea of a woman having to have a single pure life and a man being able to have a double life, one pure and one not."[118] Esther makes up her mind to lose her virginity so as not to be at a disadvantage vis-à-vis her future, undoubtedly impure, husband. As the female gatekeeper of the double standard, she feels she has been duped. She has believed she was keeping both Buddy and herself pure for each other, but he has all along been having sex with a "tarty waitress" (the other kind of girl, a "bad girl," unsurprisingly working class). Esther's experience is of a perfectly operating double standard. Buddy would in fact not be laughing in her face, since he wanted the woman he married to be a virgin. He would have had trouble if Esther "had gone all the way" with him. Taking up her own life, she calmly chooses someone for just that purpose.

Sex was a stage in which girls jockeyed for leverage, trying to minimize their vulnerability and maximize their popularity and, perhaps, their exploration. It was contested terrain. Elizabeth Ewen gives us one way to think about it: "[Sex became] a kind of putting out system or piece-work. . . . You give little pieces but not the final product. Reserving the final prize speaks to an older moral system but now the man gets a taste of the final product. Just as the consumer culture takes women's bodies and objectifies them into parts, lips, breasts, underarms . . . sex is designed this way too. The ritual of sexuality becomes compartmentalized, broken into separate parts."[119] Beth Bailey's central interpretation of dating is as a system of exchange in which money was the medium that assured access to women: "In dating, American young people sought their 'personal welfare' through dates (and later through steadies), as commodities that afforded public validation of popularity, of belonging, of success." She argues that dating was about competition and was based on notions of scarcity and abundance: Dating and going steady "valued the scarce resource over the plentiful one, and both located power in the control of scarce resources." Within this system, girls had to have veto power for the system of sexual control to function; they were responsible for sex, blamed for transgressions, and more valued the more chaste they were. Bailey points out that "cheap," the standard tag for females who "went too far," meant that such girls were of low market value. To avoid being considered cheap, it was in a girl's interest to maintain her virtue through "scarcity"; "Courtship . . . was construed and understood in models and metaphors of modern industrial capitalism."[120]

Commodification structured courtship rituals and created bizarre distinctions, for example, in the numerical quantification of women's attractiveness through the use of breast-waist-hip measurements or in the patterns of American courtship, which were "based on a series of breaks between looking and going to bed," each activity concluded because it was taboo to proceed further.[121] As if acknowledging the "putting out" system, in its dual meanings, young women displayed signs of how far they had gone with steady boyfriends. Class rings, ID bracelets, letter sweaters and jackets, fraternity pins, engagement rings, all signaled stages leading to marriage when the couple could "do it" legitimately. When her boyfriend Joe Bob gives her his class ring to wear, Ginny, the heroine of the novel *Kinflicks*, says, "Hullsport High tradition required that each new material commitment between a couple signals a new array of carnal privileges. We both knew, by the instinct that tells birds when to migrate and where, that the unexplored territories below the waist were now up for grabs."[122] In the novel *Heartbreak Hotel*, Anne River Siddons gives a detailed account of the "rules and manners which governed the matter of who did what with whom" in the world of a small Southern college:

If, for instance, you were dating a number of men, you might kiss them goodnight on the second or third date with perfect propriety. If you were going fairly steady with someone, you could certainly neck, and might pet . . . above the waist on the outside, if you had not been affiliated long; above the waist on the inside if it looked as though a pin were imminent. Once pinned, girls ceased to talk about what they did, but it was tacitly acknowledged that the field broadened considerably. If a girl was pinned and planned to marry after graduation, it was a foregone conclusion that she had probably gone all the way but it was not discussed in late-night behavioral seminars in the sorority houses.[123]

Wakefield's hero in *Going All the Way* reports on the boys' side of things, mostly about saving masculine face—since they were supposed to want to go further sexually—but similarly revealing complex distinctions:

The next day, when the guys asked you what you got the night before, you could say you got finger action inside the pants. That wasn't as good as really fucking but it rated right along with dry-humping and was much better than just the necking stuff like frenching and getting covered-tit or even bare-tit. It was really pretty much of a failure if you parked with a girl and got only covered-tit, and sometimes when Sonny just got covered-tit he actually lied if anyone asked and he said he got bare-tit."[124]

As we have seen, sexual bargaining based on market metaphors reproduced the reification of separate, distinct body parts by consumer culture. Women's bodies were fetishized and objectified, parts to be obsessed over and improved, sexualized for men and sales, and traded for love or commitment.[125] Just as industrial capitalism chopped time into pieces to be measured and bought and sold on the market, lovemaking and women's bodies were fragmented and broken into measurable parts, commodified, and quantified. Teenage girls signaled the extent of their sexual exploration or commitment through signs. The numerous distinctions (kiss, touching body parts outside clothes, inside clothes, upper body, lower body) were based on the premise that females must withhold themselves to precisely the correct degree to achieve their ends. Making sense of dating in the 1950s means recognizing the centrality of these breaks within a context of the compartmentalization of time, work, and emotional life in modern capitalist society. It also means recognizing the dramatic contrast between the sexual bargaining teenage girls became experts in and the sexual and romantic images that implied bargaining would be unnecessary. Courtship conventions condemned girls' curiosity while other postwar developments encouraged it.

Because the young women of the fifties had more leeway with regard to sex, the double standard was less relevant for them than it was for their mothers. But the unavailability of birth control was more anachronistic, the condemnation of sexual experimentation more desperate.[126] The confrontation between emergent and residual cultures was dramatic; young women were pivotal in the movement toward more autonomous definitions of feminine sexuality. In the dominant culture, gender anxiety and the insecurities of the cold war were linked through the idealization of white women's safety within domestic boundaries; contained there, they would make everything all right for men and children. Free, their whiteness and chastity might be lost forever, threatening not only white men's masculinity but sexual and racial strategies of separation and segregation designed to reassure white Americans that everything was all right.

"The Great Pretender"

Fiction, autobiographies, and social science suggest that young women in the fifties did not, perhaps could not, present their lives honestly. Themes of dissemblance were pervasive in the lives of women of this generation. Even the older generation of women committed themselves to appearances in their willingness to overlook personal distress. The 1956 rock and roll hit by the Platters "The Great Pretender," which I adored, is a fitting theme song for the era.[127]

The popularity ideal and the sexual double standard meant that white, middle-class girls had to walk a tightrope of respectability, never going (or never appearing) to go too far sexually, but giving just enough of their bodies to keep boys interested and to receive, they hoped, affection and admiration: "In real life the American girl may want to be bad but must at all costs give the appearance of being good," wrote Douvan and Adelson.[128] Girls had to hide much about themselves, especially about their bodies and sexual activity, the focus of so much public scrutiny. One way we dealt with conflicting demands was through guile. More simply, hypocrisy was encouraged by the sexual and gender norms. Benita Eisler writes, "Secrets, lies, evasions, and role-playing: As adolescents we created a precocious public persona, acceptable and accepted, in order to be left alone."[129] Often nice girls only seemed "nice" or "good." The hero of Philip Roth's short story "Goodbye, Columbus" is sleeping with Brenda, a college student, who pretends to others she is a virgin. When her mother finds her diaphragm, Brenda ends the relationship because the pretense has been exposed. Jules Henry scathingly described 1950s high school girls' efforts to make themselves sexy and attractive as misrepresentations, since they did not intend sex. These are "nymphs" who are really "pseudo-nymphs." In this charade, "the girls who best wiggle and resist, and the boys who do not press too hard and do not get angry when the girls resist, are the most mature."[130]

Girls' deceptions and contortions were strategies for coping with dramatically conflicting cues. As educational and occupational opportunities grew, the mass media exacerbated girls' double binds and doubleness by promoting oppositions: domesticity and glamor, virginity and sexuality, romance and sexual negotiation. While the terms and products with which to construct new versions of femininity were not of their making, by choosing from and embellishing products and looks, girls were engaged in creating new feminine meanings. In the process of forging new identities, they appropriated elements of the popular culture for their own uses.[131] Some rebelled by rejecting the double standard and "going all the way."

If some teenage girls conceived of fantasy and sexual experimentation as a way out of conventional feminine scripts, which many of us did, the cultural exaggeration and idealization of sex and romance made sexual disappointment likely. Nevertheless, the promotion and glamorization of sex meant that while sex could not live up to its anticipation, its growing significance served as one factor in an alternative image of self that led in the next decade to a feminine sexual revolution. Sex served, too, as a site of rebellion despite the cultural repression of the body. Media images simultaneously fostered passivity and facilitated the active pursuit of an image that could break with traditional gender norms.

Dissemblance suggests dishonesty, but the critical point is that unless we were outright rebels, we had no choice but to dissemble in order to explore new possibilities. Dissimulation was both protective and oppressive; the feeling of never being able to be oneself, of keeping up appearances, was a deep current in fifties life. Caught between old and new sexual norms, we were forging new codes the significance of which we ourselves were often unaware. As our moorings in the family loosened, we began to shape new identities for ourselves from pieces that fit together coherently neither in the culture nor in our lives.

CHAPTER 4

The Other Fifties:
Beats, Bad Girls,
and Rock and Roll

I have a memory of myself at eleven or twelve, trying to imagine my future. There would be a house with grass around it. There would be a white picket fence around the house. And there would be a married woman standing in the backyard, staring over the fence. I knew I would be unhappy. I knew I would not want to be there, but I imagined this future nonetheless.

Laurie Stone, *"Memoirs Are Made of This"* (1983)

In 1956 Paul Goodman published *Growing Up Absurd: The Problems of Youth in the Organized Society.* Early in the book he describes a growing problem: "We see groups of boys and young men disaffected from the dominant society. The young men are Angry and Beat. The boys are Juvenile Delinquents." Angry, Beat, and Juvenile Delinquents are capitalized: they were major social categories in the 1950s. Thus the "youth" in the subtitle refers to the problems of boys and young men, the usual concern of postwar social science. Work devoted to analyzing youth reproduced the male bias of work devoted to studying adults. Goodman defended his focus saying that the problems he wanted to discuss "belong primarily, in our society, to the boys: how to be useful and make something of oneself. A girl does not *have* to, she is not expected to make something of herself. Her career does not have to be self-justifying, for she will have children, which is absolutely self-justifying, like any other natural or creative act. . . . Our 'youth troubles' are 'boys' troubles."[1]. The adolescent heroine of Caryl Rivers's novel *Virgins* echoes Goodman, "I want to do things I dream about. I want to be a journalist. But I won't be. I'll just dream about it. It's different for boys. Boys *have* to do something. Girls don't."[2]

We know that Goodman was far from alone in worrying about the boys and the men; indeed, he was joined by many male observers of the American scene. Whether considering family, gender, or youth, the focus was male and often excluded, ignored, misinterpreted, or blamed females. "Deviants" such as Beats, hipsters, juvenile delinquents, homosexuals, even communists, were almost always males (psychologically damaged by "bad" mothers) in the scholarly and public mind. Social commentators took for granted Goodman's perspective: a girl did not have to make something of herself; her biology was reason enough for her existence; she would be wife and mother. If she wished to achieve outside of the family, she was discouraged, even punished.

There was, however, a barely visible cultural rebellion of some white, middle-class, girls and young women in the 1950s, in the latter case of women who were slightly older who actually lived or flirted with a bohemian life. My analysis of the attraction of the Beats and Greenwich Village is based on retrospective accounts of growing up in the postwar period and on interviews, fiction, and cultural histories and analyses.[3] My own experiences inform the account. It is East Coast-skewed data, even New York City focused, both because being a real Beat required living in Greenwich Village (or, to a lesser extent, North Beach in San Francisco) and because many of the written accounts are by women who were born, grew up in, or migrated to New York City. The women I interviewed for this chapter had some past or present connection with New York City because as middle-class Beats, bohemians, or rebels, New York City beckoned. New York City also had

the largest Jewish population, among whom were a disproporti[c]
number of people with left-wing politics; it is likely that their chil[ ],
red-diaper babies or fellow traveler babies, were also disproportionately
represented among teenaged dissenters.[4]

That being said, I also believe that my interpretations of the Beat
group and the wider significance of rock and roll for young women
provide parameters for understanding young feminine dissidence in the
1950s. The dissatisfactions articulated by the most rebellious reflected
the frustrations and tensions of the less politicized. The judgments of
those who dissented openly are crucial for understanding questions facing the others. The enormous popularity of rock and roll, while not
merely a sign of rebellion—since it was also a sign of being a teenager—
suggests that teenage girls were drawn to otherness. Interest in outsiders
and others, values and people excluded or occluded in postwar America, is the thread that connects the Beats and rock and roll, and links
both to black culture in the lives of young white women. I want to revise
the view that girls were full participants in postwar America, conformists where many boys were not. Their restlessness was significant; as in
their experimentations with glamor and sex, they were laying the
groundwork for rebellion in the years ahead. A small group of women
from a slightly older cohort were the real postwar pioneers. Younger
women, the generation in which I am interested, were restless and discontent with the life set out for them but, for the most part, still only incipient rebels. Some middle-class girls were, or wanted to be, nonconformists; frequently that inclination was a prelude to the independence
for which the women's liberation movement later fought. Often it was
early nonconformists who pioneered the social movements of the
1960s, the civil rights workers, campus activists, and youthful founders
of the women's liberation movement of the late 1960s.

Middle-class white girls' disaffection was barely discernible because no one thought to consider it and because its expression was often
oblique. In contrast to boys, stricter gender rules for girls dictated covert
dissidence. Girls' deviance was more circumspect and less dramatic
than boys', especially working-class boys', the subject of much concern
in the fifties with its alarm about juvenile delinquency. But despite the

pitfalls and constraints, some girls did find inspiration in defying sexual rules, in Beat and bohemian subcultures, and in rock and roll. When fifties defiance was and is portrayed, however, young white women are invisible. They dissembled and appeared to conform. Sexism in mainstream and alternative cultures constrained and shaped their defiance into forms not easily recognizable, especially by analysts not predisposed to discover gender rebellion. But it was gender rebellion. The stirrings prefigured its full-scale articulation a decade or so later.

Because Beat and delinquent subcultures were composed almost exclusively of males, often working-class males, and were masculine in conventional and chauvinist ways, girls' processes of identification were complex. Middle-class white girls who rejected dominant values had no choice but to utilize and adapt male versions of rebellion and disaffection.[5] For these girls, the attraction of outsiders, of hoods and greasers, of movie stars James Dean and Marlon Brando in roles of alienation and working-class defiance, and of black and black-inspired music was profound. Males who were inappropriate as boyfriends and potential mates and who represented an alternative to their bland teenage world played a significant role in girls' psychic lives. Ethnic, class, and racial differences had meaning in the lives and minds of heterosexual, middle-class white girls. Difference was ignored and denied in both adult and teenage mainstream culture, but it was alive, even thriving, for many teenage girls.

There were no female models. Analysts like Paul Goodman, Kenneth Keniston, and Edgar Friedenberg who studied youth and American culture defined male disaffection and nonconformity as a genuine social problem. Girls were conspicuously absent in their accounts.[6] Evidence from memoirs, novels, and cultural studies written later and from interviews suggest, however, that they were there. Even more suggestively, Goodman's critique of American society in *Growing Up Absurd,* with its exclusive focus on boys, inspired girls. Contrary to what might be expected, a recurrent theme surfaces in which males were the inspiration for these girls, whether as movie cowboys, delinquents, oddballs, or rebels.[7]

One of the peculiar characteristics of the 1950s, an expression of the powerful link between optimism and anxiety, was that fun-loving conformist teens existed side-by-side with disaffected teens—the delinquents, hoods, and Beatniks who loomed much larger in the cultural and psychic life of America than their numbers might suggest. The "right kind of teen" was "liberal, clean-cut, concerned about reputation, rarely kissed on a first date, never went too far sexually, avoided delinquency, studied and planned for the future, and hung around the malt shop."[8] In hindsight, these ponytailed and crew-cutted teenagers provoke some derision, but more than a little nostalgia as well, perhaps for a youthful innocence long past, undoubtedly made especially compelling by its absence today. Novels like *Vic Holyfield and the Class of 1957* by William Heyen, *Blooming* by Susan Toth, and *Virgins* by Caryl Rivers and autobiographies like *An American Childhood* by Annie Dillard and *Aphrodite at Mid-Century* by Caryl Rivers paint middle-class white adolescent lives of simplicity and love. Vic Holyfield, unlike Holden Caulfield whose namesake he is, wants only to return to his high school days and high school classmates and does so thirty years later by buying Smithtown High School and paying all his classmates to live there together for a year. It is an idyllic recreation of the best years of their lives, in which rock and roll music figures prominently, particularly the music of Elvis Presley. They have sock hops in the gym, assemblies, basketball games to their favorite rock and roll songs, rooms for slow dancing and fast dancing, 1950s movies, and concerts by entertainers popular then. The class of 1957 goes back to the golden age of teenagerdom, like the movie *Peggy Sue Got Married* and numerous other representations of the 1950s, and want it never to end. Vic Holyfield has a dream: "It was the end of the world, a nuclear cloud moving across the country like a curtain, and he was back in Smithtown, huddled in the gym with all of us, and he was happy he would be dying this way, here, with us."[9] This is a picture of innocence but, characteristically, innocence menaced by impending doom, like the science fiction movies so popular at the time. Even rock and roll, in this context, is experienced as sweet and asexual.

Another novel about teen life, very different from *Vic Holyfield*, reveals the "other," less wholesome, fifties, the attraction of which I ex-

ıere. *The Red Menace* by Michael Anania is the story of a boy
ıg up in the Midwest. Although he is white, his life is far from the
ιe-class suburbs. He lives in a racially mixed housing project, many
of whose inhabitants are on welfare. The story unfolds in the shadow of
the bomb—hence the anticommunism suggested by the title—and in-
timates the importance of the black experience for white teenagers, of
working-class boys for middle-class girls, of cars, sex, social class, delinquents, air raid drills, and machismo in the cultural matrix of teenage
life. Here the music is not romanticized. Anania is more explicit about
the appeal of its sexual content, more crude about sex. For his teenagers,
the atom bomb is linked to male sexuality (and to their nightmares),
and he suggests that the polio epidemic, "bred the same fear of contact
and association that Communism created."[10] Unlike Vic Holyfield, the
narrator of *The Red Menace* is an outsider, so alienated from America he
wants to become a communist. That he is working class is central to
his story.

It is significant that large numbers of adolescents did not feel happily engaged in typical teenage life in the historical period most remembered for its discovery and celebration of the teenager. It is worth recall-
ing in this context the mental health survey discussed in chapter 3 that
discovered that mothers in apparently happy marriages were often discontent. In an analysis of teenage culture, the sociologist Jessie Bernard
reported that a sizable proportion of high school students felt like outsiders. Citing the findings from one huge survey that indicated, in her
view, the extent of alienation among teenagers, Bernard states, "There
are the clods, the outs. And they constitute a sizeable proportion of the
high school population": 22 percent felt out of things, 11 percent felt
different, 44 percent seldom had dates, 13 percent felt they were not
wanted, 20 percent felt lonesome, and 25 percent felt ill at ease at social
affairs.[11] These figures run counter to nostalgic reconstructions of the
1950s which leave little room for feelings of teenage marginality and
exclusion. They are not surprising, however, in light of many young
women's memories.

Social analysts in the 1960s and 1970s have attempted to explain
the development of the student and youth rebellions by studying the

immediate postwar period. Richard Flacks has been one of the more perceptive among many who concur that the sources of middle-class youth discontent lay in a nexus of postwar American economic and social transformations. Like others, he has suggested that the postwar period experienced a socioeconomic crisis, as technological potentialities, the shift from entrepreneurial to bureaucratic organizations, and consumerism based on abundance rather than scarcity, outstripped the society's social and cultural arrangements and values. The most significant change for our purposes was the shift from a goods-producing to a service- and information-based white-collar economy and the resultant cultural inconsistencies.

Middle-class families were confused about how and what to teach their children when faced with new levels of consumerism and the decline in relevance of the Protestant Ethic. According to Flacks, many college-educated parents who were engaged in intellectual and service occupations had humane, not materialist, values and raised their children permissively, albeit confusedly, thereby engendering in those children a critical stance toward society. In the 1950s, these children formed the nucleus of an alternative subculture. Flacks suggests that in this period of political and economic transition and cultural incoherence, all the institutions of socialization, but especially middle-class parents who were part of a new mass intelligentsia, contributed to the creation of an alternative youth subculture: "In the schools, the media and the churches, such contradictory values as self-denial and self-expression, discipline and indulgence, and striving and being are preached, dramatized, fostered, and practiced all at once." In a study by Kenneth Keniston, young middle-class men were depicted as alienated and uncommitted; in Flacks's terms, they were intellectual and critical, a small subculture that looked "at first like a deviant group but turned out to be a vanguard" of the youth rebellion. A new generational cohort was in the making, and by the end of the decade, according to Flacks, a critical mass of alienated, intellectual youth existed.[12]

Many of these young people felt "excluded from and repelled by the prevailing youth culture" in the fifties. Their upbringing meant that they were disgusted by the "frivolity, antiintellectualism, and social indifference of the middle-class peer culture and by its stereotyped sex role definitions and superficial conventionalism." According to Flacks, they were uneasy in the dating, grooming, and peer culture. Consequently their status was low and their anxiety and self-doubt high.[13] These were some of the young people who showed up in surveys as unhappy or outsiders. Other hints of this unhappiness were the large numbers of teenage advice books and columns and educational films that simply assumed confusion on the part of teenagers; like childrearing manuals, they multiplied in the postwar period. Teenagers shared with their parents the experience of new and unclear rules of behavior.[14] Insecurity was heightened by the media celebration of the frivolous, happy-go-lucky, confident teenager; it was impossible not to define oneself in relation to popularity. Not all white, middle-class adolescents participated with ease, then, in teen culture.

Replicating other social science, most studies of youth did not utilize gender as a category. Keniston's *The Uncommitted,* for example, is about male Harvard students. Flacks makes no mention of gender in his discussion of the postwar origins of middle-class discontent. We have seen that Goodman, in concert with social commentators and sociologists of deviance, did not consider feminine rebelliousness an issue. While many of these analyses are helpful for understanding the class and generational aspects of youth discontent, they miss identifying girls' dissatisfaction as a phenomenon distinct from boys'. As we will see below, much of this dissatisfaction had its sources in the narrowness of the expectations for girls and of the latitude permitted them. Ironically, girls shared in the high expectations of the postwar generation. Over and over again, white, middle-class girls recall their sense of the new options open to them. Despite their sex, limitless possibilities seemed to stretch before them. In a collection of essays by British women who grew up in the fifties, Liz Heron writes, "Along with the orange juice and the cod-liver oil, the malt supplement and the free school milk, we may also have absorbed a certain sense of our own worth and the sense of a future that would get better and better, as if history were on our side." She continues, "It seems also that as little girls we had a stronger sense of our possibilities than the myths of the fifties allow. There general confidence in the air, and the wartime image of wome dependence and competence at work lingered on well into the decade."[15] An American girl says, "I do not remember any deprivation during the war—or at any time in my life—or any inconvenience. . . . What I do remember clearly is the burst of consumption at the war's end. It seems to me that at the very moment we were banging pots and pans . . . there was an explosion of fresh cream and strawberries."[16] Constricted feminine goals learned in the family and wider culture generated specifically feminine discontent, but the postwar expansiveness, the comfortable homes and consumer goods, the anticipation of happy futures, and media glamor counteracted and transformed that discontent (which was, for many, destructive) into the expectation of achievement and the urge to explore beyond boundaries.

Girls and "Real" Life

It is the "other" fifties, the culture that percolated underneath and around the dominant harmonious image, particularly as it relates to girls, that we want to consider. We know that some white, middle-class girls grew up anticipating what was expected of them, a life in the suburbs as a wife and mother, with great ambivalence, often expressed as ambivalence about their mothers. One woman recalls the suburbs where she grew up and "knew no white, middle-class woman with children who had a job or any major activities beyond the family. . . . During the day, it was safe, carefully limited, and female. The idea that this was all made me frantic."[17] In Caryl Rivers's novel *Virgins,* the teenage heroine tells her girlfriend that they have minds like men, which makes them, happily, different from most girls:

That was worst of all, I thought, a life where nothing ever happened. I looked around me and saw women ironing dresses and hanging out clothes and shopping for food and playing mah-jong on hot summer afternoons, and I knew I couldn't bear to spend my life that way, day

*after drab day, with nothing ever happening. The world of women
seemed to me like a huge, airless prison where things didn't change. Inside
it, I thought, I'd turn gray and small and shrivel up to nothing.[18]*

The life plan set out for these girls was unacceptable to them. Their
society's expectations and, closer to home, those of their parents', did
not coincide with their own yearnings. "I couldn't stand girls who wanted to get married and have engagement rings. I knew I was different,
and I was glad," recalls one young woman who became a beatnik.[19]
Janis Joplin, who lived in Port Arthur, Texas, during the 1950s, expressed a more earthy version of these sentiments. She describes herself
as "just a plain overweight chick": "I wanted something more than
bowling alleys and drive-ins. I'd've fucked anything, taken anything, I
did."[20] We have seen how letters to Betty Friedan from this generation
provide evidence of girls who felt trapped in the grip of the feminine
mystique. They rebelled against the bourgeois respectability and timidi-
ty of middle-class conventions that included domestic gender expectations. The banality of middle-class values was an important Beat
theme that found female adherents despite the sexism of the vision.
Girls imagined themselves as free as Beat men, domesticity (and the
women they were supposed to become) left behind. Even popular culture contained critiques of middle-class family life. The movie *Rebel
without a Cause*, for example, found a cause for the juvenile delinquency
so feared in the 1950s: pathetic parents. Nora Sayre comments about
films of the fifties: "Rarely has family life looked so repulsive as it did in
movies of the decade that also tried to uphold the family as an institution, while the parents who didn't 'understand' or cherish their children
were as guilty as the gangsters of the previous era."[21]

Domestic life provided these teenagers with little inspiration. For
them its values were materialistic, constricting, and boring. Disaffected
teenage girls longed for something significant in their lives. "Authentic,"
"genuine," "real" were words they used (or implied) repeatedly. They
felt that somehow being white, female and sheltered precluded the experience of meaningfulness. The sense that the culture was rife with
hypocrisy, everyone keeping up appearances in one form or another,

generated a yearning for genuine feeling. So did the smallness of their futures. Alienation and its inverse, a search for authenticity and intensity, ran through best-selling postwar fiction, tapping not only a youth but an American nerve.[22] Beats, bohemians, and sectors of middle-class youth shared disdain for making money at an unfulfilling job, working as a full-time housewife, conforming in the suburbs, and searching for security. "What unforeseen catastrophe would send me up the river to decorate a home in Westchester?" asks a young woman settled in Greenwich Village, referring to the prosperous New York suburb where Herman Wouk's *Marjorie Morningstar* ends up a housewife after flirting with the Village and an artistic life.[23] Concurring, I picture myself in black and army drab taking the train on Sunday morning from Long Island into Greenwich Village in order to spend the afternoon in Washington Square Park. There I listened to folk musicians and drank in the sights of bohemia. I longed to get my ears pierced, which was unheard of in my suburban high school (it was probably too close to the immigrant pasts we, and especially our parents, were determinedly shedding). I imitated a style of dress that identified me with the opposition. I recall my father grimly asking me why my clothes were always so dark and my mother encouraging me to wear pastels. My rebellion was only style, not yet anything more dangerous, but it was important to my sense of self.

In *Minor Characters,* the chronicle of her infatuation with Jack Kerouac and the Beats, Joyce Johnson, who grew up in Manhattan and was a student at Barnard in the 1950s, writes: "Moving back and forth between antithetical worlds separated by subway rides, I never fully was what I seemed or tried to be. I had the feeling I was playing hooky all the time, not from school, but from the person represented by my bland outward appearance."[24]

She is not what she appears to be; appearance disguises her real self. These themes surface again and again in memoirs and literature of the period. Girls' discontent was articulated, as it was by others in the society, as a longing for meaning, for something more real than the middle-class lives set out for them. Jan Clausen grew up in Southern California. In 1957, when she was sixteen, she read Kerouac's *On the*

Road. In it she discovers the "moral and intellectual intensity" she's been looking for: "Emerging from a childhood of many advantages, I was bitter, suddenly, against my parents, on account of certain experiences withheld from me: Smith Act trials overhanging my formative years; alcoholic binges; steamy dramas of marital infidelity; the benny-popping, reefer-puffing role models they might have been, tearing back and forth across the continent with infant me asleep in the back seat. . . . my background had been deficient."[25] Bonnie Raitt, who also grew up in Southern California, went to a summer camp in Massachusetts run by Quakers, where most of the people were Jewish or Progressives: "It counteracted the whole beach boy scene in California, which I couldn't stand. I started wearing peace symbols around my neck and listening to Odetta records." Joyce Johnson writes of herself, Jack Kerouac, and his book, "The 'looking for something' Jack had seen in me was the psychic hunger of my generation. Thousands were waiting for a prophet to liberate them from the cautious middle class lives they had been reared to inherit."[26] For Johnson, Greenwich Village and the Beats "seemed to promise . . . something I'd never tasted in my life as a child—something I told myself was Real Life. This was not the life my parents lived but one that was dramatic, unpredictable, possibly dangerous. Therefore *real,* infinitely more worth having." Johnson's central impulse was a rejection of bourgeois respectability. "Real life was not to be found in the streets around my house, or anywhere on the Upper West Side." A younger girl echoes Johnson's impatience: "Do you understand? We were hungry for experience, for some kind of real life, for some way to tap our energy."[27] Another woman describes her adolescence in the 1950s thus: "The basic awareness grew that truth, whatever it was, was something we had all our lives been protected from. Reality had been kept in quarantine so we could not become contaminated."[28]

Zane, the eighteen-year-old heroine of Alix Kates Shulman's novel *Burning Questions,* leaves her Midwest home for a more exciting life. She finds it in Greenwich Village, a place in which experimentation is permissible, where expressing oneself creatively or sexually is the highest achievement. She leaves Indiana Babbittry behind in order to find her true self. Shulman's is an ecstatic description of the mecca Greenwich Village represented for a generation of young people.

Thus Diane Di Prima, one of the few female Beats in her own right, a poet who had sexual relationships with both men and women, writes in her *Memoirs of a Beatnik* about what a good friend will miss by not living with her and a third friend in a "pad" in the Village. The opportunity for the three of them to live together means "light and freedom, air and laughter, the outside world." It means "one's blood running strong and red in one's own veins, not drawn to feed the ineradicable grief of the preceding generations."[29]

To find themselves, girls had to leave their families behind. Janis Joplin says of her adolescence,

I was raised in Texas, man, and I was an artist and I had all these ideas and feelings that I'd pick up in books and my father would talk to me about it, and I'd make up poems and things. And, man, I was the only one I'd ever met. There weren't any others. There just wasn't anybody, man, in Port Arthur. . . . I mean, in other words, in the Midwest you got no one to learn from because there's not a reader down the street you can sneak off and talk to. There's nobody. Nobody. I remember when I read that in Time *magazine about Jack Kerouac, otherwise I'd've never known. I said "Wow!" and split.[30]*

Dean Moriarity, the hero of *On the Road,* conveys the appeal of leaving, of finding life: "The only possible people for me are the mad ones, the ones who are mad to live, mad to talk, mad to be saved, desirous of everything at the same time, the ones who never yawn or say a commonplace thing, but burn, burn, burn like fabulous roman candles."[31] Annie Dillard found in books what she lacked in life as a teenager: "I myself was getting wild; I wanted wildness, originality, genius, rapture, hope. I wanted strength, not tea parties."[32] Growing up in England as part of the generation in which we are interested, Sheila Rowbotham echoes her American sisters. She describes how her image of the ultimate man was based on a mixture of James Dean, Marlon Brando, and the Beats, a man of few words but intense emotions, always on the run. (Again, *On the Road* figures significantly in a young woman's vision of herself and the men to whom she was attracted.) Such a friendly psychopath, she hoped, would notice that under her "healthy exterior" she was "in fact suitably intense and fraught for the most extended and crazed imagination." Rowbotham describes herself: "I picked up an insistence on direct experience and feeling. I was inordinately suspicious of reason and analysis. Only moments of intense subjectivity seemed to have any honesty or integrity." Above all she wanted "intense experiences where everyone spoke of intense subjects and *never* said 'pass the bread and butter.'"[33]

Talking was important for these women. For one Beat woman, moving to Greenwich Village in the fifties after college meant moving "home." Her apartment in the Village was filled day and night with people talking, eating, and drinking; many of them painters, writers and musicians—all were part of a vibrant community for which she had longed. She felt she had found "life." In all accounts of the Village in this period, of bohemian life in general, talking figures prominently. For these women who felt starved for serious talk, it was paramount.[34]

Shulman's heroine experiences her first Village meal in a tiny apartment filled with artists and talk. She is amazed at the pots filled with spaghetti sauce set directly on the kitchen table, the long loaves of garlic bread, the wine and salad to which everyone helps themselves, and the unending stream of words. Zane marvels at how much and how excitedly they can talk about one Swedish director and his movies and says, "'It's a lot better than what they talk about in Indiana.' 'What do they talk about there?' 'Cars and clothes. And communists in the government.'"[35]

Diane Di Prima describes her life in the Village in the early fifties before the arrival of masses of young people. A coffee shop for the bohemian crowd had opened up on MacDougal Street: "We all sat there in the long afternoons, reading and making each other's acquaintance, nursing twenty-five cent cups of espresso for hours, and drawing pictures on paper napkins." Joyce Johnson loved the slums: "My slums, the sweet slums of Bohemia and beatnikdom, where sunflowers and morning glories would bloom on fire escapes in the summer."[36] These women found in the Village scene what Ronald Sukenick describes as a "grungy purity . . . in its deliberate isolation from the world of Uptown." He suggests that such rebels were "confronted with the promised land of previously repressed impulses, a risky new underground landscape to explore consisting of everything deemed unreal by the dominant culture, which amounts to almost everything."[37] Di Prima captures the isolation and purity of the early days. There were only a handful, "who raced about in Levis and work shirts, made art, smoked dope, dug the new jazz, and spoke a bastardization of the black argot. . . . our isolation was total and impenetrable." Their chief concern was keeping their integrity and cool; they "looked to each other for comfort, for praise, for love, and shut out the rest of the world."[38] They sought and found for a time real life, authenticity. "I think of us trying to laugh off the fifties. . . . I think we were trying to shake the time. Shake it off, shake it up, shake it down. A shakedown," writes Hetty Jones.[39] Like Janis Joplin, Shulman's middle-class rebel says she knew from her sixteenth birthday on in Indiana what she wanted and pursued it with enthusiastic singlemindedness: "To get out."[40]

The Artistic Underground

Although it deserves more attention than it receives here, the American cultural ferment of the 1940s and 1950s is critical to this story. The underground artistic renaissance underway in Greenwich Village (and San Francisco) comes as a surprise in light of representations of postwar America culture as commercial and antiintellectual.[41] Al Young refers to a "sort of ferment in American culture that eventually rose from subterranean level" to shape contemporary art and music. Jazz, poetry, and abstract expressionist painting flourished during the decades after the war. A wildly innovative bohemian life thrived, with jazz occupying the preeminent position. The story of jazz in these years is of enormous vitality and creativity. Abstract expressionist painting and writing, particularly Beat writing, tried to create jazz on canvas and on page and to imitate the lives of jazz artists. Jazz music and jazz musicians were inspirations for white artists. Young suggests that "jazz mythology has always affected American intellectuals and artists when they were looking for a way out of what Artaud once called 'the bourgeoisification' of everything in life."[42]

Central to the story of the fifties is the powerful influence of black culture. White rebels and artists were particularly drawn to black people and black culture, often in racist and exploitative ways, which we will see when we discuss Norman Mailer below. Interracial couples were prominent in Greenwich Village, as were a "bastardization of black argot" in the Beats' language and jazz-inspired art and lives. But even in the rest of America, the denial of the black contribution to white culture—especially clear in the effort to whiten rhythm and blues for a white teen audience and in the general project of creating a homogenized white popular culture—was accompanied by its opposite, curiosity and enthusiasm on the part of young whites.

The flavor of Greenwich Village at this time comes out clearly in beatnik women's accounts. Di Prima writes,

Jazz was for us the most important, happening art; Bird in Louis' Tavern on West Fourth Street on weekday nights handed out posters for his incredible weekends at the Open Door on West Broadway, weekends when he would take us all with him, teach us all to fly. And later, Miles at the Cafe Bohemia, slick and smart as they come, exchanging sets with Charlie Mingus, cool then and cool now.... Later the jazzmen were followed by the painters, a big, bulking breed of hard-drinking men who spoke in oils and came on very paternal and sexy.[43]

For Joyce Johnson, who didn't know what she was supposed to see when she looked at abstract expressionist canvases or how to decide whether they were good or bad—"goodness or badness didn't even seem important." What she had wandered into "wasn't the beginning of something, but the coming into light of what had been stirring for years among all these artists.... Major or minor, they all seemed possessed by the same impulse—to break out into forms that were unrestricted and new." Johnson recounts the invasion of artists and would-be artists, the galleries and illegal loft living, the excitement of being where life felt intense and real.[44] The painters, writers, and musicians of the 1940s and 1950s strained against the boundaries of academic or acceptable art. Young writes, "I think that one of the things that the Beat Generation did was to take art out from under glass . . . to restore poetry and literature to the people."[45] Hetty Jones remembers that "the Beats *looked* okay to me, and I applauded their efforts, successful or not, to burst wide open—like the abstract expressionist painters had—the image of what could be (rightly) said."[46] The horrified reaction of the Columbia University literary establishment to the Beats—(writing in *Partisan Review* Norman Podhoretz referred to them as a "revolt of all the forces hostile to civilization itself," as "know-nothing bohemians")—was proof enough that the younger writers were attempting to crash the gates.[47] Johnson's insight into the artists' impulse to "break out into forms that were restricted and new" and Jones's sense the artists were "bursting wide open" described the women as well. The dramatic inclinations to which they and younger women responded flourished in them too. As women they wanted to be out from under glass.

Sexism

In the midst of the Beat scene in 1958, Joyce Johnson describes herself as she would have been seen by someone else:

With her seat at the table in the exact center of the universe, that midnight place where so much is converging, the only place in America that's alive. . . . As a female, she's not quite part of this convergence. A fact she ignores, sitting by in her excitement as the voices of the men, always the men, passionately rise and fall and their beer glasses collect and the smoke of their cigarettes rises toward the ceiling and the dead culture is surely being wakened. Merely being here, she tells herself, is enough.[48]

Johnson, Shulman's Zane, and other female bohemians became Beats by becoming the girlfriends of the "real" Beats, but ironically, in so doing they discovered themselves. Disaffected girls often became the girlfriends of male dissidents and delinquents, like Natalie Wood to

James Dean's hero in *Rebel without a Cause*. Restless teenage girls in 1950s movies were not themselves rebels but joined boys who were because they were in love. In life, as in the delinquent subculture portrayed in film, girls' identities were inextricably bound up with boys', their acceptance determined by whether they belonged to a male.[49] Nonconformity was articulated within traditional gender forms; these were the last to fall even in deviant subcultures. Shulman's *Burning Questions* explores the secondary status and exploitation of women by male Beats. In their search for liberation, Joyce Johnson and Zane, like so many other women, discovered virulent sexism.[50] But they were thrilled, nonetheless, in Johnson's words, to be near the convergence of all that was alive in America in the 1950s. Similar to women in the new left who at first often did not recognize the sexism of male radicals, Beat women found that the excitement of participating in an oppositional movement overrode all else. "We lived outside, as if, As if we were men? As if we were newer, freer versions of ourselves?"[51] The rupture with the dominant culture was enthralling. Even if one were ignored or treated shabbily, the break was initially more significant than the male chauvinism.[52]

The Beats were macho and sexist. Not intending a gendered point but making it all the same, thirty years ago Norman Podhoretz complained that "what juvenile delinquency is to life, the San Francisco writers [Beats] are to literature," adding that the Beat generation was a "conspiracy" to replace civilization with the "world of the adolescent street gangs."[53] Confirming this model of male delinquent gangs, the Beat poet Allen Ginsberg dreamed that "the social organization most true of itself to the artist is the boy gang."[54] One of the most sexist and racist eulogies to the Beats was Norman Mailer's "The White Negro" published in 1957. A romantic celebration of the outsider—a mixture of the juvenile delinquent, hipster, and black male he dubbed the "white negro"—Mailer's depiction of revolt was of the male urban outlaw who lived on the edge, searching out sex, using marijuana, appreciating jazz, finding momentary truth through his body. Mailer portrayed a nighttime adventurer who lived according to (Mailer's) black man's code of drugs, sex, and jazz, a sexual fugitive in love with violence. According to

Nelson George, Mailer and other white artists and intellectuals turned their "romance with blackness," their fascination with the alternative world of black America, into "a strange, often unintentional rape of black ideas and styles. Ironically, this was committed by some of the very people who loved (or at least claimed to love) black creativity."[55] The dehumanizing exoticization of the other, the construction of the meaning of whiteness through the romanticization of blackness, of which Ralph Ellison warned, is nowhere more obvious than in Mailer's "white negro."

Women existed in Beat culture for sexual satisfaction. No responsibilities, commitments, or roots marred the marginal man's effort to liberate himself from the superego of society (and from women, particularly their domestication of men). The Beats were about male adventure and irresponsibility. Their goal was to get women to support them so they would not have to work, so they would be free from routine and able to experience life to the fullest. Barbara Ehrenreich argues that the Beats were inspired by the underclass and underworld, by the fantasy of lower-class masculinity in a period in which the white-collar, middle-class male was seen as emasculated. We have seen how this fear and disdain for the loss of traditional masculinity was widespread in the culture, shared even by social scientists. In a culture ideologically devoted to eviscerating social class through the assimilation of everyone into middle-class whiteness, "the 'lower' class, denied a name or image, lived on in the middle-class male mind as a repressed self, primitive, dissatisfied and potentially disruptive."[56]

For some white girls, a rejection of middle-class masculinity was operating as well. This was perhaps an indirect way of exploring new versions of femininity. Although female subordination was not yet in question, an interest in sexual ambiguity or a rejection of heterosexuality may have been. James Dean, as Jon Savage observes, represented a highly androgynous sexuality. Widespread interest in young men from the "other side of the tracks" suggests an attraction to what Joyce Johnson referred to as a life that was "dramatic, unpredictable, possibly dangerous," the antithesis of white, middle-class life in postwar America. Popular teenage movies featured troublemakers like the delinquents in *Blackboard Jungle* with its rock and roll score; Marlon Brando in *The Wild One*, disrupting girls' lives; and James Dean, whose identity is so fragmented in *Rebel without a Cause* "that he appears as more than an outsider, as a sleepwalker vainly trying to learn the language of an alien landscape."[57] Girls were involved with, even created, these media heroes, as they did with Elvis Presley, another ambiguous male heartthrob. Put simply, girls were attracted to males who were different from themselves, usually meaning not middle class. Annie Dillard's idyllic and privileged childhood was characterized by odd romances: "I would give my heart to one oddball after another—to older boys, to prep-school boys no one knew, to him who refused to go to college, to him who was a hood, and all of them wonderfully skinny."[58] We have seen that Sheila Rowbotham's image of the ultimate man was "a mixture of James Dean and Marlon Brando," definitely not the man in the gray flannel suit. Alice McDermott's novel *That Night* is about the doomed romance between a middleclass girl who gets pregnant and is sent away and her hood boyfriend and his friends who invade and menace her quiet suburban street.[59] Tragic stories filled true romance and confession magazines about young women attracted to the wrong type of man. This was a middle-class fantasy, Barbara Ehrenreich argues, because it spoke to an "unassimilated corner of the middle-class psyche."[60] Girls escaped from conventional material and sexual expectations but still were only accomplices to the major actors in these narratives.

Joyce Johnson articulated what was attractive to her in these men, sardonically noting their sexism: "Some pursuit of the heightened moment, intensity for its own sake, something they apparently find only when they're with each other."[61] The Beats attempted to reconstitute male bonds, exalting in a brotherhood of male friendship and love, the "Beat Brotherhood."[62]. They were fearful of women, dichotomizing them into madonnas and whores, mothers and lovers, the latter conceptualized in terms of carnality and sexual submission. The macho masculinity they enacted was in conscious contrast to the postwar image of feminized middle-class men and provided drama and danger, and a critique of converging sex roles. In a critical analysis of the sexual politics of the Beats, Catherine Stimpson points out that they exaggerated traditional gender definitions even in their homosexual relations, suggesting "how much harder it is to be free and to extend freedom than to be sexual, and homosexual." Shulman's Zane discovers this as do other female beatniks.[63]

Despite her recognition that Beat men seemed to find intensity, which she sought too, only with each other, Joyce Johnson, like other women who lived among or were inspired by them, felt more real and alive than in her middle-class environment. In deciphering the different experiences of women slightly older than those who were adolescents in the fifties, it becomes apparent that those who actually lived among the Beat men had more complicated experiences than those who fantasized about or imitated the Beats from afar. Shulman has written a devastating portrait of what happened to Beat women at the hands of their misogynist and sexist men. But she also suggests that it should not surprise us that the dream was more inspiring than the reality.[64] A perceptive reviewer of *Minor Characters* remarks, "In retrospect we see that the young Joyce Glassman loved Kerouac's expansive male privilege to move about, see things, and write about them as much as she loved the mobile guy himself."[65] The expansiveness and male privilege of the Beats, their intensity, adventures, frenetic activity, interest in black culture, and rejection of conventional middle-class life attracted 1950s teenage girls, as did rock and roll stars. But they were interested not simply as girlfriends and fans, which was the simplest form their attraction could take; they were interested in them as models. They wanted to *be* them. The possibility of a break with domesticity was critical to this appeal. Despite the Beats' chauvinism, for girls their rejection of bourgeois respectability and the family was explosive. The "unassimilated corner of the middle-class psyche" by which the Beats were inspired and to which they spoke was as much feminine as masculine. As from other parts of sexist culture, girls took what inspiration they could get where they could get it, and as Ehrenreich suggests, it *was* threatening. Some girls' longing for adventure, for a life undefined by suburban domesticity, was fulfilled, in fantasy or fact, by sexist male bohemians. The Beats provided them with alternative images of living, even if as boyfriends they did not. For girls, they served as an early stop in the journey away from mainstream teenage culture and domesticity. Paradoxically, just as Paul Goodman did not worry about alienated young females, neither did their countercultural male heroes take them seriously, assuming, like Goodman, that their biology was all that counted.

Darkness and Difference

It is far from irrelevant that hoods and "bad girls" were portrayed as wearing black—black leather jackets, boots, and belts—and were darker in complexion than the innocent suburban teens. Reproducing the adult culture's dualism of light and dark, obvious in fair movie stars, models, and beauty standards, dissident teens chose darkness. Often they were dark because of their immigrant backgrounds. The "good" approved teen culture was light and white, the threat black. Rock and roll was the subtext for the 1950s drama of "good" versus "bad" teens, whitened versions of black rhythm and blues acceptable for mainstream white teenagers. It was a white time in America, and it is thus not surprising that dissenters were, felt, or were imagined to be dark. Hoods were not the only ones in black; the Beats wore black. Black clothes signified you were Beat or bohemian: black turtleneck shirts, black stockings, black sunglasses. "I dumped out my inheritance of pastel colours and princes and collected a new bag of black sweaters, jeans, psychopaths and beat fantasy." recalls Sheila Rowbotham.[66] Another adolescent says, "I just wanted to be a beatnik. I quit wearing pink and orange and always wore darker colors. I was one of the first people in Charleston to get dark stockings. I was in a shop once and a girl goes, 'Look, Mommy, that lady has white arms with black legs.'"[67] The fictional heroine Zane recounts a tale of her town, Babylon, Indiana, when the white, middle-class girls in her school sponsor a rummage sale in a poor, black section of town: "In Babylon certain color combinations were forbidden. Such combinations as green with blue, orange with red (or red with pink or pink with orange), brown with black, or purple with anything were considered quite untenable. Such breaches of taste, variously called loud, gauche, stupid, Italian, Jew, were simply prohibited." The room filled with people who "so consistently violated

these simple, basic rules that one could only conclude they were unaware of them. . . . Their very skin and hair violated Babylon minimal
rules of decorum."

Zane points to a fact of American cultural life in the 1950s. "Different was wrong. The wrong attitude, the wrong amount of hair . . . the
wrong color skin . . . the wrong clothes from the wrong stores, made you
unfit for Babylon."[68] A central incident in Dan Wakefield's novel *Going
All the Way* involves a beard. A friend of Sonny's grows a beard and is
refused service in bars and restaurants, is not permitted to swim in a
pool because he will contaminate it—"It's plain common sense you
can't go into a swimming pool with a beard. You'll get the water
dirty"—and he is generally ostracized. Sonny says, "Having a beard in
the summer of 1954 was like running around without any clothes on or
passing out copies of the Communist Manifesto or reading a dirty book
in a crowded bus. It was asking for trouble."[69] Hair again. A fixation on
grooming, cleanliness, on controlling the body thrived. Hair had to be
fair and light, short for males, contained and curled for women. Unruly
hair, too much hair, hair in the wrong places "was asking for trouble."
The Beats wore beards. Controlling the body was about controlling sex,
and it is not surprising that in the student, counterculture and women's
movements of the next decades hair symbolized freedom of all kinds.
(The musical *Hair*, made into a movie, enshrined it.) In the 1950s, hair,
too, had to stay in its place.

There are at least two things going on here. First, there is the issue
of difference—both the intolerance and repression of difference and its
active life in the imaginations and behavior of white, middle-class
youth. Girls expressed their dissatisfactions with domesticity and sub-
urbanism through their infatuations with boys, including rock and roll
and media stars, who could not fit into their lives. These were boys they
could not marry. The attraction to danger was more complex than that,
however. The awareness of difference was complicated by the issue of
darkness. Wearing dark or clashing colors or being dark signified difference in even more explosive ways. It meant being unable to attain, or
rejecting, prevailing values and standards of attractiveness, being an
outsider. One girl who became a beatnik moved from the Northwest to

the South: "When I heard we were moving to Georgia, I dreamed of palm trees, of having a black friend, and of everyone wearing long dresses."[70] The good taste and decorum of Babylon, the pastels and middle-classness, excluded those who did not or could not conform. As Zane says of the black people who filled the rummage sale, not only did their color combinations shock respectable people, their skin and hair were indecent. They threatened middle-class orderliness. In Philip Roth's "Goodbye, Columbus," the following dialogue takes place when Neil telephones Brenda for a date: She asks, "What do you look like?" "I'm . . . dark." "Are you a Negro?" "No." Brenda is middle class and Neil working class; both are Jews. The mixture of working class and masculine darkness reappears, amalgamating different and dark. For WASPS, Jews were dark, exercising a fascination for Christian girls. Even in this story, Jewish Brenda is effectively a WASP, so successfully has she assimilated. Assimilation entails becoming white; Brenda has succeeded, and Neil is trying, his difference undoubtedly one of his attractions. However, we have seen that many ethnic white girls (and black girls) suffered because of narrow white beauty standards. Darkness was less interesting in girls, and so they worked to disguise it while they simultaneously listened to rock and roll and dreamed of dark and different boys.[71]

"As an outsider Jew I would have tried for white, aspired to the liberal intellectual, potentially conservative Western tradition. But I never was drawn to that history, and with so little specific to call my own I felt free to choose," says Hetty Jones, who married Leroi Jones, a black man, in the 1950s. She tells how black and white were slippery divisions for her because Jews were different. She didn't "*feel* American." Her outsider status and her love of music, especially jazz, created for her more commonalities with black people than with mainstream Americans.[72] Their stultifying environments made rebellious white girls more responsive to and interested in people outside it. There is some evidence, too, that an identification with the underdog and the oppressed was common among young white people who eventually joined the civil rights and student movements. Jones was able to act on the interest in difference that other young women only dreamed of.

Blackness, darkness—symbolized for many girls by Beatnik or hood clothes, in fantasies of romance with nonconformist or outsider boys, in the love of rock and roll and interest in black culture—exerted the pull it did because whiteness was so hegemonic and the denial of difference so central to conceptions of whiteness. From this perspective, whiteness was a color defined by blackness or, rather, its denial. In a way, the young women sensed the deprivations that segregation of all kinds imposed, recognizing that they suffered from a whiteness so dominant that most white people with whom they came in contact never even noticed it.

Rock and Roll

Rock and roll was central to the white teenage experience of the 1950s.[73] Many argue that it provided the cohesiveness for this generation (and subsequent generations of youth), categorically separating young people from their parents. Ironically, packed into the phrase "rock and roll," which in the 1950s came to be a symbol of rebellious white youth, is the history of the attempt to tame and pacify the music from which it derived, rhythm and blues, for white audiences. The story of rock and roll as the badge of postwar white teenage culture is another racial story, one in which black and minority music was adapted and transformed, some would say appropriated and distorted, by white record companies and white artists into music deemed suitable for white adolescents. Here is another version of whiteness constructed against blackness, of a herculean effort to contain, transform, even erase, black culture from white life.[74] At the same time it is a story, as Eldridge Cleaver suggests, of the embrace of black music and dance by white youth:

The white youth of today have begun to react to the fact that the "American Way of Life" is a fossil of history. What do they care if their old baldheaded and crew-cut elders don't dig their caveman mops? They couldn't care less about the old, stiffassed honkies who don't like their new dances: Frug, Monkey, Jerk, Swim, Watusi. All they know is that it feels good to swing to way-out body rhythms instead of dragassing across the dance floor like zombies to the dead beat of mind-smothered Mickey Mouse music.[75]

George Lipsitz has written that rock and roll was a successful challenge by youth—crossing racial, class, and ethnic lines—to hierarchical American cultural attitudes and values. The music mobilized, and was mobilized by, youth from all sectors of the population. White youth were drawn to the music, loved it, and embraced it as their own. It defined a community and served as an expressive critique of their social environment. From this perspective, rock and roll was not simply a top-down enterprise but a contested cultural terrain.[76] Black culture, through music, was the dialectical accompaniment, the alter ego, to white, middle-class teenage life. Like the early civil rights movement that penetrated the consciousness of white America with dramas, often violent, about bus boycotts and school integration, rock and roll was a racial subtext in postwar America. Its ambiguity—mainstream but potentially disruptive, part of the dating ritual but encoded with sexual and racial meaning—hints at the complexity of young whites' enthusiasm for rock and roll. In the words of Gerald Early,

Those were the years . . . in which America recognized, and cringed before, the social reality . . . of a miscegenated culture in which, beneath the mask of inhuman racial etiquette where everyone supposedly was as separated as the twin beds in the bedroom of nearly every 1950s TV sitcom, there lurked an unquenchable thirst for mixing. And the "new" popular music helped to expose the false separation of America from itself, by revealing the culture's essential fusion all the more inescapably.[77]

Two accounts run parallel, then, and undoubtedly both are accurate. One is the effort to create white "rock and roll"—even the term itself was manufactured by a white man—from black rhythm and blues. The purpose of this, Nelson George argues, was to dull the racial identification and make young white consumers more comfortable by producing music that seemed more "universal." George refers to rock and roll as "white negroism" and suggests the point was to make as large a profit as possible by exploiting white teens.[78] Sanitized white cover versions of black records were central to this effort to maintain segregation, protect white youth (specifically white girls) from the sexuality of black music, and make huge profits for white record companies and artists (who often stole from black artists). Elvis Presley was the centerpiece of this success.

The other account is of the unprecedented interest, obsession even, of white youth with black music, rhythm and blues and rock and roll, which could be heard on black radio stations and later on white stations, played by disc jockeys like Alan Freed. Gillett's history of rock and roll chronicles how "adolescents staked out their freedom in cities, inspired and reassured by the rock and roll beat." Major white recording companies tried to keep up with the indigenous artists and independent companies. Disc jockeys like Alan Freed and Buffalo's Hounddog literally or metaphorically called for integration and encouraged a "culture invigorated by the infusion of subcultural forms."[79] George Lipsitz suggests that middle-class youths had the resources to "begin experimenting with cultural forms that challenged sexual repression, racial oppression, and class oppression. At the same time, the cultures and subcultures of seemingly marginalized outsiders held a fascinating attraction for privileged youths looking for alternatives to the secure but stifling and limited sexual roles and identities of middle-class life."[80] Janis Joplin remembers, "They were playing that fifties crap on the radio. . . . It seemed so shallow, all oop-boop. It had nothing. Then I heard Leadbelly and it was like a flash. It *mattered* to me." Bonnie Raitt says of the early 1960s, "When I heard 'Candyman' by Mississippi John Hurt on that album, I went, '*What* is that?' "[81] By that time she was already interested in Joan Baez and Odetta, but Hurt moved her deeply. She and Joplin, like many other white teens, sought out black music in record stores, on the radio, and in concert. Many of the concerts sponsored by stations that broadcast rhythm and blues were integrated; concerts at the Apollo theater in Harlem attracted white youth.[82] In Benita Eisler's *Private Lives,* a southern white man recalls his youth: "Before there was Elvis. . . . I started going crazy for 'race music.' It had a beat. I loved it. I listened to it whenever and wherever I could, first on the local black stations. I loved to dance to it. That got me into trouble with my parents and the schools, because we were not allowed to listen to this music openly." He hid his radio, which became a symbol of rebellion and a site of struggle in many families, and listened to black stations. Gerri Hirshey, a white woman whose life was changed by black music, writes, "When soul was at its peak in the 1960s, an entire generation was trying to get out of its post-Eisenhower self. Soul blew a huge hole in *Leave it to Beaver*-land. It was untrammeled, emotional, *different* music." These experiences had a common generational meaning for white teenagers who found vitality in the music. They represent a rejection of American racial codes and sexual repression and reflect the need and ability of the younger generation to find alternatives to the limited options available in middle-class life. White teens found what they were seeking in bohemians and Beats and in otherness—usually black, often working-class, culture. Elinor Lerner writes, "For teenagers like myself, there was a clear distinction between life before rock and roll and the world which had been changed by the music." Rock and roll, she says, created a sense of "alienation, rebellion, and ... affirmation/community."[83]

It is in this context that we must understand the startling popularity of rock and roll and its significance for young people. Elvis's success cannot be explained simply by the fact that he was a white, and therefore palatable, heartthrob. As we will see below, his meanings were multiple. A struggle was unfolding in which white teens chose black music while their elders tried desperately to undermine that choice. That the music was derived from black culture and made by black people, a population discriminated against and kept separate, even invisible to many white teenagers, was part of its appeal. The gatekeepers of American culture, including the white record companies, tried to make the music as forbidden for middle-class whites as were its inventors. The genuine expressiveness of rock and roll—despite so much of it having been weakened and whitened—spoke to white teenagers of another, unknown, inviting culture in America. "Black music became a means for the public expression of normally private sensations for white teenagers in the 1950s, but the institutions in which black musicians

played had always had an atmosphere of risk and excitement and promise; they offered to the young people drawn to them symbols of
rebellion," writes Charlie Gillett. Rock challenged traditional and official American culture because of its multiracial influences and contacts.
James Brown's father, much like Eldridge Cleaver, suggested that young
white folks "run *away* from America."[84]

Rhythm and blues and rock and roll thus became a lightening rod
in widening generational divisions. "We all loved Little Richard, Chuck
Berry, and Sam Cooke, and my personal favorites included the
McGuire Sisters, Doris Day, and Patti Page." Speaking is a black teenage
girl who grew up in a Detroit housing project and aspired to be in a doo-
wop singing group. She suggests the astonishing appeal of the music,
even it in its white versions, and of a culture relevant to adolescents
whatever their race and class.[85] While much of the music was trite and
accessible—records, sock hops, and dancing part of a burgeoning teen
market—it meant for some young people a break with dominant expectations.[86] The cultural duality of the music, simultaneously mainstream
and subversive, innocent and dangerous, parallels the paradox girls
faced vis-à-vis glamor and sexuality. The music was both safe *and*
potentially disruptive, more effective perhaps because of its ambiguity.
Music not obviously rebellious became a symbol of youth rebellion
against authority, with sex and race the not-so-hidden narratives. It provided a version of rebellion without requiring one to be a rebel.

In the two novels about the fifties we have compared, rock and roll
created contrasting textures for teenage life. Vic Holyfield and his
friends have warm and nostalgic feelings about Elvis Presley and other
fifties rock artists and groups; the music cemented a generational bond.
But for the hero of *The Red Menace,* rock and roll is explicitly about sex,
as it is for the writer Jane Lazarre. She describes herself listening to Elvis
Presley records in her room with the door closed when her father
storms in, "where he inevitably finds me gyrating wildly to the music,
my facial expression a perfect illustration of the dangers of loss of
reasonable self-control. I am, as they would say now, turned on. Then
we merely called it hot. I am so involved with my body that I don't hear
him come in."[87] Sheila Rowbotham writes that her love of rock music

was based on her interest in direct and intense feeling and in authenticity, which she also found in the Beats and existentialism. Rock music created a "sense of release, an explosion of pentupness" the way Beat writing did: "Every rock record simply was. The words were subordinate to the rhythm and the music went straight to the cunt and lit the bottom of your spine." Rock and roll offered Elinor Lerner an alternative to the feminine stereotype: "Visions of independence, excitement, danger, as well as temptations and promises of a life which included models other than that of the nuclear family, white house and picket fence."[88]

Anania's working-class hero describes a scene in which a middle-class girl who may be interested in him asks him to buy her a sexy rock and roll record only sold in black record stores (as a white working-class boy he has access to the black neighborhood). He believes this is a message of her sexual interest in him, but it turns out not to be. A black friend explains: "Lots of these chicks like lowdown music, man, and they like it real black . . . Now, that don't mean they're hot for some black cat or any white cat either. They just want to play dirty, man. And they ain't nothin' washes off easier than somebody else's dirt . . . Bet she likes that redneck Presley." When he answers that she does, the friend replies, "Same difference. This chick ever be caught dead with a greasehead peckerwood like Elvis?"[89] In this incident and commentary, sex, race, and class are brought together. Through music, middle-class white girls indirectly ventured into the male world of working-class blacks and whites.

Actually, the girl in question might have been "caught dead" with a boyfriend from "outside," despite the suggestion that she is hypocritical (in the privacy of her room, she could have been Lazarre). Middle-class white girls were interested in working-class boys. The girl gives signals the hero interprets as sexual, although her intentions are unclear, perhaps even to herself. She is tentative and curious. This is the common thread of girls' experiences in the 1950s: contradictory cues, ambiguity of intention, the possibility of new experiences, restlessness, hesitations, and dissemblance. The mixed messages regarding virginity and glamor and sexuality, for example, meant that girls were responding to a variety of cues and constructing selves that were conformist and questioning at the same time. Rock and roll was a principal ingredient in mainstream popular teenage culture but it was a source of rebellious inspiration too. It raised issues of sex, race, and class in a culture dedicated to ignoring them and was liberating because of it. Bodies, immediacy, fun were fundamental to the music. Its meanings hovered around the sexual. This separated young women from their families but did not necessarily translate into sex.

Analyzing fandom, particularly the adulation of Elvis, and of the Beatles in the next decade, Barbara Ehrenreich, Elizabeth Hess, and Gloria Jacobs suggest that being a fan was a way to "express sexual yearnings that would normally be pressed into the service of popularity or simply repressed. The star could be loved noninstrumentally, for his own sake, and with complete abandon. To publicly advertise this hopeless love was to protest the calculated, pragmatic sexual repression of teenage life." Being a fan implied the rejection, if fleeting, of middle-class expectations regarding appropriate boyfriends and the neat progression of courtship from dating, going steady, to getting married. It permitted irrationality and hysteria. Fandom offered girls a way "not only to sublimate romantic and sexual yearnings but to carve out subversive versions of heterosexuality." It was no accident that Elvis, a lower-class greaser singing black music, a "hood who had no place in the calculus of dating, going steady and getting married," was the object of hysteria for millions of girls. He was fantasy material precisely because he was so remote from the pragmatic ideal, an impossible partner.[90]

The hysteria about Elvis Presley revealed how deeply white America feared blacks and sexuality. Nelson George remarks that Elvis's black sound "scared white parents and the guardians of separation just as if [he himself] were black." Andrew Ross notes Presley's utilization of bits of black culture to create his stylized look: He wore Royal Pomade hair grease, "used by hep cats to create the shiny, slick hairstyles of the day. The famous rockabilly cut . . . was clearly his interpretation of the black 'process,' where blacks had their hair straightened and curled into curious shapes. Some charge that the process hairstyle was a black attempt to look white. So, in a typical pop music example of crosscultural collision, there was Elvis adapting black styles from blacks adapting white looks." Presley was the white Negro, according to Nelson George, embodying the dangerous sexuality mainstream Americans saw in blacks, a form of "reverse integration": "Elvis was sexy; not clean-cut, wholesome, white-bread, Hollywood sexy but sexy in the aggressive earthy manner associated by whites with black males."[91]

Linda Ray Pratt suggests that Elvis's appeal also consisted of the fact that he was sexually suspect, "vaguely androgynous." The sexuality Elvis projected combined masculine and feminine characteristics: masculine aggression and illicit thrills merged with tenderness, vulnerability, and romance. (This has been argued about the appeal of the Beatles too; their playful sexuality was not easily classifiable within the rigid gender distinctions that were the legacy of the fifties.) Thus, Elvis was not only racially ambiguous, but sexually ambiguous as well. This "dark androgyny," to use Thomas Doherty's description, was explosive.[92]

As fans of Elvis, teenage girls simultaneously participated in and disassociated themselves from boring and stressful courtship rituals and the prescribed wholesomeness of their futures. Their enthusiasms were tentative forays into alternative notions of femininity. Elvis and other rock and roll singers were inappropriate idols from the perspective of adult culture, neither acceptably masculine nor white enough. Even rock stars like Buddy Holly, whose "whiteness" was not an issue, sang more rhythmically and directly about sex than had previously been acceptable in white popular music. Being a fan, like taking up with or dreaming of boys from the wrong side of the tracks, boys who were wild and dark, were ways in which white, middle-class girls took advantage of the spaces that teenage popular culture provided. As fans they constructed their idols in a process of exploration, as an escape, even a protest. The racial and class component is, as usual, complicated. If whiteness in postwar American culture is framed as a question, an issue to be examined rather than assumed, then the invisibility of difference on which it was premised was interrogated by white teenagers. Their interest in rock and roll and black artists (and young women's interest in Beat men, white outsiders who were themselves drawn to black culture) was an acknowledgment of black cultural contributions. This is true despite the fact that the perception of the boyfriend or star as other was undoubtedly guilty of exoticization or phantom-creation. Thus, again, the balance is crucial between a genuine interest in and influence by another culture and way of life and a voyeuristic use as an escape from one's own. Vaguely androgynous men—playful, sexual, tender even, and often dark—provided young women with alternate visions of masculinity and femininity, of identity, and as Barbara Ehrenreich suggests, of heterosexuality. Music that spoke to young people of the body, of sex, and of people and experiences they did not know provided them with a glimpse of difference. Teenage girls used the music to imagine themselves outsiders just as they imagined themselves Beat adventurers.

Nonconformity

Carolyn Heilbrun states that what becomes obvious in studying women "who moved against the current of their times is that some condition in their lives insulated them from society's expectations and gave them a source of energy, even a sense of destiny, which would not permit them to accept the conventional female role. Some condition of being an outsider gave them the courage to be themselves." Hetty Jones says simply, "There didn't seem to be anyone like me, either where I'd come from or where I was presently."[93] Growing up in the 1950s, Caryl Rivers recognized that all she would be "offered [was] one ticket, good for a lifetime, to the bleachers," cheering for the men. The heroines of the movies she passionately imbibed cowered in the background while the good guys defeated the bad guys. Nevertheless, she says, "I had an easy solution to inequitable sex-role divisions . . . I just changed sex when I played the movie . . . I had a tough sinewy little ego that grew along with my feet," despite the fact that "the climate at mid-century was decidedly hostile to prickly ego-cacti grown by little girls. Notions about the nature of woman hovered over us like an inversion. The air we breathed was filled with carcinogens more poisonous to our inner growth than the unfiltered Camel smoke we inhaled in the bathrooms at school was to our lungs."[94]

In accounts of growing up female in the "poisonous" fifties, girls tell similar tales of changing their sex in order to achieve agency in the world. Girls playacted boys as children, and as adolescents imagined themselves men. Sheila Rowbotham's copy of *On the Road* had "Drugs, Liquor and Girls" written all over it: "The categories didn't trouble me at all. I simply switched sex as I did with Miller and Lawrence and identified with the men because they were exciting and adventurous."[95] Ellen Willis remembers finding out that she was female: "By the time I was six or so, I must have discovered the awful truth, because I made a big point of despising boys—on the grounds they were stupid and unadventurous. But when I playacted with my girlfriends, I always wanted a boy's part." As she grew up she was determined, through career aspirations, to prove she was a "perfectly good man." Women were contemptible "except for those happy few of us who were really men."[96]

A number of themes predominate in rebel girls' own explanations of their hunger for authenticity and their defiance, of their need, like Zane and Janis Joplin, "to get out." Those who felt themselves to be cultural dissidents wanted something more than their society promised them. They looked around a little harder and a bit more closely because they didn't "fit." Shulman's heroine states, only partly tongue in cheek, that even as a child a fanatical revolutionary was incubating in her everyday self. She feels she was marked early in life as "different," musing that perhaps because the name her parents gave her was so unusual, she developed into an unusual person. Hetty Jones says, "Unlike any woman in my family or anyone I'd ever actually known, I was going to *become*—something, anything, whatever that meant."[97] Such girls wouldn't or couldn't accept the rules. While it would make little sense to attempt to psychologize their dissent—given that in every historical period there are those who early in life feel out of pace with their society and time—the themes embedded in their stories reveal much about the situation for adolescents in the 1950s. These girls were among the unhappy teenagers discovered in surveys who in their discontent forged new paths for women.

The middle-class white girls who were early cultural dissidents included girls who felt homely, were smart, had leftwing or bohemian parents, or grew up in New York City. It may be, too, that girls who would later identify themselves as lesbians were, as girls and teenagers, nonconformists. Many girls felt homely or awkward. We know this is not an uncommon feeling for young women in mass-mediated and consumer culture. But in the 1950s, the emphasis on Hollywood attractiveness, on one version of female beauty—big-breasted, fair through-and-through, and conventionally feminine—generated intense feelings of inadequacy in many teenage girls. Marge Piercy suggests that the limited notion of acceptable beauty "marred a whole generation of women who grew up knowing they did not embody it (training in self-hatred) and a whole generation of men who felt they were entitled to it."[98] The Doris Day, Tuesday Weld, Marilyn Monroe, Debbie Reynolds versions of beauty were narrow and white, varying degrees of wholesomeness and sexiness notwithstanding.

Women remember longing to be part of the popular crowd and at the same time disdaining it and recognizing they didn't fit in. This duality, in tandem with a critical sensibility, appears repeatedly in rebel girls' accounts of themselves. They operated on several tracks, in more than one social scene. These adolescents remember wanting to be popular, even achieving popularity, while participating in marginal activities or social groups. Their rejection of mainstream teenage values prepared them for alternative lives despite their involvement in, or desire to be involved in, popular diversions. Zane says she had never really belonged: "I'd been branded weird for nothing more errant than playing chess . . . ; then, for my haircuts, my sox, my attitudes." But she also wanted to "win their admiration" and followed "them" after school, watched them, drew pictures of them: "And though I denounced them to my friend Dee-Dee, I was flattered whenever one of them, in an act of daring, befriended me." Sylvia Fraser recounts that as an adult she regressed to the youthful high school years she had missed and became a fifties teenager, "the Debbie Reynolds that in high school [she] refused to be while secretly yearning to be." The sense of exclusion, longing, and disdain was common among rebel girls, especially for those who came from radical families. Kim Chernin, the child of communists in Los Angeles, describes her turbulent high school years during which she "passed" as a pretty and popular girl—flattered by invitations from ordinary and privileged teenagers—while befriending and being supported by black and Mexican kids. Her ambivalence was almost palpable.[99]

Girls like these remember not liking makeup, hating the clothes because they were so uncomfortable, not being able to get the curlers right, not knowing how to flirt, feeling just plain "out of it" or sometimes just not caring enough. Vivian Gornick recalls a woman in her Bronx building who tried to teach her how to be alluring to men:

But none of it took. I was entranced during these woman-making sessions of ours. . . . I wanted to wear clothes the way she wore them, but I didn't want it enough. . . . Away from her I'd lapse into my old forgetful habits of dress, couldn't remember what went with what, how to put it all together. Certainly I couldn't remember that the way I dressed and held myself was a tool of the trade, an instrument of future gain, a vital means of achieving the image that would bring into my sphere of influence the man who could deliver up as much life-and-world as I had a right to hope for.[100]

Feeling homely or inadequate was always painful, and remembered that way, but it also provided some girls with a critique of the culture or the inspiration to escape or excel in other areas. They were able to utilize their exclusion in the service of another vision.

Perhaps of central importance was being smart and doing well in school, although as we have seen, many were discouraged by parents and teachers from excelling academically and from pursuing higher education seriously. Girls recollect with resentment their parents' and teachers' lack of interest in their intellectual pursuits. Many girls who were attracted to the Beats or who wanted to experiment were noticeably intelligent. This distinguished them in the time of the feminine mystique. Being obviously smart and excelling in school was a source of suffering for adolescent girls in the popularity-based-on-appearances teen culture. In 1950s terms, being a "bookworm" or "brain" meant that one would not easily be popular with boys. One English girl cultivated eccentricity as an adolescent because she didn't fit anywhere: "This role was made considerably easier by the fact that I was already widely regarded as something of a freak thanks to a 'braininess' which, it appeared, might have been acceptable in a boy but was most peculiar in a girl." She remarks, "From an early age I must have been aware that this quality of cleverness placed me outside any possibility of conforming to normal feminine stereotypes."[101] Many girls yearned to drop the "smart" identity in favor of popularity, since the two seemed mutually exclusive. But some understood that they might be able to use their intelligence as a way out of feminine constraints. While it was a source of discomfort, it allowed them to nurture and act on nonconformist dreams.

Having a talent or interest that set them apart provided the space to fantasize about using it to their own advantage in the world outside the family. Women speak of their reading and writing, and other interests such as music and art with enthusiasm. Many enjoyed their faculties, despite little reinforcement, clinging to a skill as a lifeline because they felt out of place, or developing it as a consequence of their discomfort, but also valuing it for the genuine intellectual and artistic satisfactions it brought. Some thought of themselves as incipient artists. Some who had access to New York City imagined a career as a stage actress (not a movie star). The theater was unconventional and thus an acceptable outlet for female artistic ambition. However, some in the slightly older cohort who considered themselves bohemian speak bitterly in retrospect about bohemian women in Greenwich Village, who had no option, because of sexism, but to pursue work as an actress or waitress. In the Village for a week, Zane has the following conversation: " 'So you're from Indiana,' he said. 'I'll bet you came to be an actress.' She doesn't understand. 'I'm a debater, but not an actress. Why do people keep asking me that?' He shrugged, then smiled. 'Why else do pretty girls come to the Village? To be actresses, or students maybe.' "[102]

According to the bohemian gender code, it was impossible for a woman to be a serious artist with genuine creative aspirations; being an actress, however, was acceptable. Furthermore, because political dissent and social movements were almost nonexistent, channeling energy into artistic expression was one available form of nonconformity. Artistic expression is not honored in American culture unless it is lucrative; thus the materialism of the 1950s made artists, Beats, and bohemians (although perhaps not jazz artists since black artists were not expected to be successful) seem particularly foolish. Within this already foolish enterprise, then, young women were further constrained by gender rules. Angela McRobbie points out that in Britain the main recruiting grounds for girls into feminism was through the arts, in postwar bohemia, despite its explicitly masculine expression. This was true, too, for the first generation of postwar feminists in the United States, many of whom nourished secret aspirations to become writers, artists, or actresses.[103]

Girls who were adolescents in the 1950s and grew up in communist or communist-sympathizing families acquired a sophistication uncommon among other girls. They were exposed to people and political issues of which mainstream girls never even dreamed. From early on, many considered themselves different, part of a dissident culture. Their family experiences meant they could never completely belong to a carefree teenage world, making them perfect examples of the dissembling so characteristic of fifties life. Ironically, the children of those who were most excoriated in postwar America—those identified as enemies and communists—experienced to an intense degree what other young people also felt, the necessity of dissimulation and secrecy. Children of communists or fellow travelers felt they didn't really fit in, were excluded, or were pressured by families not to participate in teenage life. They grew up with one foot outside the mainstream, involved in a left subculture that in many cases was all-encompassing. If they grew up in New York City, particularly Manhattan, or if they went to a private, radical, or elite New York City school, they were exposed further to a cosmopolitanism that made them less susceptible to mainstream teenage culture. There was more to draw from, more resources for the construction of alternative images and life. Going to such a school also exposed young people who did not come from left-wing families to red diaper babies, thereby broadening their horizons.[104] It is undoubtedly true that all young people growing up in major cities were exposed to a diversity unavailable to those who grew up in the suburbs or smaller cities and towns. Sociologists and historians have long pointed out that urban life breeds and makes room for difference. Exposure to a wide variety of people distanced many nonconformist girls from teenage culture.

There is evidence, and it is my informal impression, that the mothers in families who moved to the suburbs were different from those who stayed.[105] Families who remained urban did so for numerous reasons, the obvious one being financial. But some middle-class mothers either worked or had interests that the suburbs could not sustain. This meant that young middle-class women who grew up in New York or other major cities were more likely to have mothers whose identities encompassed more than housewifery and motherhood. I am not suggesting that all women who moved to the suburbs had only domestic aspirations, but rather that those who did not move understood their lives were better served in the city. The urban daughters had less conventional role models than did suburban daughters of full-time middle-class mothers.[106]

As I think about my own history, I see that probing proceeded on many fronts. I was a both a cheerleader and a beatnik, and while the dissident persona chronologically followed the teen enthusiast during my high school years, they were never clearly separate. Glamor and dissidence, apparently contradictory, both drew me. I still wanted to go to the senior prom and to have all that entailed as I boarded the train for Greenwich Village on Sundays. Popularity mattered even as I donned my black tights. I browsed the makeup counter in Woolworth's evaluating lipstick and rouge and eyelash curlers. I was hedging my bets, searching for the gaps, exploring the cultural weak spots, trying to sort out what a girl was supposed to be or might be, constructing a feminine identity for the future.

A subterranean life, acted out or dreamed about, was generated by a culture that penalized girls and young women who were unable or unwilling to fit the model of the happy-go-lucky teenager eagerly anticipating marriage and motherhood. The rigidity of what was acceptable in that culture made some of us feel discontent and unreal, as if our lives had not yet begun. The parameters of feminine beauty, personality, intelligence, and ambitions were so narrow that a minor deviation meant exclusion and discomfort and, often unintentionally, became a wedge that grew into insurgence. As young women, we looked to the Beats and bohemians and to rock and roll with an interest that betrayed our dismay at the thought of a life of suburban domesticity. Our at times articulated and other times mute rebelliousness led us to men who broke the rules. It also led us to break the rules ourselves. As beatniks and even as fans of rock and roll, young women were curious about what lay outside the family, their towns, and suburbs. Like young women who were drawn to glamor and the promises of movie and media culture—and none of these interests were mutually exclusive— we latched onto signs of otherness in music and subcultures, in effect, rehearsing lives we hoped would be different from our mothers'.

Alone in the Fifties:
Anne Parsons
and the Feminine Mystique

The unmarried individual occupies a position in society generally considered by social theorists as dysfunctional in the societal structure, a position that is out of step with the normative patterns of living.

Gerald Gurin, Joseph Veroff, and Sheila Feld,
Americans View Their Mental Health *(1960)*

A book of essays by Anne Parsons, entitled *Belief, Magic, and Anomie: Essays in Psychosocial Anthropology,* appeared in 1969. It was edited by a number of well-known social scientists: Rose Laub Coser, the main editor, Renee C. Fox, Louisa P. Howe, Sidney Mintz, Jesse Pitts, and David Schneider, and one psychiatrist, Merton J. Kahne.[1] From the editors' introduction, we learn that Anne Parsons worked on the staffs of a number of Boston-area hospitals and in Naples, Italy; that she had many colleagues and friends there and in France and Italy, particularly anthropologists and psychiatrists; and that she died in 1964 at the age of thirty-three. We do not learn from the introduction that she was the daughter of the famous sociologist Talcott Parsons; nor that she committed suicide.

Anne Parsons is remembered by only those who knew her personally. This is not surprising since her scholarly career, although brilliant, was brief and yielded no major book or synthesis. It was her friends and colleagues who brought out her book of essays posthumously. In this chapter, I want to rescue her from an undeserved anonymity by reconstructing some of her painful personal experiences and by articulating their relation not only to her own history but, more important, to the complex pressures confronted by her generation of educated and professional women in the 1950s, and indirectly, by those younger than she. Her life is a case study that reflexively captures in her insights and dilemmas critical cultural dissonances for elite, white women of the 1950s. Anne Parsons was in her twenties, not an adolescent, in the 1950s. In many ways she is not a representative woman. Nevertheless I include her story here because it is revealing of the climate in which girls grew up.

She suffered in a culture that women of my generation were able to subvert; her story dramatizes the significance of those changes. The extremity of her experiences and pain provide a vivid glimpse into the psychological and social conflicts experienced by professional women in the 1950s. Unlike the Beat rebels and nonconformist adolescent women who purposively explored outside mainstream culture, Anne Parsons was a grim prisoner of that culture. If she had been able to break with it, she would have been provided some relief. Ironically, by remaining single and committing herself to her career she challenged gender norms profoundly, perhaps more profoundly than rebel or "bad" girls did. Anne Parsons's deviations translated into an aloneness that is the sobering counterpoint to the excitement of the younger generation's impending rupture with dominant expectations.

Early Years

Anne Parsons was born in 1930 in Cambridge, Massachusetts, where her father, Talcott Parsons, taught at Harvard and her mother, Helen Walker Parsons, worked at the Russian Research Institute. The family lived on Brattle Street, the center of Harvard Cambridge, until she was seven years old, when they moved to the suburb of Belmont.[2] She grew up with a strong sense of her family history and of her place within it: "Through the lineage of her mother . . . as well as her renowned sociologist father . . . Anne was a descendent of Yankee sea captains, clergymen, physicians, college professors, and of the courageous women who were their mothers, sisters, wives and maiden aunts."[3] Talcott Parsons, who had joined the Harvard faculty in the late 1920s, was in the 1940s and 1950s the most famous and influential sociologist in America. He was a liberal grand theorist and defender of advanced capitalist society. He wrote copiously and his eminence, personality, and position at Harvard were critical factors in Anne's development. She says of herself that she was happy before she moved, but in the public schools in Belmont life became more complicated for her. Although there were Protestant-Catholic divisions at school, her unhappiness was due primarily to her feelings of being on the outside. She desperately wanted to belong, but she was not skilled socially. The skills that might have enabled her to fit in were not encouraged by her family and were perhaps not even of concern to them.

In the autobiography she wrote for entrance to the Boston Psychoanalytic Institute in 1959, she refers to herself as a "brain" who nevertheless dreamed of being a cheerleader or going out with the captain of the basketball team. She says however, that by her senior year in high school, she had begun to see herself as a free thinker and mild political radical and to like that identification. From 1949 to 1951, she went to Swarthmore College. She was not happy there but she studied hard "as usual," in part because it helped her loneliness. She later learned that people thought she was unapproachable because she was so studious, but in truth she says, "I was so studious because I was afraid to approach people." She praised Swarthmore for its high standards and values that questioned materialism, affirmed female intelligence, and assumed that girls were in college for more than "husband-getting": In 1963, she wrote of her college years to Betty Friedan:

Even then my initial conscious refusal to follow the feminine mystique was not too difficult: I come from an intellectual family where an interest

in the outside world is taken for granted and in her quiet and modest
way my mother has managed a house, three children, and a steady job
without ever having talked about Femininity or How to Ensnare a
Man. However the feminine mystique did even then effect (sic) *me in*
various insidious ways, for example, in my now-regretted decision
not to take fourth-year high school math for fear of being called a
brain and in my more important failure to ever make a real and
substantial career choice.

After two and a half years, Parsons transferred from Swarthmore to
Radcliffe in order, she says in her letter to Friedan, to get married: "During college I came close to marrying for security's sake but at the last
minute called the wedding off: the world seemed so much bigger than
split-level houses, and I thought I had better start off to see it which I
did." This decision is one that marks her as more independent than
many young women in 1952. Her decision to go to Swarthmore, which
in the 1950s had a reputation as a pacifist and radical college, suggests
this as well.

After her graduation, she remained in Cambridge for a year and
then went to study in Paris on a Fulbright. In 1955 she received her
Docteur d'Universite with a thesis written in French on the diffusion of
psychoanalytic ideas in France and the United States, signalling her
lifelong interest in psychoanalysis. In Paris she studied with Lacan,
Piaget, and Lévi-Strauss; anthropology and psychiatry were her con-
centrations.

She returned to Boston at the age of twenty-five, and there
followed three years that she later referred to as miserably unhappy.
From 1955 to 1958 she was affiliated with the Harvard Medical School
and undertook cross-cultural research on patients in a number of
Boston-area mental hospitals, but mainly at McLean Hospital. Funded
by a fellowship from the National Institute of Mental Health, she
worked with and collected case histories of female schizophrenic
patients, Italian-American and Yankee, in order to compare them. She
also began to think about marriage again. Writing to Friedan she says,
"At the ripe old age of 25, I found it was already too late: most of my

contemporaries were already on the third child and too busy mowing lawns and buying things to be much interested in existentialism or the political situation in Algeria."[4] A second profound disappointment of these years is expressed in a letter written shortly before her death. She regrets the absence of political movements in which to be involved: "Nearly ten years ago I got back from being a student in Paris, and for lack of anything better and a feeling that the thirties that I had always wished I lived in had died, I got a hospital research job." She continues, "My advice to the next generation is that there are still perfectly good reasons for starving in the Village with nothing but a first name and a typewriter. . . . there is no point at all to allowing one's soul or one's language to be corrupted" by foundation grant applications and professional life.[5] Clearly a bohemian life in Greenwich Village offered an appealing contrast to the Puritan traditions of her upbringing. It was a world she was drawn to but never approached, although as we have seen, other women of her generation were able to find a home of sorts in that culture.

Although her life was not entirely without reward in this period—she writes in her autobiography of feeling more human in her work at the hospital and of pleasing her father, who was "immensely proud" of her Paris degree—she felt overall that she had sacrificed too much for her career. In her letter to Friedan, she says that she had managed to stay out of psychoanalysis so far by rejecting the idea that she "was avoiding (her) basic femininity by being more interested in seeing Paris than having children at 22" and that she had "paid a very high price for a rather rapid career advance." She continues: "I know that a life devoted wholly to work in a mental hospital was an impossible one, but no matter how I tried I couldn't find a way out." She tells Friedan of the extreme difficulties faced by those in her situation:

Life for the unmarried person after 25 or so is simply not very easy because by this fact one is thrown out of all the better-worn social grooves so that even relatively simple things as what to do on Sunday become impossibly difficult. Probably the worst of the unpleasant results the situation creates is that it becomes difficult to remember that love is an

*intimate personal emotion that depends purely on chance, not a social
obligation (as proof of one's normalcy) or an abstract search for an
"object."*[6]

Parsons received further funding from the NIMH, and in 1958 she
went to Naples, Italy, to continue her cross-cultural research on schizo-
phrenia. Her two years in Naples seem to have been her happiest. In her
letter to Friedan, she refers to them as an escape, adding, sardonically,
"[I lived] happily for two years with a man who had only a fifth-grade
education but was much less phased by my 'aggressive and competitive'
personality than most of the American M.D.'s and Ph.D's that I had
known." The interest in difference is evident here too: Parsons finds
contentment with an inappropriate man—uneducated, Catholic, and
undoubtedly, dark. She studied Southern Italian families, mental
patients, and culture. Parsons had always had the fantasy of living in a
different social world from the one she was born into. From her
autobiography we learn, for example, that she had thought of taking a
year off from college to do factory work because, she says, she didn't
know what she was studying for. Her parents refused permission. As we
have seen, she was attracted to the bohemian life of Greenwich Village.
In Naples, she was able to realize this longing. Italy was her most intense experience of an alternative to the white Anglo-Saxon culture in
which she had grown up. Among other things, she says, she had the
chance to be young in Italy: "Perhaps I more than most people have
deliberately sought an early heavy responsibility but from all sides one
is pressured by the responsibility to make one's major life choices and
settle down at an early point—if one doesn't, that's neurosis. But I never
wanted to be a permanent Bohemian, only to see the world a bit." In
Naples she learned to see her own world with more distance, realizing
her mixed feelings about the ambition and careerism that drove everyone in Boston and that made her feel less human and whole, not in
touch with all of herself. She worried about returning and not being
able to be both a professional and a human being.[7]

The autobiography from which I am quoting was written in Italy in
October 1959 as a part of Parsons's application to the Boston Psy-

choanalytic Institute to enter a training analysis there. In that spring and fall of 1959 while making plans for her return, she was full of ambivalence. She did not want to leave Italy and was especially unsure about entering psychoanalysis. During that fall, she also applied for a Foundations' Fund for Research in Psychiatry fellowship for training social scientists in psychiatry. The goal of the Foundations' Fund was interdisciplinary enrichment. Recipients were encouraged to become analytic candidates; indeed, her fellowship (or the way Parsons wrote it) was predicated on the analysis. The sponsoring institution for this fellowship was McLean Hospital, her "main career advisor" there, Dr. Alfred Stanton, psychiatrist-in-chief at McLean.[8] She postponed her departure from Italy several times and wrote both then and later about how torn and confused she was, recognizing that to leave a place where she was happy in order to return to Boston and a work situation that might recreate the unhappy three years prior to Italy made little personal sense.[9] In retrospect, it is clear she made herself vulnerable by entering psychoanalysis and the Boston professional psychiatric and social scientific communities.

From the time she chose to write her thesis in France and embarked on a career incorporating psychoanalytic interests, psychoanalysis loomed large on her horizon. The world of her father, Harvard, and psychoanalytically inclined social scientists overlapped with the psychiatric community and the Boston Psychoanalytic Institute.[10] This was a close-knit and conservative world in which her identity as Talcott Parsons's daughter was perhaps the most significant fact about her. Given that and given what she knew about herself, she seems to have entered analysis innocently, drawn intellectually but unprepared psychologically and socially.[11] In the autobiography that was part of her application, she expresses her reservations, saying that while she respects the theory and method of analysis, she is not sure it is right for her: "I still do not feel that the personal values involved are wholly sympathetic, for I have retained a strong sense of the importance of working things out for oneself even if via deviant paths, of the value of real as opposed to couch experience even if the reality is conflictual or difficult, and the importance of personal privacy and reticence."

This last point is important in understanding Parsons's subsequent sense of betrayal at the hands of her psychoanalyst and therapists. The value, and need, of privacy was basic to her personality and to the family from which she had come. Moreover, her father's sociological work was, not surprisingly, characterized by a concern for proper differentiation of spheres of social life. She utilized his analytic categories in her work and life. Thus her sensitivity to the complicated personal and public relationships in therapeutic situations had both personal psychological and intellectual sources.

In a poignant, even ironic, letter to her parents written that same fall of 1959, she explains why she is having second thoughts about returning.[12] According to Parsons, when people in their social scene are unhappy the solution is to get analyzed and her decision to go for analytic training has been made under such pressure. She doesn't really want to commit herself to it, and thinks that what is responsible is "more [her] Puritan conscience than [her] professional judgement." Of course, analysis is written into the terms of her fellowship. Thus social pressure and her enormous sense of responsibility draw her to the psychoanalysis that will further undermine her emotional and mental health.

In fact, she says, she has learned in Italy that she has always tried to do too many things well: "For me it means that I can't be both a good theorist and a good researcher in two fields, fulfill the practical responsibilities that Stanton expects at McLean, keep an apartment and accounts with the precision I learned as a child, be attractive, well dressed and gracious as the present environment expects of a woman, and still have time to be a human being." She counterposes all her responsibilities, including being a woman, with being a human being. Being a woman (attractive, well-dressed, and gracious) was work that did not come easily to Parsons. It was also an effort that did not make her feel like a human being; rather, it fell into the large responsibility category that, for her, was opposed to good feelings. She tells her parents that Naples has enabled her to relinquish some of her ambition:

Mostly I want to continue to live a bit longer at the slower pace with the more limited and absorbable intellectual life I have found here as a way of consolidating some kind of inner freedom before I have to go back and face all the cross-pressures of Boston.... When children have difficulties adapting to life, it is generally said now that this has something to do with the parents. In any basic sense there is no reason for you to feel hurt or guilty in relation to me. One thing I do have is a kind of basic optimism and I think even a quite consistent set of values underneath my various girations. Otherwise I would have given up long ago. Nor do I feel I am fighting any kind of cruel and unreasonable external authority although I am certainly revolting against something and it has taken a long time to figure out just what. If there is one thing I got it is certainly a sense of responsibility and a set of instrumental values. But the thing about responsibility is that is it only relevant when you know to whom, how and for what meaning you are being responsible. And although at certain points in history instrumental values alone may have been meaningful in their own context, I think in ours something has really changed. I first noted it when in high school I learned you don't get dates because you are good and know how to keep accounts but because you curl your hair right and know how to make social conversation.... For me the problem that came to a head in the very unhappy time I spent in Boston was that working, doing well, trying to please the people I respect was incompatible with having any real emotional life, i.e., the main problem that I got into a stew about was not being married and thanks to my upbringing, I have always thought marriage is a good thing. But at that point marriage was impossible for me and I suffered from it.... No one wants to marry a woman who is continually involved in professional obligations or wholly absorbed by mental patients or theory since it just isn't professional achievement men look for in marriage.

Finally, she says, "Also, damn it expressive values are here to stay and you just have to have the social graces." She also tells her parents that when she returns to Boston, she hopes for the best in unattached males. "Why don't you keep an eye out for people you might invite to dinner in the spring? I wouldn't want interfering Italian parents but you carry the principle of noninterference to an extreme."

Here, then, is Anne Parsons, characteristically apologizing to her parents for the burden she feels she is to them (and utilizing her father's categories to analyze her life). Also characteristically, she is engaged in a dialogue with her father about the conflict between expressive and instrumental values, a dialogue as much with herself as him. She articulates her own turmoil over the recognition that what she has been taught in her family—what many young women were taught in postwar families, that is, to do what was expected of them—has not made her happy or successful. She notices that expressive skills and values are what really count. In a number of her key personal writings, Anne Parsons says she was never taught how to be conventionally feminine (for example, her mother never taught her how to curl her hair) because her family stressed other sorts of values. Although she admires this, she also has begun to understand how she has suffered from it. Her life as a woman would have been easier if she had been easier about such things. As she put it to her parents, "For me the problem that came to a head. . . . was that working, doing well, trying to please the people I respect was incompatible with having any real emotional life." Again, she articulates the Beat and bohemian challenge to middle-class respectability and the work ethic, although those subcultures appeared inaccessible to her.

Clearly, both Parson's desire for marriage and the familiar feminine conflict between work and love, so exaggerated in the 1950s, were great. There is no doubt that she wanted desperately to get married—it would have been hard not to in the 1950s, and she believed in marriage, "thanks to [her] upbringing." Most painfully of all, perhaps, Anne Parsons appeals to her parents for love. This is a theme that surfaces at different points, sometimes in the complaint that they are so independent as to not need any help from their children, other times in the accusation that they were uninvolved and noninterfering. It is noteworthy, too, that she enlists her parents' aid in her search for a mate, although it seems clear she needed more from them than help in finding a husband.

In the years after her return from Italy, Parsons's life took the shape of a dreadful isolation and sense of marginality that eventually overcame her. To be sure, her isolation was not all culturally inflicted. From early on she had felt herself an outsider, and although she longed to be part of a group, she separated herself from people. Not only was she often uncomfortable with others; she did not really want to be nor feel like those who did fit in easily. This is important because, while it is clear she was hurt by her choices and by who she was, she also insisted on being that person. Marginality and rebelliousness were critical components of her identity. Significantly, there were other women who felt as she did, other academics and professionals, artists and bohemians, and the politically active. Thus while much can be made of her self-imposed isolation or psychological problems—and they should not be denied—Anne Parsons was a woman whose struggles tell us about being alone in the 1950s.

The Feminine Mystique

Like so many other young women, Anne Parsons wrote to Betty Friedan after reading *The Feminine Mystique.* The difficulties intelligent women faced were described in many of the letters received by Friedan. In her letter of September 1963, Parsons emphasizes the conflict she has experienced between the immorality of not being interested in the world around her and the singleness that has been the outcome of her wide interests. As a result, she says, she has not had a serious relationship with an American man since the age of twenty-two. Furthermore, echoing a theme of Friedan's, she complains that in most upper-middle-class circles the unmarried career woman is scapegoated:

Nobody needs to look at her as a person at all since it is so well known in advance that she is aggressive, competitive, rejecting of femininity and all the rest. Thus being in that category is like being a Negro or Jew—with the difference that the prejudices are manifest in such subtle ways that it is very hard to pin them down, and that the feminine mystique is so strong and attractive an ideology that it is very hard to find a countervailing point of view from which to fight for oneself. The one resource the unmarried woman has is the psychoanalyst . . . but he will probably tell her she is aggressive, competitive, rejecting of femininity.

Parsons's last point is especially bitter, for by the time she wrote to Friedan, she was herself a patient at the Yale Psychiatric Institute. Her letter includes descriptions of extremely painful personal incidents with "budding psychoanalysts" in which Parsons was excluded and discouraged by her male colleagues. In her dealings with colleagues she tells of being cut off or in some way made to feel inappropriate, probably, she suggests, because she was too intellectual and single, or both. Potential friendships never developed. People communicate to the unmarried woman that

she is some sort of poison in the social system that has to be cast out: all I do know is that my own life became more and more of a void symbolized by the long spaces between my apartment and the suburban houses where I occasionally got invited for dinner to hear about the local school system and within which none of the messages from myself which I sent out in increasingly desperate ways ever came back with more than an echo of "you, you, you just don't want to be a woman at all." I began to wish that someone would call me names or throw stones or threaten to send me to a concentration camp so that at least I would know for certain that the world was against me.

The idea that Parsons's problems stemmed from her denial of her basic femininity cruelly united the Freudian and feminine mystique identification of femaleness with motherhood. She referred to this diagnosis often after she began the analysis required by her fellowship, maintaining that it just did not seem to fit who she was. The accusation that she had rejected her true self blamed the victim. That she was not married, had no lover, and pursued a career were used as proof of her lack of femininity. She tried desperately to defend herself against the charge and clearly she later found some help in Friedan's book, but the judgment unnerved and wounded her deeply. In a period that exaggerated conventional femininity and marriage as the only acceptable routes for women, an identification as unfeminine (dooming one to the fate of the most pitied of all women, the "old maid") was the ultimate failure. In such a cultural configuration, women had no option but to embrace a femininity that subordinated work and interest in the world to heterosexual love and marriage. The parochialism of the gender norms was profound, Parsons's inability to find alternative support extreme. She wrote to Friedan that she had lacked enough courage "to face the fact that if [she] wanted a world of [her] own, [she] would have to go out and find it" and to accept the idea that the kind of men she found worthwhile would not provide traditional marriage, that she would have to face "long periods of loneliness."

During Parsons first year as a nonmedical candidate in training analysis at the Boston Psychoanalytic Institute, she was not actively involved because of the requirement that a year of personal analysis be completed before the candidate entered the seminars. During the second year, she did attend seminars regularly. During the third year, her contact with the institute tapered off because she was not admitted to the clinical seminars that make up the most important part of that year's program. By a decision of the institute, her candidacy was terminated in March 1963. This was blow from which she never recovered.

In her progress report to the Foundations' Fund, written after her admission as a mental patient at the Yale Psychiatric Institute, Parsons explained why her work during the second and third year of the fellowship had been less productive than expected. She felt that one critical reason was the interdisciplinary nature of the work. While interdisciplinary work can be exciting, she noted, it can also result in "identity diffusion, or a failure to achieve or maintain the real and solid kind of professional identity and professional ties that are an important part of the self in the contemporary world." Despite the fact that she could clearly see the objective barriers faced by those who work within several disciplines, she always tended to take the blame upon herself. She suggested that her broad focus, which she believed prevented a clear professional identity, was a personal failure.

However, she argued, the central cause of her lowered work capacities had to do with her own analysis. If she had not been in analysis, she believed, she could have found more constructive ways of dealing with the problems she faced. For about a year the analysis had gone moderately well and offered some relief from depression. At the end of that year, however, she reports she went through a "severe panic episode," which she could only explain by reference to world events since it came at the time of the 1961 Berlin crisis and centered on fear of nuclear war. One of the effects of the episode was to make her doubt her professional commitments. In a letter to Dr. Jerome Frank, she says that during this time she did a great deal of reading that "crystallized" in her mind a "political image of the world . . . [the military-industrial complex] against the rest of humanity."[13] She describes her panic as very vivid, an overwhelming sense that "imminent destruction was actually possible," and relates that during the most acute phase she repeatedly

discovered the existence of some new evil: for example, a friend told me of developments in biological and chemical warfare making it possible to kill a man by flicking a drop of fluid and for a day or two I felt that such fluids were all around. Also I was extremely sensitive to sirens: in fact, the whole affair began one day when I heard fire sirens on the way to my analytic session after a lunch table conversation in which I learned that a colleague had built a shelter.

In Parsons, widespread postwar fears about nuclear war became a palpable, individual panic.

Parsons tells Dr. Frank that during this period, she "was both living alone and at the end of first year of analysis with an extremely orthodox analyst whose reaction to [her] panic experience was to say nothing at all." In her progress report to the Foundations' Fund, she describes herself as removed from any "social reciprocity." She confesses how she became more and more disturbed during the year after the panic and developed increasingly negative feelings about the analysis, trying desperately to get away from it and from Boston, looking for jobs in New York: "I did not attempt to hide the extent of the disturbance from Dr. A: through the entire period he maintained almost total silence and when I did force the issue of leaving insisted that this would be a form of acting out of impulses that should be analyzed on the couch. One of the factors that restrained me from leaving was a sense of responsibility towards the Foundations' Fund and the completion of the professional program which I had accepted."

At the beginning of the third year she had in fact terminated analysis. This was a desperate and dramatic step for Parsons, given her sense of duty, career plans, and personal and professional connections with individuals linked to her analyst and the Boston Psychoanalytic Institute. Her progress report states that she felt a "process of intra-psychic deterioration" had begun, and that she was fighting to protect herself.

The dismissal of Anne Parsons from the Boston Psychoanalytic Institute in March 1963 is critical to her story, although I will only outline it here. In the Foundations' Fund report, she says she had not communicated the facts earlier because of their embarrassing personal nature but believes they are important. She was shocked to have been dismissed as a psychoanalytic candidate with the stated reason that she was suffering from "serious neurotic difficulties not treatable by means of psychoanalysis." Parsons acknowledges that she may have been suffering from untreatable difficulties: "However, scientific knowledge is supposed to entail some predictive power and while one can understand mistakes being made on the basis of one or two interviews, it seems difficult to see why it was necessary to wait until six months after I had terminated a two-year analysis to communicate this to me. Being given the diagnosis of operable cancer after the time in which the operation could be carried out has passed must have about the same effect." She says that the timing of the dismissal indicates it was political, the result of her questioning the institute's policies.[14] At no time, she argues, did her analyst give her any indication that her status as a candidate was in doubt. Concluding her report to the Foundations' Fund, Parsons says apologetically that their expenditure on her behalf has resulted in the undoing in the course of analysis of whatever capacity she had for continued research. She describes her bitterness at the length of her ordeal and the handling of her case: ["It was only after two years of] such an unhappy analysis at such a great cost to myself that I was informed that it was not the appropriate treatment for me and in the grossness and obviousness of the way in which psychoanalytic politics quite independent of my personal life were involved in the time of the communication of that information." Finally, Parsons points out that it is much easier to stand up for oneself against disagreement when that disagreement involves external matters such as professional status or views "than when it hinges on an analysis in which one has communicated about 400 hours of one's private life."

This last point echoes one she made to Betty Friedan about the feminine mystique, namely, that her rejection and exclusion were not based on her ideas or politics but rather on her person, who she was, so that there was no way to defend herself. Both as a single woman and in her rejection from the institute, her core identity was at issue. She believed that her politics were unacceptable at the institute, although there was no confirmation of this. In neither case, did she have any control over the situation. Parsons said to Friedan that in her culture the one resource the single woman has to defend herself against the norm of marriage and children is the psychoanalyst. Ironically, when she did enter psychoanalysis she had the same terrible experience: she was rejected because of her personality and situation.[15] She felt utterly defenseless, especially as she had believed the analysis was confidential.

Between 1960 and 1963, Anne Parsons felt dreadfully and inescapably isolated. Whatever her personal difficulties, the fact is, she was a single professional woman with unfashionable approaches to mental illness without a regular position in a high-powered, mainly male, work world. She was a victim of the conservative, formal, and reticent politics of the Boston Psychoanalytic Institute and of her analyst. Furthermore, those affiliated with the institute included analysts who were acquaintances, superiors at hospitals where she worked, and well-known social scientists. Her situation was further complicated by being Talcott Parsons's daughter. She had neither anonymity nor support at the institute. She felt trapped in her failure since the analysis was central to her work, to the fellowship, and to her self-esteem. She was humiliated: after two years of a destructive analysis in which her analyst silently watched her deteriorate, she was rejected as an analytic candidate by that analyst and by people who knew her personally, were known to her, and were her father's and her own colleagues. To use a term she herself employed more than once, not only in regard to psychoanalysis, but of life in general, she had been "cast out."

Hospitalization, September 1963–June 1964

Diary of a Mental Patient (September 1963)
First day: well here I am, at last it happened, I got awfully scared about long John rockets and short range missiles and long range missiles and they said we had a lot more than the Russians anyway and biological warfare and chemical warfare and they say you can kill a man by flicking a drop of acid at 100 feet and it looked like the whole order was cracking at the seams and then I was an intellectual and a woman to boot, isolated and all that, so I tried the couch and he kept saying why can't you come to terms with your basic feminine instincts so I kept on trying on his couch and it wasn't much fun and I thought about it and I was really awfully scared about the missiles and live now while you have the chance and weren't we going to have any resistance and I was resisting insight into my feminine instincts and who the hell could marry one of those pompous medical students anyway it wasn't so much fun on the couch and think about cafes in Paris and Vienna and students in Africa fighting for freedom and who the hell can find the real repression in suburban houses no it is just that you CANNOT COME TO TERMS WITH YOUR BASIC FEMININE INSTINCTS *but I don't want an automatic washing machine electric dryer electric roaster think abut peasants working with their men in the fields and Hungarian freedom fighters a lot of them were girls and I know an Israeli who has two babies and fought the Arabs besides she's pretty with red hair and talks about how men act under combat and all those medical students just sit there of course they know all about* SAFE PAINLESS CHILDBIRTH *and* CHILDREN NEED ENOUGH LOVE *and if somebody doesn't do something about it they are going to blow up too but it was* YOU *that* COULD NOT COME TO TERMS WITH YOUR BASIC FEMININE INSTINCTS *and want to run that electric waxer around all day and then suddenly I cracked or as they would say in the jargon around here I flipped and here I am. Today they wrote my name on a list and I belong to a* THERAPEUTIC COMMUNITY.

*... and I was isolated from the group but nobody every beat me up
or called me names because I came from the best New England families
and I wasn't taught to be suspicious of anyone except maybe Irish
Catholics from Boston and my father thought it was clear that everyone
should be against Nazis and he kept pounding on the typewriter all day
about it so he was isolated from the group and I guess that's where I got
it from.*

*... Then there is me. My name is Anne and I come from the best
New England families Mayflower and all that I never put up my hair in
rollers every night or used hair-spray because my mother never taught me
how and the Irish Catholic cheerleaders who wrote up the yearbook at
Elmtown High School had dates every night and I was isolated from the
group.*

*... Anne is isolating herself from the group resisting insight throw
the pills in the sink smuggle in the Nation or at least change your
subscription address.*

These words, including the title, were written by Anne Parsons in
September 1963 when she was hospitalized at the Yale Psychiatric Institute in New Haven, where she spent the next nine months until her
suicide there. All the problems and pain of her life come together in one
heart-rending cry: fears about the bomb and war, conflict between the
focus on private troubles and social conscience, the difficulty of being a
single professional and intellectual woman, the pressures from outside
and within to marry and have children, the psychoanalytic diagnosis of
her problems as a failure to accept her femininity stemming in part
from the lack of training and ordinary feminine socialization for an
American girl, and her tremendous isolation, which she attributes to her
father as a role model, both as an intellectual "pounding on the typewriter all day" and as part of her upper-middle-class Protestant heritage
of independence.

In the nine months between "Diary of a Mental Patient" and Parsons's last letter to her father a month before she died, quoted below,
she achieved and suffered much. Her experience in the hospital raises
many questions, the most obvious being whether if her treatment had

been different she would have survived (this should be asked about her analysis as well: psychoanalysis with a completely silent analyst was probably not only not appropriate for Parsons, but destructive). I cannot answer these or several other salient questions about her hospitalization and death, although her civil liberties are certainly an issue since she tried desperately to get out of the hospital. My central concern is how the internal and external pressures she experienced in her life conspired to rob her of a future, my focus the inhospitality of the environment that led to such utter isolation and loneliness (and eventually to hospitalization and death). In what follows, I highlight themes from her writing that echo those she developed before her hospitalization. They take on a terrible poignancy here as her enormous intelligence spotlights her own dilemma.

In mid-April of 1964, Parsons wrote to her parents and wished them a wonderful trip to Europe and Moscow.[16] Her father was on his way to Heidelberg to give the keynote address at the Max Weber Centennial, a great honor. In contrast, she tells them, all her efforts to find a position, grant, or professional affiliation after the hospital have been discouraging; nothing has come through. But even in this letter she has some other ideas. In fact, she had been awarded a fellowship to go to the University of Chicago for the previous fall, but she says she does not want to pressure David Schneider, the anthropologist, because "he might feel he had do something on personal grounds, but I don't really think that that is the way for me to go about earning my living." Sadly and ironically, Schneider had written to her father at the time of her hospitalization to say he would almost definitely be able to hold the fellowship for her.[17] Around this time, she also wrote to Stanley Diamond at Syracuse University to tell him of her unsuccessful search for grants or affiliation and of her minimal needs, concluding that "it seems difficult to get much of anything from the booby-hatch." She would, she says, be glad for information about almost anything that came to mind as a possibility.[18]

In her last letter to her father, written on May 3, 1964, she congratulates him on having reached the pinnacle of his career but continues with a discouraged report of her own. She had tried to run away to New York, but says she asked the staff not to tell him "for the sake of your European peace of mind." A number of things had happened to undo the stability she had achieved over the winter, one of which was the impossibility of finding a professional affiliation, another her sudden inability to write: "I found myself facing the fact that if you have lived 33 years without having built up a real intellectual discipline (which is quite different from just having bright ideas), it doesn't suddenly come. Especially not with a brain like mine that still feels like there is a big hole in the middle of it." A final factor were the restrictions imposed by the hospital for her impulsive trip to New York, one of which was that she couldn't get out to the library. She feels she has been "unfairly restricted and told about getting along with the group by fiat, rather than being allowed to run to my individual friendships or outside interest." She does not think she has it in her to work back to where she was before, blaming both the hospital and herself ("a bit more intelligence on my part about when to ask for help and when to do things on my own"). Although the doctors will no doubt recommend extending hospitalization and psychotherapy, she no longer feels therapy is of use to her.

She suggests that she look around in New Hampshire, near their farm, for a family that would be willing to take in a boarder, since she does not think she can survive alone in the city. It simply does not make sense, she argues with her father, for her to stay in the hospital, a burden on him:

You asked me a year ago what it is that I really want. Then I had no idea, six months ago I began to get the hope that if I could be allowed to live quietly in the hospital building up my own work and set of friends I could do it here in New Haven, but neither I nor the powers that be could manage that without my getting thrown off course. Now I think I want much less; only a chance to live near the farm which is what I most love.

Especially, I would appreciate your thinking over the problem while you are in Moscow. For the cost of the extra year's hospitalization here, which is what the staff will certainly recommend, three Russians could study in the United States. Many people there do not have even a room to

*sleep in. Is any single individual in this world then worth the
expenditures of various sorts (I don't mean just money either) that have
gone into my unsuccessful treatment? I do not believe so and I wish I had
been born somewhere where there is less gadgeteering optimism or trying
something new than here. Too much of me.*

This last point is one she had made continually during her hospitalization and is a source of her criticisms of psychotherapy and the
hospital. She told her father repeatedly that political and social issues
were more important than her individual situation and that her parents
should not waste time on her "personally ill-fated soul." In a letter written to him the previous fall, she had criticized her therapists, "This is
what an . . . important part of my conflict with Dr. A . . . was about,
since when I was in such a panic about nuclear war and the possibility of
American fascism, he simply could not or did not see that people ever
have strong emotions about anything but their immediate personal
relationships or whatever it is that happens before one is six years
old."[19]

In the nine months between "Diary of a Mental Patient" and her
resigned May letter, Anne Parsons wrote copious letters, articles, essays,
notes, and manifestos in the hospital. Reading through them, it is impossible not to be moved by her productivity, energy, and struggle, her
insight into her own and others' situations, her coherence and ar-
ticulateness, the wide range of her intellectual interests, her political activism, and her moral integrity. She fought for her life and for what she
thought was right; she struggled over the inequality she found in the
hospital as she had in the world outside. She battled, as a woman, to
find a place for herself.

Much of her unpublished writing and many of her letters, most to
her father and to Rose Coser, are about politics, indicating the close attention she paid to world and national events: the Kennedy assassination, militarism, war and Cuba, her fears about a right-wing shift in
America. Parsons became increasingly radical during the last years of
her life. From the time of her "acute nuclear panic" in 1961, she was pre-

occupied with nuclear proliferation and the preparations for war that, in her opinion, made war more likely. Many of the letters to her father accuse him of being too conservative.[20] She was in contact with a pacifist organization, in part because she hoped they might have room for her in their community. An interest in Rosa Luxemburg grew. Within the hospital, she organized a Thanksgiving fast in spite of the fact that the doctors tried to talk her out of it by saying that all her personal motivations would have to be examined in therapy. She defended her right to interpret events in political ways, objecting to the "overpersonalization" of therapy. The prestige of psychoanalysis in the United States, she believed, encouraged people to discuss issues in personal rather than cultural or political terms, a form of depoliticization she objected to.[21]

As a patient she fought for her integrity: her right to her own room and solitude, to study and write, to receive and send mail uncensored, not to continually participate in the group, to protect herself from what she felt was the destructiveness of the psychiatrists' approach (she went "on strike" from therapy), and to get out of the hospital. Much of her time was spent writing and struggling with the hospital about her treatment. Themes in her letters and petitions echo themes in her articles: a critique of psychiatry and of the culture of psychotherapy, with a focus on how therapy does not work for some people, the authoritarian values involved, and how the therapist must understand and respect the patient's values. She felt she was a virtual prisoner by the end. Often inspired by larger political and moral issues, she organized patients around conditions in the hospital. Like a good anthropologist (and weirdly, in the same setting in which her own fieldwork had taken place, with herself now a patient instead of a researcher), she took extensive field notes about the individual and group behavior of patients and staff, probably intending to use them as data for a book on the "culture of psychotherapy."

Most of her letters were about incidents and struggles in the hospital. One of the main conflicts was over the doctors' criticisms that she isolated herself too much. Referring to her identification with Rosa Luxemburg, she says that it is easier to know what real difficulties are "in the face of restrictions than in the face of silence behind the couch."[22] She battled unsuccessfully for uncensored mail, objecting to the staff knowing all the details of her life regardless of whether she wished to confide in them. She stated she had a right to privacy and asked her father to intervene, pointing out there was self-interest involved since they read his letters too: "It and my various other battles around here just seem like the small personal contributions I can make to the ideals of freedom and human dignity within the limitations of my present status."[23]

In a December letter, she tells her father she is no longer taking psychotherapy seriously. Consequently, it is terrible to have it compulsory. In fact, she says, there is little doubt in her own mind that her improvement comes from this decision since she believes she managed to function relatively well before she had any treatment and "this was simply not true afterwards." At least two of her difficulties with the psychiatric profession she believes her father should understand, "considering where (she) got the values":

The first comes from the doctrine of the individual conscience in relation to God, one which many of us have perhaps abandoned. . . . In the 16th century some people who have since had important effects in history said that one of the troubles with a confession is that it gives too much power to the priests who then tend to use it towards their own ends. . . .

. . . The second difficulty you should understand best of all, and this comes from the anti-intellectualism . . . that is often built into psychoanalytic values. Here it takes an even more gross and obvious form than anything to be found in Boston. . . . Dr. B on a number of occasions has given as proof of my abnormality and lack of human feeling the fact that I spend long hours alone in my room either reading or writing rather than perpetually socializing as part of "the group." But would you want me to take him seriously and adjust my behavior accordingly?[24]

Parsons did not believe there were good enough reasons for her to stay in the hospital, and from late December until her death in June tried heroically to get released and to find a position for herself. She wanted to put the Boston difficulties behind her and live in the present, and she believed the hospital staff would not let her do that. They would not let her inquire about grant money because, as she explained in a letter to her parents, the doctors were

reluctant to let me go into any new situation unless by establishing a long-term psychotherapeutic relationship I could prove that I could depend on someone and allow myself to be taken care of. However, to assume that a professional relationship with a doctor can substitute for the husband or lover that one does not have seems to me now to be sheer nonsense, or even perverse. I am alone in the world and sometimes I find it unbearably difficult. . . . Thus facing the fact of loneliness makes much more sense than "learning" to build my emotional life around Dr. B just because he happened to get assigned to me as a case.[25]

She repeatedly charged the therapists with wanting to create a "paternalistic dependency" on them and to change her values "in directions which are congruent with theirs."[26] In a memorandum to the hospital, she calls "immoral or even perverse" the expectation that "an adult single woman build her emotional life around a professional relationship which by definition cannot include the satisfactions that people ordinarily look for as a consequence of closeness."[27] The project to get Parsons to depend on someone and allow herself to be taken care of, which she attributes to therapeutic goals, has gender implications as well. The dependency they encouraged was the centerpiece of femininity. Parsons comes close to a feminist critique of therapy here but never develops it, her orientation being class and cultural biases.

In her New Years' Day letter to her parents, Parsons reiterates that she will do everything possible, including legal action, to secure her release. Her parents' help is enlisted. Suggesting they write to the hospital supporting her plans for release, Parsons even argues they should not pay her bill. As it becomes clear she will not be released and that many of the conditions imposed on her will not be altered, she raises the issue of her civil liberties and goes "on strike," by refusing to participate in psychotherapy sessions. She states she will no longer make personal confidences to a therapist who does not understand or respect her need and desire to read and write, and demands to know what it means to be "voluntarily" committed to the hospital since she cannot even get them to discuss her release.[28] In a memorandum to the hospital, she suggests that given the fact that after three years and $10,000 dollars at the Boston Psychoanalytic Institute she was told she was unsuited to psychoanalytic treatment, she feels she has a legitimate interest in "insuring myself against the possibility that after three years and $36,000 . . . I will not be referred to a state hospital for lobotomy on the grounds that I am unsuited to hospital psychotherapy."[29] Thus Anne Parsons became more and more critical of her personal treatment and of psychiatry in general, and her last energies were spent in struggle against what she believed was futile and immoral treatment. Personal letters and memorandums parallel the intellectual essays published in *Belief, Magic, and Anomie.* Together they provide a record of a woman in trouble who used that trouble as a source for remarkably astute perceptions about the world in which she found herself.

She was extremely productive throughout the winter of 1963 and 1964. A number of articles accepted for publication at this time were published after her death. Some of her professional correspondents did not know she was a patient since she used a return New Haven street address. Some of them assumed she was on the faculty of Yale. Her main personal correspondents during this period were her parents and the sociologist Rose Coser, a true friend before and during Anne's hospitalization. It is striking at this time, as it is earlier in her life, how isolated she was. Many of the people concerned about her were her father's colleagues. She simply had no close friends, no woman friend, other than Coser, with whom she corresponded or who visited her.

From the time she was hospitalized until her death, Anne Parsons selflessness was expressed through her worry about the burden she created for others, especially her parents. In a November letter to her parents, Parsons says,

I think the fact of my being a mental patient is much harder on you than it is on me . . . I do worry about your side of it quite a bit, just because you did not deserve the kind of pain I inflicted with no real reason by my behavior . . . it was my life that failed, not your lives. But I do not think that there is very much I can do about it besides staying away and leaving you in peace to do whatever makes most sense to you to do. I do not mind if that entails some neglect or exclusion.[30]

Her parents' independence, self-containment (noninterference, as she had called it earlier) made her feel her needs were inappropriate. Their stoicism made her failures more abnormal and exaggerated.

Parsons reflects in a letter to Rose Coser on the anti-Puritan tensions so critical to her life, noting that in Italy she did, "have the real opportunity of using the outgoing capacities which, you are right, I do have." She tells Coser that the pressures put on patients are another version of the "cold, and intellectualistic Boston ethic."[31] In this vein, Parsons again expresses her feelings of being an exile in Boston. Explaining to her parents why she does not want to return for Christmas, she says that with all the modern differences in language and content of thought, Boston is still the

same old Puritan community that it always was... But the nature of the Puritan community is that people who violate its norms get cast out, and it seems to me that I have been cast out of Boston just as surely as if I had a scarlet letter graven on my arm ... when you have been cast out of a community there is no point going back to it; it's just quite a different situation from having social status and a real position of leadership ... and in a way I have been cast out of the family too—though not with same kind of coldness I have noticed elsewhere.[32]

Anne Parsons's isolation was great; her sense of rejection profound; her feelings of failure overwhelming. Yet her intellectual gifts and skills enabled her to see the historical, sociological, and political explanations for many of her difficulties. Although this did not diminish her pain, it helped her to put her life in perspective.

In 1992, the twenty-eighth anniversary of Anne Parsons's death, it is possible to see her as a victim of the 1950s, of the culture of the feminine mystique that considered marriage and motherhood the only legitimate goals for white women, a culture in which she did not participate. Educated white women of her generation went to college in the late forties and early fifties. They were too old to take part in the student movement or to make immediate use of the social movements of the 1960s, and their lives were influenced only over time by the women's liberation movement. In thinking about Parsons it is hard to escape the thought that if she, who so much wanted to be part of a movement for social justice and who struggled toward a radicalism that did not yet exist as a broad social phenomenon, had participated in the movements of the sixties, or even the subcultures of the 1950s, she might have been able to make a new life for herself. Her inability to participate, to connect with other people and to belong, however, was part of her problem.

Parsons suffered from the inhibitions and narrow advice that constrained all but unusually strong and adventurous women of her class and race. In 1977, twenty-five years after their graduation, the class of 1952 of Radcliffe College, of which Parsons was a member, looked back on the discouragement and bad advice they had received about careers and career planning. The alumni report suggested that, even if the role of women had not undergone major changes since that time, the message would have been "perverse," fostering as it did a lack of self-esteem in women: "The prevailing view of the Radcliffe administration in our day was clearly to seek a successful husband on whom to piggy back for the rest of our lives, while remaining well read and interesting to husband and children." College ended for many with "misgivings, lack of confidence, uncertainty and without goals."[33] American culture in the 1950s undervalued the vast majority of women who became wives and mothers almost immediately after graduation, but it also devalued the minority who did not; it is the harshness of this devaluation and of the choices available to women that form the context for the story of Anne Parsons.

Parsons was not alone in her sacrifice. There are of course the famous suicides of Sylvia Plath and Anne Sexton, but there are also many others of her generation who had trouble surviving undamaged. Most of them married, had children, and had to give up more intellectual and creative ambitions. Those like Parsons, who did not "piggyback" on a husband for the rest of her life, were unable to experience the intimate and nurturing aspects of their personalities. This was the underside of the feminine mystique; single, professional women were seen as deviant. They suffered because they did not fit the prevailing social categories, which defined women uncompromisingly as mutually exclusive types—mother versus career woman, working mother versus good mother, glamorous female versus domestic female, good girl versus bad girl—making difficult and dangerous the satisfactory combination of work, family, and sexual life that later would seem possible and desirable. The repressiveness of the time took its toll on many women, not least those who did pursue a professional life and have never yet been properly recognized.

As the daughter of an eminent sociologist, Anne Parsons's intellectual inheritance was impressive. As the first child in a family that valued and exemplified their Protestant heritage, she was burdened in her efforts to create a satisfactory life for herself. She was in many ways her father's daughter, as the themes in her work and her private accounts of her own situation demonstrate. Her interest in the cultural shaping of personality, mental illness, and professionalism are inherited from her father's work, but her feminine and outsider status provided a different vantage point and different conclusions. Although she was in many ways enlightened and privileged, her legacy, in conjunction with her anomalous position as a single career woman, undermined her.

Anne Parsons was an unusually talented intellectual, bringing passion, integrity, and insight to her research, the interdisciplinary nature of which worked against her professionally. Her studies of religion, mental illness, family dynamics and social change, and psychoanalytic theory, all from a cross-cultural and vigorous anti-ethnocentric perspective, should be studied. If she were writing today she would surely be widely known. As a forgotten intellectual, as a forgotten woman, as a casualty of our immediate past, she deserves recognition.

The peculiarities of her Puritan and elite environment should not blind us to the fact that many women were prisoners in a culture in which they could not thrive in the 1950s. Although Anne Parsons internalized the conventional expectations of her time and suffered from her failure to achieve them, she fought against them with integrity and passion. Concluding with the story of Anne Parsons situates her as a bridge between girls growing up in the 1950s and the second wave of feminism. The misery of the 1950s for women who challenged the gender codes was a central factor in the development of the women's liberation movement. The girls' stories are linked to Parsons's, and both are linked to the story of the women's movement. Her life exemplifies the choices and sacrifices girls eventually refused. Their stories and hers are intelligible in tandem as narratives that tell of women's efforts to shape lives of dignity and freedom. Although unknown to the younger women, Anne Parsons's ultimately unsuccessful struggle is deeply connected with theirs.

Conclusion

By the mid-1960s, women who were active in the new left, antiwar, and student movements had begun to realize that their positions in those movements were subordinate. They were discriminated against by male activists—their comrades, lovers, and coworkers. As women began to articulate their concerns, they were most often met with incomprehension and derision. Young white women born during or soon after World War II, who had been moved by the civil rights and student movements and by radical cultural critiques of American society, coalesced into the youthful and radical wing of the women's liberation movement.[1] These were the most politicized women of their class and generation, and in their questioning of gender relations in the movement and American society, they were giving voice to themes that structured their early lives.

At first their rage was directed at men in their own milieu who ignored, used, or mistreated them. They argued that movements for social change must embody equal and respectful relations, that women must be recognized as capable of all the skills and talents men brought to the movements. Women, in other words, could and should be leaders and intellectuals, activists and spokespeople, and not relegated to the sidelines for sex, housework, support, and service. Female activists came together in consciousness-raising groups and learned how similar their concerns were and how much they had in common. In one of the central insights of the women's liberation movement, they discovered that many of their most intimate and personal problems had social and political sources. This book has relied on that early insight by interrogating the social and cultural factors that contributed to "private troubles," in C. Wright Mills's phrase.

Women's view widened to encompass an analysis of American society from the perspective of gender. Young radical women began to see that every institution in American society discriminated against women, but their most passionate concerns centered on personal life and sexuality. In part, this focus on personal concerns was due to the fact that most were privileged and had not faced a discriminatory labor market, nor did they have children. They were also white and had not faced racial discrimination. But their focus had other sources, too. The interest in sexuality, their bodies, and their personal relationships had roots in their growing-up years in the fifties and early sixties. Girl culture, consumer culture, and changes in the economy all converged in such a way as to put personal, individual, and sexual fulfillment high on their agenda. Issues such as control of one's body, in the form of available birth control and abortion, were understood in individual sexual terms as much as in women's rights terms. Early women's liberation activists verbalized problems that were fundamental to their generation's early experiences. As children and teenagers, they had learned the vocabulary that they needed to make sense of themselves. But their movement also entailed a rupture with their past. This book has investigated that break with traditional definitions of femininity and the struggle for a freer and more autonomous life. In both cases, the most political women articulated concerns that white, middle-class women were grappling with as they worked their way toward new feminine identities.

Lynn Ferrin recalls how she had dreaded the idea of becoming like her mother, "Mrs. Him." She speaks of how exhilarating the women's movement was for those who had tried to imagine a different future:

I was among the women in that whole vanguard of sexual freedom who were very excited by being free women. For me it was like, "God, this is wild. You can have lovers. You don't have to be married. You can have different men, and experience different men's lovemaking." It seemed really avant-garde and exciting; we were in the front lines. In my circles, you wouldn't think of getting married, settling down with one person. The suburbs and the station wagon full of Cub Scouts became something you didn't want anything to do with.

She continues that all this was still kept a secret. Your family could not know if you lived with a man. Her mother, she says, (and we have seen other daughters who felt the same thing) would not have been able to accept the idea of her being actively sexual or intimate outside of marriage. "That was something I didn't think my family could handle. If I did that my mother would check into a hospital."[2] Ferrin's is a dramatic statement of opportunities and enthusiasms that distinguished young women who grew up in the fifties from their mothers' generation. The rupture is remarkable. What is striking is how unambivalent Ferrin was, how upbeat and spirited about her new life despite the insecurity it held, and how intent she was on escape from the life her mother led. Many women were discontent or restless but fearful, too, even envious of those who had fewer choices, but Lynn Ferrin couldn't wait for the future that beckoned to middle-class women. Despite her enthusiastic embrace of a bohemian identity, even historian Sheila Rowbotham remarks that contradictory values surrounded her generation of women in England: "Freedom and smirks, honesty or making yourself cheap," made it "painfully difficult to hew out another course. Yet all my friends wanted to find another way of being. We wanted reason and mischief, danger and trust, love and freedom."[3]

The roots of the dramatic sexual revolt of Lynn Ferrin and women like her lie in the fifties. Girls' efforts to create new feminine meanings out of contradictory texts regarding attractiveness, sexuality, marriage, and popularity began early and eventually found public expression in the feminist movement. Paradoxically, girls' apparently conventional engagement with postwar commercial popular culture also framed feminist issues. Numerous commentators have remarked on second-wave feminists' emphasis on intimacy and personal fulfillment, their critique of the family, and their conviction that sexual liberation was central to equality.[4] The women's liberation movement politicized the changes young women were making under cover of the old culture. In the 1960s, women began articulating and attempting to resolve the gender contradictions of the 1950s; they undertook to codify the modernization of gender. These tensions have not disappeared; in fact they have intensified and changed, especially for young women, but the terms of the discussion are different because of my generation's articulation of the problems and, especially, our political struggles.

As young, white women in the fifties, we were both victims of our culture and agents of our own invention. We straddled the old and the new in a period that was fearful about changing gender and racial definitions. Challenges to whiteness and masculinity in the postwar period were preparing the ground for the political struggles of the 1960s. We were a privileged part of our generation, uneasy about what our elders wanted for and from us. We grew up in a relaxed culture whose subtext was anxiety and whose sexual and gender rules for young, single women were stringent. We tried to resolve these contradictions, to find solutions to what it meant to be a woman in such a time. One of our strategies was dissemblance, required in a culture so committed to conventional femininity. We, along with many Americans, were keeping up appearances. Like those accused of communist or leftist sympathies during the cold war, many of us led double lives, hiding feelings, thoughts, and behavior that were unacceptable. Except for the most rebellious, it was only years later that the hidden parts of ourselves that had been generated, and denied, by the culture could be explored. We decided we didn't want to be miserable, that we didn't have to be, which is probably what set our generation and class apart from those before us. We were women of privilege. We were not deprived. We were discriminated against, but rarely brutally. We were girls at the center, not the periphery or margins. Only our gender distanced us (and does still) from arrogance and power.

But sometimes it has not. I mention this because lately I have spent a good deal of time reading and thinking about writing by feminist women of color and by postmodern theorists who argue that those on the margins, those engaged in minority discourse, have not been heard from and must finally be listened to. Their interventions into the white, male, Western intellectual traditions provide perspectives and voices that we clearly need to hear if we are to construct a culture that empowers all of us and that values sexual, racial, and ethnic diversity. Much feminist writing today emphasizes the differences between women, especially between white, middle-class women and women of color. This is in sharp contrast to the early days of the women's liberation movement when women's commonalities were celebrated (although class and race did not go unrecognized) and men constituted difference. We have learned over the years that women's experiences are structured, not simply by sex, but by race, class, ethnicity, and culture as well. I have wondered, in this context, where the value lies in reconstructing and listening to the voices of white, middle-class girls?

I raise this because I agree with those who try to dislodge comfortable hegemonic attitudes such as assuming that one group's experience is typical of all women's experience, being deaf to those different from oneself. While it is important to acknowledge individual female writers for these insights, it is just as important to acknowledge the ongoing significance of feminism for raising such questions, for injecting the politics of difference into intellectual life. Further, I believe the continuity is strong, if complex, between the discontent of middle-class white girls of the fifties and the questions feminists, including women of color, raise even today. Racial diversity was on the American agenda in the 1950s and despite its low visibility then, girls like me were shaped by it. But my awareness of the significance of race, my interpretation of the fifties as a time in which whiteness and white masculinity (and thus white femininity) were contested issues, owes most to the movements of the sixties—to the heterogeneity those movements fought for, especially in the academy, and to feminists who have argued that race and class structure women's lives and that white women have much to learn from women of color. Although it is often obscured, the vitality of feminism is unbroken between the early women's liberation movement, which was never exclusively white, and the concern with difference of contemporary feminist intellectuals and activists. And that vitality includes both the affirmation of difference and the recognition of connectedness. Thus my commitment to both women's particularities and commonalities, or at least to their historical connectedness, owes much to feminism.[5] I still believe that the stories of some women, despite class, race, and ethnic differences, teach us something about all women.

I began this book with questions about how it was that young, secure, and middle-class white women, who had all the advantages American society could provide, became feminists? While writing it, I thought not only of my mother, who imparted to me many of the norms and forms of the fifties, but also of my daughter, now in her mid-twenties. It occurred to me that I had implicitly contrasted my experiences with hers, or more accurately, what I took to be hers. This would have been a more difficult book to write if I had not had a daughter of young adult age. As I wrote, I often thought, Do white, middle-class women of every generation have this experience? How is what I am discovering or remembering different from her memories? Aren't all white, middle-class women miserable as they grow up? I almost always concluded that while all women who have grown up in the past fifty years in America have had to confront similar issues, my daughter's generation encountered something new, namely, my generation of women — women who grew up in the 1950s and were changed by the sixties, especially by feminism. Considering three generations of women, my mother, myself, and my daughter, highlights the peculiarities of my growing-up years. As my daughter was growing up, I was a very different sort of mother than my mother was while I was growing up, not least because my notion of family responsibility and women's place had shifted dramatically.

Paying attention to the kinds of concerns I had as a mother—how to instill confidence and strength in my daughter in order to help her to become an independent woman—enabled me to notice the differences between my mother's and daughter's generations. Many of our mothers were strong and wanted us to be strong, but they did not want us to be so independent that men would not want us. My own daughter was the recipient of enthusiastic feminist ideas from early in her life; I became a feminist when she was small, and although I didn't insist on karate lessons (common then) I did believe that encouraging her to feel physically and mentally powerful was important. (I should also add that while I was eagerly reading her *Firegirl* and dressing her in overalls, she was coveting dresses and drawn to romance and stereotypical family images.) My assumptions about desirable traits and skills for a girl could not have been the same as my mother's or the women who raised my generation; their situations were very different. Of course, this does not mean that there were not fifties mothers with athletic, educational, and career aspirations for their daughters. But on balance, the mothers of my generation raised us in a conservative gender culture and believed, based on their own experiences, that girls would have to marry if they were to lead reasonable lives. For the most part, they did not entertain the possibility of serious careers, long periods of singleness, or single or no parenting. We do. This, to me, is a substantial change.

Women of my class and generation stand between two dramatically contrasting generations. The older was defined by the Depression and a culture that reinforced a scarcity mentality, conventional femininity, and a family focus. The younger generation, that of my daughter, inherited the benefits and drawbacks of changes in the American economic and social structure as well as changes brought about by feminism. Put simply, our daughters take for granted freedoms and burdens that we did not and could not, but that we were instrumental in shaping and that we struggled to forge out of our family legacies and the images and opportunities the culture provided us.

The transformations in American society of which white, middle-class women could take advantage accelerated in the postwar period. Women who grew up in the fifties and early sixties benefited from those changes, and this meant lives lived differently from their mothers'. They were forerunners, even if unintentionally, of what postwar advanced capitalist society made possible: the development, really the requirement, of women's participation in the labor force, the potential equality in intimate heterosexual relationships, and more generally, sexual freedom. In fact, most middle-class women have no choice now regarding whether they work. (Working-class and poor women never did.) Thus, in three generations, middle-class women have moved from being (or expecting or hoping to be) full-time housewives and mothers dependent on their husbands to the realization that they cannot count on marrying or on bringing up children in a two-parent family—a monumental shift indeed.

The change reinforces the point made throughout this book that as young women, my generation of white, middle-class girls linked an older traditional world of feminine expectations with a newer world of abundance and promises of fulfillment. Consumer society, mobility, abundance, tempting images of glamor, sex, and romance, opportunities in school and work, and teen culture all meant that girls' links to their families were looser and future possibilities more fluid than they ever had been. This is even more true for our daughters. While girls' growing up is never easy in a society dominated by men who devalue women (and growing up with a newly feminist mother may not be easy either), our daughters have not had to face the anxious and narrow constraints that we did. Many of our memories of the fifties and early sixties are of being squelched, of longing for other routes. Some of us learned to try not to impose restrictions on our daughters, whether biological or metaphorical. There was, of course, less reason to do so. Though many of us were not in the forefront of agitation for social change in the 1960s, we nevertheless pioneered in our life choices, and perhaps in our ambivalent explorations, movement toward a freer life for women.

Notes

Introduction

1. Molly Haskell, *From Reverence to Rape: The Treatment of Women in the Movies* (New York: Penguin Books, 1974), p. 234. Also see Brandon French, *On the Verge of Revolt: Women in American Films of the Fifties* (New York: Frederick Ungar, 1978), p. 154: "America in the fifties was on the verge of a revolution which challenged many of the fundamental ordering principles of Western culture: Not only male supremacy, but white supremacy, and an economic system in which one sector of society benefits at the expense of another."

2. In addition to written accounts, I informally interviewed twenty women, seven of them bohemians in the 1950s. I used the interviews to formulate my ideas and as corroboration of other data and cite them accordingly.

3. William Chafe, *The Unfinished Journey: America since World War II* (New York: Oxford University Press, 1986), pp. 111, 144.

4. Joseph Satin, ed., *The 1950s: America's Placid Decade* (Boston: Houghton Mifflin, 1960), p. 16.

5. See Chafe, *The Unfinished Journey*, pp. 111–17; Marty Jezer, *The Dark Ages: Life in the United States, 1945–1960* (Boston: South End Press, 1982), ch. 5. Also see George Lipsitz, *Class and Culture in Cold War America: "A Rainbow at Midnight"* (South Hadley, Mass.: J. F. Bergin, 1982), for a consideration of the working class in this period. See Judith Stacey, *Brave New Families: Stories of Domestic Upheaval in Late Twentieth-Century America* (New York: Basic Books, 1990), for the argument that the working class pioneered what she calls the postmodern family revolution, which middle-class women began to emulate in the post–World War II era.

6. William L. O'Neill, *American High: The Years of Confidence, 1945–1960* (New York: Free Press, 1986). This is a conservative and very positive interpretation of the postwar period.

7. Doug McAdam, *Freedom Summer* (New York: Oxford University Press, 1988), pp. 14, 15. Also see Landon Y. Jones, *Great Expectations: America and the Baby Boom Generation* (New York: Ballantine Books, 1980).

8. Ellen Maslow, "Storybook Lives: Growing Up Middle Class," in *Liberation Now* (New York: Dell Publishing, 1971), p. 172. A black, working-class woman makes a similar point: "Though the average person might automatically think of anyone living in public housing as being deprived, we barely knew the meaning of the word. Our parents constantly reminded us that we were far better off than they had been at our age, and the camaraderie and freedom we felt as kids contributed to making mine perhaps the first generation of black youths to believe their individual potential was unlimited" (Mary Wilson, *My Life as a Supreme,* with Patricia Romanowski and Ahrgus Juilliard [New York: St. Martin's Press, 1986], p. 25). Also see Angela Davis on a similar theme, quoted in Paula Giddings, *When and Where I Enter: The Impact of Black Women on Race and Sex in America* (New York: Bantam Books, 1984), p. 271.

9. Alice McDermott, *That Night* (New York, Harper and Row, 1987), p. 163. For the broad relevance of fiction in historical writing, Barbara Melosh says, "In the subjective medium of fiction, we can read the afterimage of history, its imprints on the writer's consciousness and way of seeing the world. In this sense, novels are themselves primary sources, historical evidence of ideology" ("Historical Memory in Fiction: The Civil Rights Movement in Three Novels," *Radical History Review* 40 [1988]: 64–76). Also see James William Gibson, *The Perfect War: The War We Couldn't Lose and How We Did* (New York: Vintage Books, 1988), pp. 470ff., for an argument that fiction deserves as much consideration as nonfiction for understanding the war in Vietnam.

10. For example, see George Chauncey, Jr., "The National Panic over Sex Crimes and Cold War Sexual Ideology, 1947–1953" (paper presented at the Organization of American Historians meetings, New York City, April 1986); Estelle Freedman, "'Uncontrolled Desires': The Response to the Sexual Psychopath, 1920–1960," *Journal of American History* 74 (1987): 83–106; James Gilbert, *A Cycle of Outrage: America's Reaction to the Juvenile Delinquent in the 1950s* (New York: Oxford University Press, 1986); Warren Susman, with the assistance of Edward Griffin, "Did Success Spoil the United States? Dual Representations in Postwar America," in *Recasting America: Culture and Politics in the Age of Cold War,* ed. Lary May (Chicago: University of Chicago Press, 1989), pp. 19–37.

11. C. Wright Mills, *The Sociological Imagination* (New York: Grove Press, 1959), pp. 11, 12.

12. Dale Carter, *The Final Frontier: The Rise and Fall of the Rocket State* (London: Verso, 1988), pp. 85, 103. See Elaine Tyler May, *Homeward Bound:*

American Families in the Cold War Era (New York: Basic Books, 1987), on enthusiastic portrayals of newlyweds and families in fallout shelters, pp. 3–5.

13. Norman Mailer, "The White Negro," in his *Advertisements for Myself* (London: Transworld Publishers, 1959), p. 242. Ironically, World War II was responsible for both American prosperity and hegemony *and* the mass murders that haunted dreams and imaginations in ways that undercut that well-being.

14. Andrew Ross, "Hip, and the Long Front of Color," in his *No Respect: Intellectuals and Popular Culture* (New York: Routledge, 1989), p. 88.

15. Harriet Gilbert, "Growing Pains," in *Truth, Dare or Promise: Girls Growing Up in the Fifties,* ed. Liz Heron (London: Virago, 1985), p. 46. This is a collection of British women's recollections about growing up in the 1950s.

16. Michael Rossman, *The Wedding within the War* (Garden City, N.Y.: Doubleday, 1971), p. 94. For accounts of reactions to the atom bomb, see Todd Gitlin, *The Sixties: Years of Hope, Days of Rage* (New York: Bantam Books, 1987), pp. 21–24; Paul Boyer, *By the Bomb's Early Light* (New York: Pantheon Books, 1985), discusses anxiety about the atom bomb; Evan Stark, in *History and the New Left: Madison, Wisconsin, 1950–1970,* ed. Paul Buhle (Philadelphia: Temple University Press, 1990), p. 167, mentions having to wear dog tags in grade school (in order to be identified if you were incinerated) and worrying whether the tags would survive the blast. The film *Desert Bloom* explores a teenage girl's life in Nevada during the 1950s with the desert atomic bomb tests as a significant theme. Also see the film *Atomic Cafe* for reactions to the bomb. E. L. Doctorow wrote in the mid-1980s, "Every small loss of moral acuity, I see collectively as the secret story of American life under the bomb. It was first our weaponry and then our diplomacy, and now it's our economy. How can we suppose that something so monstrously powerful would not, after forty years, compose our identity? The great golem we have made against our enemies is our culture, our bomb culture—its logic, its faith, its vision" (*Nation,* February 21, 1987, p. 330).

17. William Chafe, *The Unfinished Journey,* p. 128.

18. See May, *Homeward Bound,* pp. 109–13, on the civil defense pamphlets of "bombshells" and pin-ups which utilized images of female sexuality to sell atomic power.

19. Chafe, *The Unfinished Journey,* p. 125. See also Chauncey, "The National Panic over Sex Crimes and Cold War Sexual Ideology"; Freedman, "Uncontrolled Desires"; John D'Emilio, *Sexual Politics, Sexual Communities: The Making of a Homosexual Minority in the U.S., 1940–1970* (Chicago: University of Chicago Press, 1983); Estelle Freedman and John D'Emilio, *Intimate Matters: A History of Sexuality in America* (New York: Harper and Row, 1988); and Jeffrey Escoffier, "Sexual Revolution and the Politics of Gay Identity," *Socialist Review* 15, nos. 4 and 5 (1985): 119–53.

20. Edgar Z. Friedenberg, *The Vanishing Adolescent* (Boston: Beacon Press, 1959), p. 115.

21. See Nora Sayre, *Running Time: Films of the Cold War* (New York: Dial Press, 1978), pp. 25-26.

22. Andrew Ross, "Containing Culture in the Cold War," *No Respect,* p. 47.

23. See Michael Rogin, *Ronald Reagan: The Movie* (Berkeley: University of California Press, 1987), ch. 8, "Kiss Me Deadly: Communism, Motherhood, and Cold War Movies"; also see May, *Homeward Bound,* on the links between communist and domestic containment.

24. Rogin, *Ronald Reagan: The Movie,* pp. xiii, xiv. See Richard Slotkin, *Fatal Environment: The Myth of the Frontier in the Age of Industrialization, 1800–1890* (New York: Atheneum, 1985); and Joel Kovel, *White Racism: A Psychohistory* (New York: Columbia University Press, 1984). Also see Minnie Bruce Pratt, "Identity: Skin Blood Heart," in *Yours in Struggle: Three Feminist Perspectives on Anti-Semitism and Racism* (Ithaca, N.Y.: Firebrand Books, 1984), pp. 3-63, for a powerful indictment of the white Southern Christian culture in which she grew up, where the exclusion and suppression of others had their source in the sexual, racial, and religious terrors of the men of her group.

25. See Orlando Patterson, "Toward a Study of Black America," *Dissent* 36 (1989): 476-86 for a recent articulation of the argument that American democracy was and is based on slavery and racism.

26. See Christina Simmons's review of Beth Bailey's *From Front Porch to Back Seat* in *Women's Review of Books,* January 1989, pp. 21-22, for a discussion of the punishment of women as a backlash to gains made in the early twentieth century and again in the postwar period. Many authors argue versions of this point, with which I agree, suggesting, for example, that dating etiquette, the campaign against sexual deviance, and the feminine mystique were all forms of boundary setting in order to control women and sex.

27. Kathleen Gerson, *Hard Choices* (Berkeley: University of California Press, 1985), p. 10.

28. Joyce Carol Oates, *Because It Is Bitter, and Because It Is My Heart* (New York: Plume Books, 1991), pp. 93, 291.

29. See Cornel West, "The New Cultural Politics of Difference," in *October* 53 (1990): 93-109. He says that Black cultural workers must "investigate and interrogate the other of Blackness/Whiteness. One cannot deconstruct the binary oppositional logic of images of Blackness without extending it to the contrary condition of Blackness/Whiteness itself." Social theory is needed to *"explain* the historically specific ways in which 'Whiteness' is a politically constructed category parasitic on 'Blackness' " and to conceive of the "hybrid character of what we mean by 'race,' 'ethnicity' and 'nationality' " (p. 105).

30. See August Meier and Elliott Rudwick, *CORE: A Study in the Civil Rights Movement, 1942-1968* (New York: Oxford University Press, 1973), ch. 2; and Chafe, *The Unfinished Journey,* 105-8. See also Aldon D. Morris, *The Origins of the Civil Rights Movement* (New York: Free Press, 1984), pp. 30-35, for anticommunist attacks on the NAACP.

31. See Joyce A. Ladner, "A Sociology of the Civil Rights Movement: An Insider's Perspective" (paper given at the American Sociological Association meetings, Atlanta, August 1988), where she refers to the "Emmett Till generation," black people of approximately Till's age, fourteen in 1955, for whom his murder was formative. She suggests their subsequent activism in SNCC was in part a response to Till's death.

32. Michelle Wallace, "Modernism, Postmodernism, and the Problem of the Visual in Afro-American Culture," in *Out There: Marginalization and Contemporary Cultures,* ed. Russell Ferguson et al. (Cambridge, Mass.: MIT Press, 1990), p. 41.

33. Alice Walker, "Choosing to Stay at Home," *In Search of Our Mother's Gardens* (New York: Harcourt Brace Jovanovich, 1984), pp. 161, 162.

34. Assata Shakur, *Assata* (Chicago: Lawrence Hill Books, 1987), pp. 42, 34.

35. I do not want to suggest that girls of different races and classes had nothing in common. Black girls were shaped by the mass media and popular culture as were white girls; they longed for the glamorous and romantic lives no American girl could ignore. Popular culture and the mass media were great levelers. But white girls often felt too safe and black girls were often not safe enough. Story after story tells of being exploited and preyed upon by white people, often men, sometimes black men. For stories of cruelty and exploitation see, for example, the autobiography of Ann Moody, *Coming of Age in Mississippi* (New York: Dell Publishing, 1968); and fiction by Jean Wheeler Smith, "Frankie Mae," in *Blackeyed Susans,* ed. Mary Helen Washington (Garden City, N.Y.: Doubleday, 1975), pp. 3–20; Alexis Deveaux, "The Riddles of Egypt Brownstone," in *Midnight Birds,* ed. Mary Helen Washington (Garden City, N.Y.: Doubleday, 1980), pp. 19–29; Grace Edwards-Yearwood, *In the Shadow of the Peacock* (New York: Ivy Books, 1988).

36. Hazel V. Carby, *Reconstructing Womanhood: The Emergence of the Afro-American Woman Novelist* (New York: Oxford University Press, 1987), p. 18; Jane Flax, "Postmodernism and Gender Relations in Feminist Theory," *Signs* 12 (1987): 629. When race and sex are discussed as separate categories, it makes black women invisible, as if one person could not occupy more than one category. It also implies that whiteness is not a racial category. For a discussion of this issue, see Frances M. Beal, "Double Jeopardy: To Be Black and Female," in *Liberation Now,* pp. 185–97; Valerie Smith, "Split Affinities: The Case of Interracial Rape," in *Conflicts in Feminism,* ed. Marianne Hirsch and Evelyn Fox Keller (New York: Routledge, 1990), pp. 271–87; and especially Elizabeth V. Spellman, *Inessential Woman: Problems of Exclusion in Feminist Thought* (Boston: Beacon Press, 1988).

37. See Lillian Smith, *Killers of the Dream* (New York: W. W. Norton, 1978), for a moving exploration of the distortions segregation and racism wreak on white people. Her focus is the South. Also see "Disloyal to Civilization: Feminism, Racism, Gynephobia," in Adrienne Rich's *Lies, Secrets, and Silences* (New York: W. W. Norton, 1979), pp. 275–310.

38. *Seventh Heaven* (New York: G. P. Putnam's Sons, 1990), a white suburban novel of the early 1960s by Alice Hoffman, revolves around the turmoil
caused by a divorced mother moving into a conventional two-parent family
suburb. She is a pariah; no one socializes with her since she does not fit their
domestic categories. More than that, she is threatening, and several settled
characters project onto her (subversive) longings that have no place in the suburbs. Her entry into their lives disrupts their tranquility, which turns out to be
only superficial.

39. Ralph Ellison, *"An American Dilemma:* A Review," in *The Death of
White Sociology,* ed. Joyce A. Ladner (New York: Random House, 1973),
p. 82.

40. Timothy Maliqalim Simone, *About Face: Race in Postmodern America*
(New York: Autonomedia, 1989), p. 19.

41. Oates, *Because It Is Bitter, and Because It Is My Heart,* p. 155.

42. See Nathan Irvin Huggins, *Harlem Renaissance* (New York: Oxford
University Press, 1971), for an exploration of the ways in which black people
were used by whites during the Harlem Renaissance. He says, "Harlem was a
means of soft rebellion for those who rejected the Babbittry and sterility of their
lives, yet could not find within their familiar culture the genius to redefine
themselves in more human and vital terms. The Negro was their subversive
agent" (p. 91). I want to thank Herman Gray for this reference, his patience, and
help in thinking about this issue, and for insisting on the importance of black
people's voice and subjectivity in white representations of black people.

43. See George Lipsitz, "Against the Wind: Dialogic Aspects of Rock and
Roll," in *Time Passages: Collective Memory and American Popular Culture* (Minneapolis: University of Minnesota Press, 1990), pp. 99–132.

44. I quote from Andrew Ross, "Containing Culture in the Cold War,"
p. 64; and Doug McAdam, *Freedom Summer,* p. 143.

45. See William Graebner, *Coming of Age in Buffalo: Youth and Authority in
the Postwar Era* (Philadelphia: Temple University Press, 1990), for evidence of
adult social control of high school students.

46. Lynn Lauber, *White Girls* (New York: W. W. Norton, 1990), quotes
from pp. 9, 10, 156. The heroine in Oates's novel *Because It Is Bitter, and Because
It Is My Heart* "stares greedily" at the black boys' skins and dark eyes, is attracted
to their "honeyed and melodic" words (pp. 23, 101–2).

47. Anne Rivers Siddons, *Heartbreak Hotel* (New York: Ballantine Books,
1976), p. 165.

48. See Susan S. Lanser, "Feminist Criticism, 'The Yellow Wallpaper' and
the Politics of Color in America," in *Feminist Studies* (1989): 415–41, for a fascinating racial interpretation of Charlotte Perkins Gilman's essay that bears on
my points here. She asks, "Is the wallpaper, then, the political unconscious of a
culture in which an Aryan woman's madness, desire, and anger, repressed by the
imperatives of 'reason,' 'duty' . . . and 'proper self-control' . . . , are projected
onto the 'yellow' woman who is, however, also feared alien?" (p. 429). Lanser's

interpretation of the story suggests that the constricted meaning of white femininity for an early twentieth-century upper-middle-class white woman in a racist society shaped her images of escape in racial (and racist) terms. Again, the subjectivity of the "yellow other" is invisible. Also see Marianna Torgovnik, *Gone Primitive: Savage Intellects, Modern Lives* (Chicago: University of Chicago Press, 1990); and Susan Hawthorne, "The Politics of the Exotic: The Paradox of Cultural Voyeurism," *NWSA Journal* (1989): 617-29.

49. See Minnie Bruce Pratt, "Identity: Skin Blood Heart," where she criticizes herself for identification with victims and her use of them to mourn for herself: "Then I understood that I was using Black people to weep for me, to express *my* sorrow at my responsibility, and that of my people, for their oppression: and I was mourning because I felt they had something I didn't, a closeness, a hope, that I and my folks had lost because we had tried to shut other people out of our hearts and lives" (p. 40).

50. Ellen Maslow, "Storybook Lives," pp. 174-75.

51. Mirra Komarovsky, *Women in the Modern World* (Boston: Little, Brown, 1953), p. 48.

52. Susan Hartmann, *American Women in the 1940s: The Home Front and Beyond* (Boston: Twayne Publishers, 1982), p. 204.

53. The "dry tinder" image comes from Sara Evans, *Personal Politics* (New York: Alfred A. Knopf, 1979), p. 23. Also see Robert K. Merton and Elinor Barber, "Sociological Ambivalence," in *Sociological Theory, Values, and Sociocultural Change,* ed. Edward A. Tiryakian (New York: Free Press, 1963). Here a statement by Jo Freeman is relevant: "The major impetus of the postwar feminine mystique was to urge women to overcompensate psychologically for what they no longer were structurally" (*The Politics of Women's Liberation* [New York: David McKay, 1975], p. 26).

CHAPTER 1   **The Experts' Fifties**

1. David Riesman, *The Lonely Crowd* (New Haven: Yale University Press, 1950); William H. Whyte, *The Organization Man* (New York: Simon and Schuster, 1956); John Seeley, R. Alexander Sim, and E. W. Loosely, *Crestwood Heights* (Toronto: University of Toronto Press, 1956); Jules Henry, *Culture against Man* (New York: Vintage Press, 1963); and Talcott Parsons, "The Social Structure of the Family," in *The Family: Its Functions and Destiny,* ed. Ruth Anshen (New York: Harper and Row, 1949), pp. 241-73; "Age and Sex in the Social Structure of the United States," *Essays in Sociological Theory* (New York: Free Press, 1954); "The American Family: Its Relations to Personality and to Social Structure," in *Family, Socialization, and Interaction Process,* ed. T. Parsons and R. Bales (Glencoe, Ill.: Free Press, 1955). This chapter is based on two published articles: "The 1950s: Gender and Some Social Science," *Sociological Inquiry* 56 (1986): 69-92; and "Domineering Mothers in the 1950s: Image and Reality," *Women's Studies International Forum* 8 (1985): 601-8.

2. The most important book on race relations in the postwar period was

Gunnar Myrdal's *An American Dilemma: The Negro Problem and American Democracy* (New York: Harper and Row, 1944), which utilized the talents of many of the most prominent black sociologists of the interwar years, including E. Franklin Frazier, Charles S. Johnson, St. Clair Drake, Horace Cayton, and Alison Davis. Although Nathan Glazer wrote in the foreword to E. Franklin Frazier's *The Negro Family in the United States* (1939; Chicago: University of Chicago Press, 1966) that "there was scarcely an American social scientist from the late thirties on who was not in favor of radical changes in the political, economic, and social position of the Negroes of the United States" (p. xi), almost no sociology of the black community was undertaken in the 1950s. See John Bracey, August Meier, and Elliot Rudwick, eds., *The Black Sociologists: The First Half of the Century* (Belmont, Calif.: Wadsworth Publishing, 1971). Also see Joyce A. Ladner, ed., *The Death of White Sociology* (New York: Random House, 1973), for a study of black sociology in the 1960s.

3. Many sociologists at the time considered it controversial because the analyses were neither narrow nor neutral. The authors had strong opinions about what was happening in the postwar period and, unsurprisingly, made big mistakes. In the 1961 volume of responses to *The Lonely Crowd*, edited by Seymour M. Lipset and Leo Lowenthal, *Culture and Social Character: The Work of David Riesman Reviewed* (New York: Free Press, 1961), essays by Lowenthal and Paul Kekskemeti defend the book and its sociology as "humanistic" and "interpretive," as does Lipset's preface, indicating the debate generated about its methodology and conclusions. In the same vein, William H. Whyte, Jr., refers approvingly to an "older" social science that had strong opinions, to which he links *The Organization Man*, contrasting it to the work of younger practitioners who "collaborate" in becoming narrow technicians (p. 68).

4. Arthur Miller's portrait of Willy Loman in his play *Death of a Salesman* (New York: Viking Press, 1949) depicted the profound need for recognition and approval generated by an other-directed society. See Eric Fromm, *The Sane Society* (New York: Rinehart, 1955), and Robert Lindner, *Must You Conform?* (New York: Grove Press, 1956), for discussions of conformity. Also see Seymour Martin Lipset's essay "A Changing American Character" (in *Culture and Social Character*, pp. 142ff., 158-71), in which he disputes whether there is any more conformity than there ever was in America, suggesting that Americans have always been other-directed, to be expected in a democracy.

5. Riesman, *The Lonely Crowd*, p. 75.

6. See chapter 2 for a discussion of changing childrearing goals in this period.

7. See Whyte, *The Organization Man*, pp. 382-92, for this point.

8. See Sloan Wilson's novel *The Man in the Gray Flannel Suit* (1955; Cambridge, Mass.: Robert Bentley, 1979) for a discussion of this problem in the 1950s, and see Joseph Heller's *Something Happened* (New York: Alfred A. Knopf, 1974), for a more recent exploration of similar themes.

9. Riesman, *The Lonely Crowd*, with a new preface (New Haven: Yale Uni-

versity Press, 1961), pp. xvii, xx, xxi. In "A Changing American Character" in *Culture and Social Character,* Lipset characterizes the period and many of the intellectuals, including Riesman, as conservative. He argues that Riesman disapproved of the democratization of taste not from a radical but a conservative perspective, that he was worried primarily about declining standards. Also see Bennett Berger, "Adolescence and Beyond," *Social Problems* 10 (1963): 407, where he defends the adaptability and flexibility of an other-directedness required in a rapidly changing society of unfamiliar life situations. He characterizes other-directedness as having imagination, a talent for role-taking, and a sensitivity to others. For a similar point, see Berger's *The Survival of a Counterculture* (Berkeley: University of California Press, 1981), p. 221.

10. See Kenneth Keniston, *The Uncommitted* (New York: Dell Publishing, 1960), pp. 183ff., for an examination of alienated young men suffering from, among other things, the effects of rapid social change. Into this anomic situation stepped new guides to behavior, in particular, mental health professionals. In Crestwood Heights, the mental health workers were continuously called upon to give guidance of all sorts. See Seeley et al., *Crestwood Heights,* ch. 11. See also Maurice Stein, *The Eclipse of Community* (New York: Harper and Row, 1964), p. 209, for a discussion of the depth of social disorganization underneath the affluent surface of life. See Beth Bailey, *From Front Porch to Back Seat* (Baltimore: Johns Hopkins University Press, 1988), pp. 119ff., and Christopher Lasch, *Haven in a Heartless World* (New York: Basic Books, 1977), on the role of experts and social scientists in this period. In *Rabbit Run* (New York: Alfred A. Knopf, 1960), a novel by John Updike, an older minister says to a new-style minister who is no longer giving moral guidance but the psychological and behavioral counseling people look to him for now, "Do you think your job is to meddle in these people's lives? I know what they teach you in the seminary now: this psychology and that. But I don't agree with it. You think your job is to be an unpaid doctor, to run around and plug up holes and make everything smooth" (p. 169).

11. Henry, *Culture against Man,* p. 133; Margaret Mead, *Male and Female* (New York: Dell Publishing, 1949), pp. 271, 292, 295; Daniel Miller and Guy Swanson, *The Changing American Parent* (New York: John Wiley and Sons, 1958), p. 200; Parsons, "Age and Sex in the Social Structure of the United States," p. 90; Riesman, *The Lonely Crowd* (1961), p. xii; Seeley et al., *Crestwood Heights,* p. 103.

12. See Robert Blood, Jr., and Donald Wolfe, *Husbands and Wives: The Dynamics of Married Living* (New York: Free Press, 1960); Ernest W. Burgess and Harvey Locke, *The Family: From Institution to Companionship* (New York: American Book, 1945); Keniston, *The Uncommitted,* pp. 239–69; Miller and Swanson, *The Changing American Parent,* pp. 196–206; Parsons, "The Social Structure of the Family," pp. 263–64, and "Age and Sex in the Social Structure of the United States," pp. 99–100.

13. Erik Erikson, *Childhood and Society* (New York: W. W. Norton, 1960),

pp. 288–98; Geoffrey Gorer, *The American People* (New York: W. W. Norton, 1948), pp. 23–69; John Keats, *The Crack in the Picture Window* (New York: Ballantine Books, 1956), pp. 123–24; Keniston, *The Uncommitted*, pp. 253–69; David Levy, *Maternal Overprotection* (New York: Columbia University Press, 1943); Ferdinand Lundberg and Marynia Farnham, *Modern Women: The Lost Sex* (New York: Harper Brothers, 1947); Edward A. Strecker, *Their Mother's Sons* (New York: J. B. Lippincott, 1946; revised 1951); Philip Wylie, *Generation of Vipers* (New York: Holt, Rinehart and Winston, 1942; revised 1955).

14. Seeley et al., *Crestwood Heights*, p. 103; Riesman, Introduction to *Crestwood Heights*, p. xii; Henry, *Culture against Man*, pp. 131, 133.

15. Parsons, "Age and Sex in the Social Structure of the United States," pp. 89, 90.

16. Miller and Swanson, *The Changing American Parent*, p. 198. See William Graebner, "The Unstable World of Benjamin Spock: Social Engineering in a Democratic Culture," *Journal of American History* 67 (1980): 612–29, and Michael Zuckerman, "Dr. Spock: The Confidence Man," in *The Family in History*, ed. Charles Rosenberg (Philadelphia: University of Pennsylvania Press, 1975), for discussions of new personality norms and childrearing behavior. Also see chapter 2 for discussion of families and childrearing.

17. Riesman acknowledges the femininity of other-directedness in only one passage: "One may see the tendency of some women to assume a role, particularly vis-à-vis men, which looks like extreme other-direction—with men being 'the others'—but which is actually rooted in a much older tradition of female self-abnegation. A regimen of complaisance, or service to others, does not of course constitute other-direction. At the same time, however, the deep internalization of an ethos whose content requires constant attention to others will undoubtedly produce a type which while still recognizably inner-directed, appears to be closer to other-direction" (*Faces in the Crowd* [New Haven: Yale University Press, 1952], p. 19).

18. Barbara Ehrenreich and Dierdre English, *For Her Own Good: One Hundred Fifty Years of the Experts' Advice to Women* (Garden City, N.Y.: Doubleday, 1978), p. 215, and Ehrenreich, *The Hearts of Men* (Garden City, N.Y.: Doubleday, 1983), pp. 31–32.

19. Lynn Spigel, "The Domestic Economy of Television Viewing in Postwar America," *Critical Studies in Mass Communications* 6 (1989): 337–54; Gerhardt Saenger, "Male and Female Relations in the American Comic Strip," *Public Opinion Quarterly* 19 (1955): 195–205. For other popular culture studies that consider gender, see George Lipsitz, "The Meaning of Memory: Family, Class, and Ethnicity in Early Network Television," in his *Time Passages: Collective Memory and American Popular Culture* (Minneapolis: University of Minnesota Press, 1990); Ehrenreich, *Hearts of Men*, ch. 3, "Early Rebels"; Norman Podhoretz, "Our Changing Ideas as Seen on TV: The Father on the Hearth," in *The Scene before You: A New Approach to American Culture*, ed. C. Brossard (New York: Rinehart, 1955); Peter Biskind, *Seeing Is Believing: How Hollywood Taught*

Us to Stop Worrying and Love the Fifties (New York: Pantheon Books, 1983); E. Ann Kaplan, "Motherhood and Representation: From Post World War II Freudian Figurations to Postmodernism," *Minnesota Review* 29 (1987): 88–102; Sonya Michel, "Danger on the Home Front: Motherhood, Sexuality, and Disabled Veterans in Postwar American Films" (manuscript).

20. Friedenberg, *The Vanishing Adolescent,* p. xii.

21. D'Emilio, *Sexual Politics, Sexual Communities,* p. 49. Also see Allan Berube and John D'Emilio, "The Military and Lesbians during the McCarthy Years," *Signs* 9 (1984): 759–64; and David Riesman, Introduction to Friedenberg's *The Vanishing Adolescent* (1964 edition), p. xix.

22. There is widespread evidence of a crisis of masculinity in the postwar years, which sometimes entailed hostility toward women. See Joseph Pleck, *The Myth of Masculinity* (Cambridge, Mass.: MIT Press, 1981), p. 159; Peter Filene, *Him/Her/Self* (New York: New American Library, 1974), pp. 176–83; Douglas Miller and Marion Nowak, *The Fifties: The Way We Really Were* (Garden City, N.Y.: Doubleday, 1975), pp. 168–77; and Susan Gubar, "This Is My Rifle, This Is My Gun," in *Behind the Lines: Gender and the Two World Wars,* ed. Margaret Higonnet et al. (New Haven: Yale University Press, 1987), pp. 227–59. See Jeffrey P. Hantover, "The Boy Scouts and the Validation of Masculinity," in *Men's Lives,* ed. Michael Kimmel and Michael Messner (New York: MacMillan, 1989), pp. 158–66, regarding white-collar male anxiety about masculinity in the early twentieth century that led to the founding of the Boy Scouts and suggests continuity from the late nineteenth century to the present.

23. Margaret Allen, "The Domestic Ideal and the Mobilization of Woman Power in World War II," *Women's Studies International Forum* 6 (1983): 401–2; Karen Anderson, *Wartime Women: Sex Roles, Family Relations, and the Status of Women during World War II* (Westport, Conn.: Greenwood Press, 1981); Joe L. Dubbert, *A Man's Place: Masculinity in Transition* (Englewood Cliffs, N.J.: Prentice-Hall, 1979), pp. 230–69; Susan Hartmann, *American Women in the 1940s: The Home Front and Beyond* (Boston: Twayne Publishers, 1982); Leila Rupp, *Mobilizing for War: German and American Propaganda, 1939–1945* (Princeton: Princeton University Press, 1978).

24. Seeley et al., *Crestwood Heights,* p. 162.

25. In Parsons's jargon, "The functional importance of the solidarity of the marriage relationship to our kinship system may therefore be presumed to be a major factor underlying the segregation of the sex roles in American society, since sex is the primary basis of role differentiation for marriage partners" ("The Social Structure of the Family," p. 264).

26. Ibid., p. 265. See also "Age and Sex in the Social Structure of the United States," p. 95. In the former essay, Parsons argued for the importance of avoiding competition between spouses and pointed out that career women were usually unmarried, a fact that was not irrelevant in his own daughter's life, as we shall see. He also suggested that employed middle-class women were often secretaries in order not to compete for status with their husbands and that

working-class marriages in which the wife's occupational status was equivalent to their husband's were unstable.

27. Seeley et al., *Crestwood Heights*, pp. 142, 106.

28. Margaret Mead, *Male and Female*, p. 301; Henry, *Culture against Man*, p. 170.

29. Parsons, "The Social Structure of the Family," pp. 260, 274; "Age and Sex in the Social Structure of the United States," pp. 99. See Mead, *Male and Female*, for clear articulation of the damages and binds created for women and men. Also see Mirra Komarovsky, *Women in the Modern World* (Boston: Little, Brown, 1953). For a somewhat unfair critique of Mead and for her own analysis of these issues, see Betty Friedan, *The Feminine Mystique* (New York: Dell, 1963), pp. 117-41.

30. Riesman, *The Lonely Crowd*, pp. 280, 258. See A. C. Spectorsky, *The Exurbanites* (Philadelphia: J. B. Lippincott, 1955), for a description of the phenomenon among affluent exurban wives, and Maurice Stein on Spectorsky, *The Eclipse of Community* (New York: Harper and Row, 1964), pp. 199-204. See also Riesman, "Two Generations," in *The Woman in America*, ed. Robert J. Lifton (Boston: Houghton Mifflin, 1964), pp. 72-97, for a discussion of greater sex segregation in an earlier historical period, and Barbara Ehrenreich, *The Hearts of Men*, for the suggestion that men in the 1950s desperately wanted to escape their family and work responsibilities.

31. Parsons, "Age and Sex in the Social Structure of the United States," p. 270.

32. Henry, *Culture against Man*, pp. 142-43. Cultural expectations of an exclusively family-centered existence encouraged this trend. See Edna Rostow, "Conflict and Accommodation," in *The Woman in America*, pp. 211-35; David Riesman, "The Found Generation," *American Scholar* 24 (1956): 421-26.

33. Parsons, "The American Family," p. 11; "Age and Sex in the Social Structure of the United States," pp. 99, 100.

34. Seeley et al., *Crestwood Heights*, p. 222. See also p. 177.

35. Parsons, "The Social Structure of the Family," pp. 261-62.

36. Seeley et al., *Crestwood Heights*, p. 217.

37. Parsons, "The American Family," p. 21-22.

38. Riesman, Introduction to *Crestwood Heights*, p. vi; Seeley et al., *Crestwood Heights*, p. 194.

39. Philip Wylie, *Generation of Vipers* (New York: Holt, Rinehart and Winston, 1942; revised 1955). See Margaret Mead, *Male and Female*, pp. 288-90, for a critique of the attack on women. Also see Friedan, *The Feminine Mystique*, pp. 180ff.; Ehrenreich and English, *For Her Own Good*, pp. 203-17; Gubar, "This Is My Rifle, This Is My Gun." For black women, see Paula Giddings, *When and Where I Enter* (New York: Bantam Books, 1984), pp. 250-56. Also see Rickie Solinger, *Wake Up Little Susie: Single Pregnancy and Race in the Pre-Roe v. Wade Era, a Cultural Study* (New York: Routledge, 1992), for psychiatrists' at-

titudes toward white unwed mothers. Among their explanations for unwed pregnancy in daughters were aggressive mothers and passive fathers.

40. Edward A. Strecker, *Their Mother's Sons* (New York: J. B. Lippincott, 1946), p. 6.

41. Susan Contratto, "Psychology Views Mothers and Mothering, 1897–1970," in *Feminist Revisions*, ed. V. Patraka and L. A. Tilly (Ann Arbor: University of Michigan Press, 1983), p. 163, also pp. 149–78. For more on the new theories of child development, see Christopher Lasch, *Haven in a Heartless World: The Family Besieged* (New York: Basic Books, 1977); Nancy Pottishman Weiss, "Mother, the Invention of Necessity: Dr. Spock's Baby and Child Care," *American Quarterly* 29 (1977): 519–46; Michael Zuckerman, "Dr. Spock: The Confidence Man," in *The Family in History*, pp. 179–207.

42. See Ilene Philipson, "Heterosexual Antagonisms and the Politics of Mothering," *Socialist Review* 12 (1982): 55–77, who argues that "maternal overinvolvement," stemming from isolation of mothers, was responsible for the inadequate psychological development in the baby boom generation, impairing their ability to maintain adequate heterosexual relationships as adults.

43. Parsons, "The Social Structure of the Family," p. 256. See also Friedan, *The Feminine Mystique*, p. 180.

44. Riesman, Introduction to *Crestwood Heights*, p. xiii. On the suburban matriarchy theme, see Rose L. Coser, "Authority and Structural Ambivalence in the Middle-Class Family," in *The Family: Its Structures and Functions*, 2d ed., ed. R. L. Coser (New York: St. Martin's Press, 1974), pp. 362–73; John Keats, *The Crack in the Picture Window;* Parsons, "The Social Structure of the Family," p. 251; Seeley et al., *Crestwood Heights*, p. 200.

45. Mead, *Male and Female*, p. 290.

46. There is contradictory evidence about isolation in the suburbs. Keats calls them a "vast communalistic female barracks" in *The Crack in the Picture Window*, p. 57, and Whyte's description of Park Forest is of a communal and neighborly way of life (*The Organization Man*, p. 356). Others who confirm an extensive social life are Herbert Gans, *The Levittowners* (New York: Vintage Books, 1967), and Marilyn French, in her novel *The Women's Room* (New York: Summit Books, 1977). The important point may be the isolation of women from men but not each other.

47. Ehrenreich and English, *For Her Own Good*, p. 214.

48. See Michael Rogin, "Kiss Me Deadly: Communism, Motherhood, and Cold War Movies," *Representations* 6 (1984): 26. See also Regina Markell Morantz, "The Scientist as Sex Crusader: Alfred C. Kinsey and American Culture," *American Quarterly* 29 (1977): 563–89.

49. Nancy Chodorow and Susan Contratto, "The Fantasy of the Perfect Mother," in *Rethinking the Family*, ed. B. Thorne (New York: Longman, 1982), pp. 54–71.

50. See Christopher Lasch, *Haven in a Heartless World*, for the argument that the development of the family in the twentieth century has entailed the

replacement of parental authority by the norms of consumer society, peer groups, and human relations experts. Also see Jacques Donzelot, *The Policing of Families* (New York: Pantheon Books, 1979); Frankfurt Institute for Social Research, *Aspects of Sociology* (Boston: Beacon Press, 1972).

CHAPTER 2   Family Legacies

1. The sources for the discussion of the mothers are based primarily on mothers who were born in the 1910s and 1920s, women who could be the mothers of adolescents and young women in the 1950s. When I refer to mothers who were born around 1930, young mothers in the 1950s, I make that clear. In this and the next two chapters, thirteen informal interviews with members of the cohort are utilized as background evidence and confirmation of other data. The research also used the *Correlates of Participation and Non-Participation in the Women's Liberation Movement, 1972-1974*, data set (made accessible in 1980, raw data files), collected by D. Franklin; *Patterns of Child Rearing, 1951-1952*, data set (made accessible in 1979, raw and machine-readable data files), collected by R. Sears, E. Maccoby, and H. Levin; *A Follow-up of the Patterns of Child Rearing Subjects, 1977-1978*, data set (made accessible in 1979, raw and machine-readable data files), collected by D. McClelland; *Lives in Progress, 1938-1965*, data set (made accessible in 1981, raw data files), collected by R. White: all data are available through the archive of the Henry A. Murray Center of Radcliffe College, Cambridge, Massachusetts (Producer and Distributor).

2. Elaine Tyler May, *Homeward Bound: American Families in the Cold War Era* (New York: Basic Books, 1988).

3. Judith Stacey, *Brave New Families: Stories of Domestic Upheaval in Late Twentieth-Century America* (New York: Basic Books, 1990), p. 10. Stacey suggests that this aberrant family set the terms for the rebellion against and nostalgia for the passing family and gender order. For a similar point also see Carol A. B. Warren, *Madwives: Schizophrenic Women in the 1950s* (New Brunswick: Rutgers University Press, 1987), p. 17, and Steven Mintz and Susan Kellogg, *Domestic Revolutions: A Social History of American Family Life* (New York: Free Press, 1988), p. 190.

4. Mintz and Kellogg, *Domestic Revolutions*, p. 178.

5. Peter Filene, *Him/Her/Self: Sex Roles in Modern America*, 2d ed. (Baltimore: Johns Hopkins University Press, 1986), p. 166.

6. Mintz and Kellogg, *Domestic Revolutions*, p. 179, and see pp. 178-81.

7. See Suzanne M. Bianchi and Daphne Spain, *American Women in Transition* (New York: Russell Sage Foundation, 1986), especially chs. 1 and 2; and Andrew Cherlin, *Marriage, Divorce, Remarriage* (Cambridge, Mass.: Harvard University Press, 1981), pp. 6-44.

8. Gerald Gurin, Joseph Veroff, and Shiela Feld, *Americans View Their Mental Health* (New York: Basic Books, 1960), and Joseph Veroff, Elizabeth Douvan, and Richard Kulka, *The Inner American: A Self Portrait from 1957 to 1976* (New York: Basic Books, 1981). In 1957, 2,460 Americans over the age of

twenty-one were interviewed They were a representative sample of the total population in age, sex, education, income, occupation, and place of residence, a miniature, normal, stable adult population of the United States (p. xi). The Veroff, Douvan, and Kulka 1976 study replicated this, with the samples having a high degree of correspondence.

9. "Did Success Spoil the United States? Dual Representation in Postwar America," Warren Susman with the assistance of Edward Griffin, in *Recasting America: Culture and Politics in the Age of the Cold War*, ed. Lary May (Chicago: University of Chicago Press, 1989), pp. 21–22.

10. W. D. Wetherall, *The Man Who Loved Levittown* (Pittsburgh: University of Pittsburgh Press, 1985), p. 7. The cowboy imagery is interesting for two reasons. First, because it suggests the suburbs as the last frontier in America, which in many ways they were. Second, because as a frontier the suburbs were settled by white people. The implications are numerous, not least that suburban development replicated the white man's seizure of the Native American's land and the larger point that white people's prosperity was predicated on racial exploitation and exclusion. Kenneth Jackson's *The Crabgrass Frontier: The Suburbanization of the United States* (New York: Oxford University Press, 1985), a history of the American suburbs, utilizes the frontier imagery in its title.

11. Mintz and Kellogg, *Domestic Revolutions*, p. 183; Mintz and Kellogg note that in the ten years after 1948, of thirteen million homes built in the United States, eleven million were built in the suburbs. Also see, William Chafe, *The Unfinished Journey: America Since World War II* (New York: Oxford University Press, 1986), p. 117).

12. Clifford E. Clark, Jr., "Ranch-House Suburbia: Ideals and Realities," in *Recasting America*, pp. 173–74. See Gwendolyn Wright, *Building the Dream: A Social History of Housing in America* (New York: Pantheon Books, 1981), especially ch. 13, for a history of American housing and of its meanings. Also see John Seeley et al., *Crestwood Heights* (Toronto: University of Toronto Press, 1956), for a discussion of the home as the site of conspicuous consumption and status striving in a new, upper-middle-class suburb.

13. Susman, "Did Success Spoil the United States?" p. 22. Also see Dana Polan, *Power and Paranoia: History, Narrative, and the American Cinema, 1940–1950* (New York: Columbia University Press, 1986), ch. 6, where he discusses images of the home in films of the 1940s.

14. Gurin et al., *Americans View Their Mental Health*, pp. xvi, 117; also Jessie Bernard, *The Future of Marriage* (New York: World Publishing, 1972), for a summary of studies of the family, many from the postwar period, that show that men and women have different experiences of the same marriage, with women more unhappy than men. Also see Bernard's "The Paradox of the Happy Marriage," in *Women in Sexist Society*, ed. V. Gornick and B. Moran (New York: Signet Books, 1971), pp. 145–62.

15. Robert O. Blood and Donald M. Wolfe, *Husbands and Wives: The Dynamics of Married Living* (New York: Free Press, 1960), p. 118.

16. For esteem at work, see Filene, *Him/Her/Self*, 2d ed., p. 168. Female employment continued to rise after the war with more middle-class wives and mothers working than ever before: "By 1960 twice as many women were employed as in 1940 and 40% of all women over sixteen held a job.... The proportion of wives at work doubled from 15% in 1940 to 30% in 1960 ... the number of mothers at work leaped 400% ... and 39% of women with children aged 6 to 17 had jobs by the end of the fifties" (Chafe, *The Unfinished Journey*, p. 126).

17. Warren, *Madwives*, p. 59. Warren's reanalysis of the case records of women diagnosed as schizophrenic in the 1950s indicates that some of them were not mentally ill but were suffering from dependence and isolation. These housewives had almost no communication with other adults, including their husbands. The gender segregation in their families was extreme, as it was in most families of the period. Their husbands and others around them considered the women ill because they could or would not perform housework and childcare adequately. Many received electroshock therapy. Some found the mental hospital a refuge and did not want to leave to resume the domestic situations that had driven them "mad" in the first place. Also see Lucy Rose Fischer, *Linked Lives: Adult Mothers and Their Daughters* (New York: Harper and Row, 1986), pp. 107-8, for a similar point about low educational achievement and the absence of career opportunities that reinforced mothers' commitment to motherhood.

18. John Modell and John Campbell, "Family Ideology and Family Values in the 'Baby Boom': A Secondary Analysis of the 1955 Growth of American Families Survey of Single Women" (Minneapolis: Minnesota Family Study, Family Study Center, University of Minnesota, 1984), p. 18.

19. May, *Homeward Bound*, pp. 28-36. The numbers are from my own and May's computations of the E. L. Kelly data, "Personality, Marital Compatibility, and Married Life: A Twenty Year [1933-1955] Study," which are at the Murray Center for the Study of Lives at Radcliffe College, Cambridge, Mass. Three hundred white, middle-class couples were surveyed first in the late 1930s and periodically until 1954-55, when they filled out extensive questionnaires about their marriages and lives. May reproduces the questionnaire in the appendix to her book. The figures are based on the Personal History and Report on Marriage to Research Partner, Time II, 1954-1955. Two-thirds of the husbands and one-half of the wives said they sacrificed nothing due to marriage (page 18, B.V. Question 7). Twice as many husbands as wives said they had gained happiness through marriage (page 19, B.V. Question 8).

20. May, *Homeward Bound*, p. 158.

21. Blood and Wolfe, *Husbands and Wives*, p. 222.

22. Modell and Campbell, *Family Ideology and Family Values*, p. 29.

23. John Modell, *Into One's Own: From Youth to Adulthood in the United States, 1920 to 1975* (Berkeley: University of California Press, 1989), p. 261. See Gurin et al., *Americans View Their Mental Health*, p. 130, where women's satis-

factions from parenthood were couched in their importance to their growth as persons, their stability, maturity, and purpose in life.

24. May, *Homeward Bound,* p. 136.

25. For grim recollections about marital sex manuals and marital sex, see Benita Eisler, *Private Lives* (New York: Franklin Watts, 1986), ch. 7, "Is Sex Dirty?" On the encouragement of marital sex in the 1950s as a way to stabilize the family, see Barbara Ehrenreich and Dierdre English, *For Her Own Good: One Hundred Fifty Years of Experts' Advice to Women* (Garden City, N.Y.: Doubleday, 1978), pp. 217–22; Birmingham Feminist History Group, "Feminism as Femininity in the 1950s?" *Feminist Review* 3 (1979): 52; Carol Smart, "Law and Control of Women's Sexuality: The Case of the 1950s," in *Controlling Women: The Normal and the Deviant,* ed. B. Hutter and G. Williams (London: Croom Helm, 1981), pp. 40–60.

26. May, *Homeward Bound,* p. 132. See pp. 132–34 for May's discussion of these findings. My own computations of the Kelly data confirm May's finding that it was more important to please one's spouse than to please oneself and indicate this was more true for women than men, although it was high for both. See Kelly data, page 14 of questionnaire B.II., "How important is it to you that . . . " (Report on Marriage to Research Partner, Time II, Murray Center for the Study of Lives, Radcliffe College, Cambridge, Mass.).

27. It is worth pointing out that Alfred C. Kinseys's 1953 study of female sexuality mentions women's regrets about not having had intercourse before marriage because they believed their sex lives would have been better later. (*Sexual Behavior in the Human Female* [Philadelphia: W. B. Saunders, 1953], pp. 316–17). See May, *Homeward Bound,* on this and also her discussion of women who regretted having had intercourse before marriage because they believed their husbands did not respect them (pp. 125–26). All studies imply that the focus on premarital restraints and virginity until marriage or its violation, in conjunction with the double standard, badly affected marital sexual relationships.

28. Patricia Frazier Lamb and Kathryn Joyce Hohlwein, *Touchstones: Letters between Two Women, 1953–1964* (New York: Harper and Row, 1983). Page references for the letters are given in the text.

29. Lynn Lauber, *White Girls* (New York: W. W. Norton, 1990), p. 68. The heroine, Loretta, also observes, "It was only we younger girls who admitted to the discontent that grew in us like the tumors our mothers whispered about" (p. 35).

30. May, *Homeward Bound,* p. 202–3.

31. Nancy Pottishman Weiss, "Mother, the Invention of Necessity: Dr. Benjamin Spock's *Baby and Child Care,*" *American Quarterly* 29 (1977): 537, 541. In addition to the sources already cited, the characterization of dissatisfaction is based on my own evaluations of the Kelly questionnaires, Report on Marriage to Research Partner, Time II, Questionnaire page 18, B.V. question 7 ("What did you sacrifice because of marriage?"), page 19, B.V. question 10 ("How

happy has your marriage been?"), and page 20, B.V.I. question 1, open-ended question ("Anything else?"), Murray Center, Radcliffe College, and on Elaine Tyler May's conclusions in *Homeward Bound,* based on the same data.

32. Vivian Gornick, *Fierce Attachments* (New York: Simon and Schuster, 1987), p. 32. See Carol L. Glickfield, *Useful Gifts* (Athens: University of Georgia Press, 1989), for a fictional account of the extreme differences in opportunities, experiences, and attitudes, in this case between a New York City working-class mother and her daughter who grew up in the 1940s and 1950s. It is an account that emphasizes the restricted and painful life of the mother.

33. Marital childlessness fell to its biological minimum. See Modell, *Into One's Own,* p. 256.

34. Modell and Campbell, "Family Ideology and Family Values," p. 19.

35. Gurin et al., *Americans View Their Mental Health,* p. 128. Gurin and his colleagues state, "As people question what kinds of parents they have been, as they list the sources of their inadequacies as parents, they appear much more concerned with failures in their relationship with the child than in their failures as providers or in caring for the child" (p. 141). See chapter 5 on parenthood. See note 8 above for details about the sample used in the mental health study. Also see Weiss, "Mother, The Invention of Necessity," for a discussion of mothers' feelings of inadequacy.

36. For this characterization of Dr. Spock's advice see Weiss, "Mother, The Invention of Necessity."

37. Lois Meek Stolz, *Influences on Parent Behavior* (Stanford: Stanford University Press, 1967), p. 281. This was a 1958 California study of seventy-eight parents, mothers and fathers, and their attitudes toward childrearing.

38. Nancy Mairs, "Conspiracies of Silence," *Women's Review of Books* 6 (1989): 7–8.

39. Robert Sears, Eleanor Maccoby, and Harry Levin, *Patterns of Child Rearing* (New York: Harper and Row, 1957). The discussion of the Sears data is based on the published book of 379 interviews of mothers of kindergarten-aged children and on 75 (20 percent) of the original questionnaires, which are stored at the Henry A. Murray Center for the Study of Lives, Radcliffe College. I include quotations in order to illustrate my points. When referring to other childrearing studies, I so indicate. The published book did not control for class, although when the authors did compare middle-class and working-class mothers, they found that the latter were "more punitive" and "less permissive"; even so they downplay the significance of class differences (pp. 480–82). While my discussion is based on the percentages of all the mothers studied as reported in the published volume, it is informed by my own evaluation of the original data that unpermissive attitudes were characteristic of both working- and middle-class mothers. For the article based on their data that compared mothers by class, see Eleanor Maccoby, Patricia K. Gibbs, and Staff of the Laboratory of Human Development, Harvard University, "Methods of Child-Rearing in Two Social Classes," in *Readings in Child Development,* ed.

W. E. Martin and C. B. Stendler (New York: Harcourt, Brace, 1954), pp. 380–96.

40. Sears et al., *Patterns of Child Rearing*, p. 44. Seven percent had never worked, 30 percent had worked before marriage and not after, 43 percent had worked after marriage but not since the child was born, 17 percent worked at least part time since the child was born, 3 percent not ascertained. When giving Sears statistics, if the numbers do not total 100 percent, they were not ascertained. Examples from the Sears study are hereafter cited by case numbers, which have been changed.

41. Sears case 10B; Many of the fathers of those born during the war were in the army when they were born. Some of the mothers in this study attributed fathers' difficulties in relating to these babies and small children to their wartime absence and experiences. A study of families, both during and after the war, in which fathers were away during the war, would undoubtedly yield interesting results.

42. Seeley et al., *Crestwood Heights*, p. 190.

43. May, *Homeward Bound*, p. 53.

44. Sears, cases 11B, 12B.

45. Sears, *Patterns of Child Rearing*, pp. 400, 397.

46. Ibid., p. 397. When asked about sex-role expectations, on a range from 1 (low: mother believes little or no difference exists between boys and girls) to 7 (high: mother stresses and trains for wide differentiation in dress, games, toys, manners), 36 percent were on the low end (1–3), 43 percent were on the high end (5–7), with 20 percent in the middle at 4.

47. Ibid., p. 407; See also, Stolz, *Influences on Parent Behavior*, pp. 177–78, about attitudes toward aggression, and p. 62, for how important manners were to parents. See Melvin L. Kohn, *Class and Conformity: A Study in Values* (1969; Chicago: University of Chicago Press, 1977), p. 106, for working-class mothers' gender differentiation of their children.

48. Sears cases 13B, 11B, 14B, 15B.

49. Daniel R. Miller and Guy E. Swanson, *The Changing American Parent* (New York: John Wiley and Sons, 1958), p. 228. Also see Stolz, *Influences on Parent Behavior*, p. 133, where she says that two-thirds of the parents believe there are differences between boys and girls in behavior.

50. See Sears, *Patterns of Child Rearing*, pp. 71, 76–77, on breastfeeding; p. 109, for the toilet training data: 6 percent began bowel training before the children were five months old, 41 percent began between the ages of five and nine months, 30 percent began between the ages of ten and fourteen months, 10 percent between fifteen and nineteen months, and 5 percent between twenty and twenty-four months. For severity of toilet training scale, see p. 119, for sexual anxiety, p. 112 and p. 76.

51. Seeley et al., *Crestwood Heights*, p. 89.

52. Miller and Swanson, *The Changing American Parent*, p. 219. Miller and Swanson found 57.6 percent began bowel training between six and nine

months, 84 percent began by the end of the twelfth month, 97.7 percent by the end of the eighteenth month, and an additional 2.3 percent during or after the nineteenth month.

53. Sears, *Patterns of Child Rearing*, p. 199. For modesty training and masturbation, see ibid. pp. 193, 197–201, and Miller and Swanson, *Changing American Parent*, pp. 225–26. Both Sears and Miller and Swanson express doubts about actual tolerance of masturbation and about mothers who claim never to have seen their children touch their genitals. In both the Sears and Miller and Swanson studies, the researchers suggested that mothers did not notice masturbation because they were anxious about it. The relationship of (mostly male) researchers to mothers must be analyzed for unstated judgments, particularly regarding sexual matters and in light of the postwar condemnation of mothers.

54. Sears case 16B; also see cases 17B and 18B about cleanliness. See Sears, *Patterns of Child Rearing*, pp. 213–14, 189, for quotations and discussion of sex training. See Miller and Swanson, *The Changing American Parent*, pp. 218–19, for conclusions about comparisons with nonliterate societies that are similar to those of the Sears study as stated in the epigraph to this chapter.

55. Alice McDermott, *That Night* (New York: Harper and Row, 1987), pp. 60, 108.

56. Lauber, *White Girls*, pp. 100, 75. Another novel about the late fifties and early sixties, *Grown Up Fast: A True Story of Teenage Life in Suburban America* (New York: Poseidon Press, 1988), by Betty Israel, is the story of a suburban girl who is pregnant but denies it to herself and everyone else. Her parents cooperate in this charade as do all those around her until finally in the seventh month a doctor breaks their bubble of denial. Also see *Cat's Eye* by Margaret Atwood (New York: Bantam Books, 1988), the story of a girl of this generation growing up in Canada. Her mother ignores every sign of distress as if by not acknowledging it, it will go away.

57. Sears, *Patterns of Child Rearing*, pp. 216–17.

58. Richard Flacks, *Youth and Social Change* (Chicago: Markham Publishing, 1971), pp. 25–26.

59. Sears, *Patterns of Child Rearing*, p. 404. Sixty-one percent of mothers expected boys to go to college, only 34 percent had the same ambitions for their daughters. See also pp. 404–5 and p. 401. Also see Elizabeth Douvan and Joseph Adelson, *The Adolescent Experience* (New York: John Wiley and Sons, 1966), p. 326, and James Coleman, *The Adolescent Society: The Social Life of the Teenager and Its Impact on Education* (New York: Free Press, 1961), pp. 244–65.

60. Sears cases 20B, 13B.

61. See Barbara Ehrenreich and Dierdre English, *For Her Own Good: One Hundred Fifty Years of Experts' Advice to Women* (Garden City, N.Y.: Doubleday, 1978); William Graebner, "The Unstable World of Benjamin Spock: Social Engineering in a Democratic Culture, 1917–1950," *Journal of American History* 67 (1980): 612–29; Jules Henry, *Culture against Man* (New York: Vintage Books,

1963); Christopher Lasch, *The Culture of Narcissism* (New York: W. W. Norton, 1978); Seeley et al., *Crestwood Heights;* Weiss, "Mother, The Necessity of Invention"; Martha Wolfenstein, "Fun Morality: An Analysis of Recent American Child-Rearing Literature," *Journal of Social Issues* 7 (1951): 15–25; Zuckerman, "Dr. Spock: The Confidence Man," pp. 179–207.

62. William H. Whyte, Jr., *The Organization Man* (New York: Simon and Schuster, 1956), p. 392; See also Stolz, *Influences on Parent Behavior,* pp. 54–55, 75.

63. Miller and Swanson state of the new child, "Not only is he free, but the confident, smooth social relations of the great organizations of which he must become a part will require him to get along well with other people and to take their feelings as well as his own into account with skill and confidence" (*Changing American Parent,* p. 55). It is worth reiterating that the use of the male pronoun, while not unusual, accurately reflected their and other social scientists' concern about the effects of the new corporate personality requirements on men and specifically their meaning for masculinity. See also pp. 97, 105–6, for a description of the more rigid childrearing behavior of entrepreneurial mothers.

64. "That getting married, having children, and staying married are now matters of choice, rather than things taken for granted, creates a new atmosphere for marriage and a new meaning for family life," say Robert Bellah, Richard Madson, William M. Sullivan, Ann Swidler, and Steven M. Tipton in *Habits of the Heart* (New York: Harper and Row, 1986), p. 110.

65. See Fischer, *Linked Lives,* especially pp. 81–116, for an interesting treatment of mothers and daughters and a discussion of mothers as negative role models. This will be discussed further below.

66. The sources for the portrait are 1978 follow-up interviews by David McClelland of thirty-eight middle-class daughters (out of the fifty-eight women interviewed) of the Sears mothers interviewed in 1951 and 1952. In this case, they are the actual daughters of 1950s mothers already discussed. See David McClelland, *Follow-up Patterns of Childrearing Subjects,* 1978. Other sources include interviews by social scientists of women of this generation for a variety of research purposes. A 1974 study by Diane Franklin of women who grew up in the 1950s in order to ascertain the factors that led, or did not lead, to participation in the women's liberation movement included forty-seven interviews of this cohort. See Diane Franklin, *Correlates of Participation and Nonparticipation in the Women's Liberation Movement,* 1974. Extensive interviews of two Radcliffe seniors, whose names have been changed, are in the Robert White study, *Lives in Progress,* White-Riggs Group, 1963–1965. These three studies are at the Henry A. Murray Center at Radcliffe College, Cambridge, Mass. I also utilized letters to Betty Friedan from this cohort which are in the Friedan Papers at the Schlesinger Library of Radcliffe College, Cambridge, Mass.

67. See Modell, *Into One's Own,* pp. 283–84, 270; see also pp. 266 and 280 for these points.

68. Veroff et al., *The Inner American*, p. 203; also pp. 224, 374. See Kathleen Gerson, *Hard Choices* (Berkeley: University of California Press, 1985), p. 17.

69. Approximately one-third of the McClelland respondents, daughters of the Sears mothers considered in the first part of the chapter, did not have children in 1978 when they were thirty-two years old (three-quarters of them were married by that time), and approximately 30 percent of the Franklin respondents, the women involved in the study of women's liberation, all of whom were married, were childless. See Modell, *Into One's Own*, pp. 282ff., for data about later childbearing and smaller families.

70. See McClelland cases 625, 325, 348.

71. Modell, *Into One's Own*, p. 278.

72. Gerson, *Hard Choices*, p. 10.

73. See especially chs. 11, 14, and 24 in F. Ivan Nye and Lois Wladis Hoffman's *The Employed Mother in America* (Chicago: Rand McNally, 1963).

74. McClelland cases 304, 723.

75. In the original 1951–52 Sears study, 22 percent of the mothers and 37 percent of the fathers were college graduates while 14 percent of the mothers and 10 percent of the fathers had not finished high school (*Patterns of Child Rearing*, p. 26). Their children achieved more education, on the average three years of college (McClelland 1978). The Franklin respondents had an unusually high educational attainment: 64 percent had completed college and of these an extremely high 47 percent had attained a graduate degree. Their parents, too, had much less education. Fifteen percent of the mothers and 23 percent of the fathers graduated from college and over 50 percent of the mothers and fathers each received a high school education or less (Franklin 1974). In Fischer's study, *Linked Lives,* daughters were almost four times as likely to have completed a four-year college degree than mothers (p. 108). See p. 228 in May, *Homeward Bound,* for educational statistics for the women in the Kelly study (the older generation). In the United States, college attendance doubled from the early 1960s to the early 1980s; the number of women aged 25–34 with less than a high school education has dropped steadily since 1940. In 1940, over one half of all women had not graduated from high school, but by 1981, less than 15 percent had not. Since the 1950s, the number of women earning degrees at every level has increased steadily. Bianchi and Spain, *American Women in Transition,* pp. 114ff., and Steven D. McLaughlin et al., *The Changing Lives of American Women* (Chapel Hill: University of North Carolina Press, 1988), pp. 32ff., especially pp. 35, 37.

76. Letter from eighteen-year-old (n.p., nd.); Anne Parsons letter to Friedan, September 1963.

77. Sally Kempton, "Cutting Loose," in *Liberation Now! Writings from the Women's Liberation Movement* (New York: Dell Publishing, 1971), p. 43.

78. Franklin case 103, and Franklin report (1975), pp. 151–52.

79. See D. M. Avery (1979, 1981) at the Murray Center for Research on Lives, Radcliffe College, for a late 1970s study of crisis in women's lives. The

crises described by almost all the women of this cohort entailed having done what they believed they "should" do and realizing later with alarm and guilt that they were not happy. This precipitated turning-points in their marriages and self-images, with many deciding to work or prepare for careers despite the opposition of family members. Because the older generation had different standards of fulfillment, they were more able to avoid crises of conflicting loyalties, even needs. Also see letters to Friedan, Schlesinger Library, Radcliffe College.

80. Letter to Friedan, September 4, 1964, Freeport, Texas.

81. Robert White, *Lives in Progress*, Vaigle Interviews 2, 7, 1965.

82. Harriet Gilbert, "Growing Pains," *Truth, Dare, or Promise: Girls Growing Up in the Fifties*, ed. Liz Heron (London: Virago, 1985), p. 54.

83. Fischer, *Linked Lives*, p. 113.

84. The Kelly Longitudinal Study questionnaire, question 4, Report on Marriage to Research Partner, 1954–1955, p. 9. A.VIII, question 4, asked 1950s mothers to rate the importance of three statements: (1) parents should teach children what is right; (2) parents should give children freedom to express themselves; (3) parents should guide children in learning to get along in the world. A large majority gave "least important" to no. 2 and almost all the other women divided "most important" between no. 1 and no. 3 (author's evaluation of Kelly data at the Murray Research Center, Radcliffe College).

85. Franklin case 3.

86. McClelland cases 610, 740, 304, 642, 732.

87. Bellah et al., *Habits of the Heart*, p. 103.

88. See, for example, the Franklin and McClelland studies at the Murray Center, as well as the Friedan letters at the Schlesinger Library.

89. McClelland case 658.

90. Letter to Friedan, July 23, 1970, Kansas City, Mo.; Franklin case 106. Another wrote to Friedan, "My mother had lived the mystique and tried to break away but was unsuccessful. My brother suffered deeply from it and I was fortunate enough to learn from it even though she wanted me to commit myself to a fate like hers . . . This has severed our relationship" (July 13, 1968, North Haven, Conn.).

91. Fischer, *Linked Lives*, pp. 81, 83. Also see Diana Grossman Kahn, "Lessons of Their Mothers' Lives: Imitation and Avoidance by Contemporary College Women," *International Journal of Women's Studies* 5 (1): 58–74 (n.d.).

92. Quotes from Barbara Raskin, *Hot Flashes* (New York: St. Martin's Press, 1987), p. 330; and Lauber, *White Girls*, pp. 52, 110.

93. See Fischer, *Linked Lives*, pp. 88–91, for this and other explanations of why resemblance with mothers was viewed negatively.

94. Annie Dillard, *An American Childhood* (New York: Harper and Row, 1987), p. 194. See the review of Marianne Hirsch's *Mother/Daughter Plot* by Gayle Green, *Women's Review of Books*, February 1990, pp. 8–9, for similar observations. Also see "Black Eve or Madonna? A Study of the Antithetical Views of the Mother in Black American Literature," by Daryl C. Dance, in *Sturdy Black*

Bridges: Visions of Black Women in Literature, ed. Roseann P. Bell, Bettye J. Parker, and Beverly Guy-Sheftell (Garden City, N.Y.: Doubleday, 1979); Gloria Joseph and Jill Lewis, *Common Differences: Conflicts in Black and White Perspectives* (Garden City, N.Y.: Anchor Books, 1981), sec. 2, "Mothers and Daughters"; Patricia Hill Collins, *Black Feminist Thought* (Boston: Unwin Hyman, 1990), ch. 6, "Black Women and Motherhood."

95. Letter to Friedan, May 22, 1965, San Jose, Calif.

96. Letters to Friedan: May 2, 1963, Westminster, Mass.; January 9, 1964, New York City; May 17, 1963, Sioux Falls, North Dakota. See May, *Homeward Bound,* p. 213–14 for the point that mothers wrote to Friedan hoping their daughters lives would be different from theirs.

97. Barbara Melosh with Linn Shapiro and Judy Kaplan, "Growing Up Red: Children of the Left Meet and Remember," *Radical History Review* 31 (1984): 80.

98. Jan Clausen, *Sinking Stealing* (Trumansberg, N.Y.: Crossing Press, 1985), p. 55.

99. Assata Shakur, *Assata* (Chicago: Lawrence Hill Books, 1987), p. 37. She remarks that when she was growing up every white man on television was able to support his family with no strain so there was no reason for his wife to work. "Her job was to stay home and take care of the kids. Black people accepted those role models for themselves even though they had very little to do with the reality of their existence and survival" (p. 74).

100. These include Bellah et al., *Habits of the Heart;* Herbert Hendin, *The Age of Sensation* (New York: W. W. Norton, 1975); Christopher Lasch, *Haven in a Heartless World* (New York: Basic Books, 1977) and *The Culture of Narcissism* (New York: W. W. Norton, 1978); Richard Sennett, *The Fall of Public Man* (New York: Vintage Books, 1976); Philip Slater, *The Pursuit of Loneliness* (Boston: Beacon Press, 1970).

101. Bellah, *Habits of the Heart,* p. 76.

102. Thomas Hine, *Populuxe* (New York: Alfred A. Knopf, 1986), p. 173.

103. For the story of Jewish women who have rejected the ambiguity and returned to an extreme family-centeredness, more extreme than that of their mothers, see Debra R. Kaufman, *Rachel's Daughters: Newly Orthodox Jewish Women* (New Brunswick, N.J.: Rutgers University Press, 1991).

CHAPTER 3 **Sexual Puzzles**

1. In this chapter, as in the previous chapter and the next, I have used informal interviews with women of the cohort to explore issues related to growing up in the fifties. They contributed in general to my interpretation and confirm data from other sources.

2. Marty Jezer, *The Dark Ages: Life in the United States, 1945–1960* (Boston: South End Press, 1982), p. 247, cites a study of movie advertisements that found the use of sex appeal before the war was never more than 50 percent while in

1951, 70 percent of all movie ads emphasized sex. See Diane Barthel, *Putting on Appearances: Gender and Advertising* (Philadelphia: Temple University Press, 1988), pp. 115ff., for a discussion of glamor and its relationship to industrial capitalism.

3. In Michel Foucault's terms, the postwar explosion of talk and print about sex (Alfred Kinsey's studies of male and female sexuality were bestsellers) by experts such as therapists, counselors, and teachers produced a new sexual personality—the teenager—who was at once subject to what Foucault would call the multiple disciplines of the discourse on sex and subject of efforts to subvert those disciplines. See *The History of Sexuality*, vol. 1 (New York: Vintage Books, 1980).

4. For historical studies of sexual behavior of youth, see Beth Bailey, *From Front Porch to Back Seat: Courtship in the Twentieth Century* (Baltimore: Johns Hopkins University Press, 1988); Paula Fass, *The Damned and the Beautiful: Youth in the 1920s* (New York: Oxford University Press, 1977); Joseph F. Kett, *Rites of Passage: Adolescence in America, 1790 to the Present* (New York: Basic Books, 1977); Robert S. Lynd and Helen Merrill Lynd *Middletown* (1929; New York: Harcourt, Brace and World, 1956); John Modell, *Into One's Own: From Youth to Adulthood in the United States, 1920–1975* (Berkeley: University of California Press, 1989).

5. Quoted in Barbara Ehrenreich, Elizabeth Hess, and Gloria Jacobs, *Remaking Love: The Feminization of Love* (Garden City, N.Y.: Doubleday, 1986), p. 21, by a sociologist in a *Life* magazine article on teenage girls.

6. John D'Emilio and Estelle Freedman, *Intimate Matters: A History of Sexuality in America* (New York: Harper and Row, 1988), p. 280, and especially ch. 12.

7. Raymond Williams, *Marxism and Literature* (Oxford: Oxford University Press, 1977), pp. 122, 123.

8. See Kathy Peiss, *Cheap Amusements: Working Women and Leisure in Turn-of-the-Century New York* (Philadelphia: Temple University Press, 1986), for a study of an earlier time that addresses similar issues. As argued in a collection of feminist essays, the debates about popular culture are characterized by tension and ambivalence regarding the "political implications of the will and motives of the producers and consumers of popular culture." See *Becoming Feminine: The Politics of Popular Culture*, ed. Leslie Roman, Linda Christian-Smith, and Elizabeth Ellsworth (Falmer Press, 1988), p. 12. The essays in this volume set forth competing interpretations of popular culture, which on the one hand emphasize the contestation, resistance, and creation of their own meanings by subordinate groups and on the other hand concentrate on the "ways in which popular culture bears the inscription of the interests of the dominant classes whose cultural forms are constituted through the concentra-

tion of capital and cultural power within the enterprises of mass communication that comprise multinational corporate capitalism" (p. 12).

9. Benita Eisler, *Private Lives: Men and Women of the Fifties* (New York: Franklin Watts, 1986), p. 127.

10. Sara Davidson, Introduction to Dan Wakefield's *Going All the Way* (New York: Dutton, 1970, 1989), vi.

11. See Robert R. Bell, *Premarital Sex in a Changing Society* (Englewood Cliffs, N.J.: Prentice-Hall, 1960), for a discussion of the discrepancy between stated values regarding sex and behavior.

12. For female sexual disappointment, see Simone De Beauvoir, *The Second Sex* (New York: Alfred A. Knopf, 1953), ch. 14, especially pp. 359ff. In her study of contemporary teenage girls' sexuality, Sharon Thompson argues that first intercourse is not about pleasure. See "Search for Tomorrow: On Feminism and the Reconstruction of Teen Romance," in *Pleasure and Danger: Exploring Female Sexuality*, ed. Carole Vance (Boston: Routledge and Kegan Paul, 1984), pp. 365–67. Rosalind Petchesky states that in 150 recent interviews with teenage girls, she "found that they never mentioned anything concerning *pleasure* (although they might say, 'it didn't hurt')". See *Abortion and Woman's Choice: The State, Sexuality, and Reproductive Freedom* (Boston: Northeastern University Press, 1984), p. 218. Also see Ira Reiss, "Sexual Codes in Teen-Age Culture," *Annals* 338 (1961): 53–64.

13. Sylvia Plath, *The Bell Jar* (New York: Bantam Books), p. 187.

14. Caryl Rivers, *Virgins* (New York: Pocket Books, 1984), p. 214.

15. Lisa Alther, *Kinflicks* (New York: New American Library, 1975), p. 130.

16. Kate Stimpson, *Class Notes* (New York: Avon Books, 1979), p. 129.

17. Mark Bego, *Cher!* (New York: Pocket Books, 1986), p. 32.

18. Joyce Johnson, *Minor Characters* (Boston: Houghton Mifflin, 1983), p. 85.

19. Ibid., p. 30. Numerous observers pointed out that to engage in sexual intercourse *was* a form of rebellion. See, for example, Winston Ehrmann, *Premarital Dating Behavior* (New York: Henry Holt, 1959), pp. 203–4, where he says that girls with liberal standards who had intercourse with boys they didn't love were expressing feelings of rebellion. Nora Johnson wrote in 1959 how "promiscuity . . . demands a certain amount of nerve," in comparison to going steady (*Atlantic Monthly* 204 [1959]:57).

20. For more on the subject, see Stuart Ewen, *Captains of Consciousness: Advertising and the Social Roots of Consumer Culture* (New York: McGraw-Hill, 1976), for a study of how advertising linked the definitions of democracy and freedom to brand names and consumer goods. See also Barbara Ehrenreich, *Fear of Falling: The Inner Life of the Middle Class* (New York: Pantheon Books, 1989), for an analysis of middle-class aspirations and consciousness since World War II.

21. Valerie Walkerdine, "Dreams from an Ordinary Childhood," in *Truth,*

Dare, or Promise: Girls Growing Up in the Fifties, ed. Liz Heron (London: Virago, 1985), p. 63.

22. Thomas Doherty, *Teenagers and Teenpics: The Juvenilization of American Movies in the 1950s* (Boston: Unwin Hyman, 1988), p. 54; Paul Carter, *Another Part of the Fifties* (New York: Columbia University Press, 1983), p. 203. Also see Jessie Bernard, "Teen-Age Culture: An Overview," *Annals* 338 (1961), for data on how teenagers spent their money.

23. Cited in George Lewis, *Side-Saddle on the Golden Calf: Social Structure and Popular Culture in America* (Pacific Palisades, California: Goodyear Publishing, 1972), p. 224. Robert and Helen Lynds' *Middletown,* a study done in the 1920s, discovered growing separation of youth from their families and orientation toward peers, but the explosive market construction of teenagers came after World War II.

24. Jon Savage, "The Enemy Within: Sex, Rock, and Identity," in *Facing the Music,* ed. Simon Frith (New York: Pantheon Books, 1989), p. 139. See also Doherty, *Teenagers and Teenpics,* p. 46.

25. See Doherty, *Teenagers and Teenpics,* p. 46, and Jon Savage, "The Enemy Within," p. 139.

26. For an argument about the weaknesses of a hegemonic reading of postwar culture, see T. J. Jackson Lears, "The Concept of Cultural Hegemony: Problems and Possibilities," *American Historical Review* 90 (1985): 567–93, and "A Matter of Taste: Corporate Cultural Hegemony in a Mass-Consumption Society," in *Recasting America: Culture and Politics in the Age of the Cold War,* ed. Lary May (Chicago: University of Chicago Press, 1989), pp. 38–57. See William Graebner, *Coming of Age in Buffalo: Youth and Authority in the Postwar Era* (Philadelphia: Temple University Press, 1990), for an emphasis on the local, assimilationist meanings of teen culture, and George Lipsitz, *Time Passages: Collective Memory and American Popular Culture* (Minneapolis: University of Minnesota Press, 1990), for an approach that stresses the subversive creation and uses of popular culture. For a collection of the most influential 1970s authors studying subcultures, the pioneers of "cultural studies," see Stuart Hall and Tony Jefferson, eds., *Resistance through Rituals: Youth Subcultures in Post-War Britain* (London: Hutchinson, 1975), especially "Subcultures, Cultures, and Class" by John Clarke et al. and "Girls and Subcultures" by Angela McRobbie and Jenny Garber. Also see *Becoming Feminine,* Roman et al., and Elizabeth Long, "Feminism and Cultural Studies," *Critical Studies in Mass Communication* 6 (1989): 427–35.

27. For rationales for studying the middle class, see Herve Varenne, "Doing the Anthropology of America," in *Symbolizing America,* ed. H. Varenne (Lincoln: University of Nebraska Press, 1986); Bailey, *From Front Porch to Back Seat,* and Elaine Tyler May, *Homeward Bound: American Families in the Cold War Era* (New York: Basic Books, 1988).

28. James Gilbert, *A Cycle of Outrage: America's Reaction to the Juvenile Delinquent in the 1950s* (New York: Oxford University Press, 1986), pp. 203, 204,

205. See pp. 204–11 for the development of a teenage market. Also see Joe Austin, "The Public Discourse of the 'Youth Problem,' 1939–1960" (manuscript).

29. I quote from Savage, "The Enemy Within," p. 140, and Bernard, "Teen-Age Culture," p. 4. For historical discussions, see Robert and Helen Lynd, *Middletown*, pp. 241–42, 266; Simon Frith, *Sound Effects: Youth, Leisure, and the Politics of Rock and Roll* (New York: Pantheon, 1981).

30. Savage, "The Enemy Within," p. 142; Bernard, "Teen-Age Culture," p. 3.

31. Marjorie Rosen, *Popcorn Venus: Women, Movies, and the American Dream* (New York: Coward, McCann and Geoghegan, 1973), pp. 296, 267.

32. *Photoplay* was the circulation leader of thirty magazines, with a monthly circulation of 1.2 million. See *This Fabulous Century, 1950–1960* (Alexandria, Va.: Time-Life Books, 1970), p. 204. Also see Maureen Honey, "The 'Celebrity' Magazines," in *New Dimensions in Popular Culture*, ed. Russel B. Nye (Bowling Green, Ohio: Bowling Green University Press, 1972), pp. 47–58, where she says by the early 1960s two dozen celebrity magazines had a monthly circulation of 8 million readers. The readership was female.

33. Marge Piercy, "Through the Cracks: Growing Up in the Fifties," in *Parti-Colored Blocks for a Quilt* (Ann Arbor: University of Michigan Press, 1982), p. 114. She continues, "Even the lawns were Christian."

34. Graebner, *Coming of Age in Buffalo*; see George Lipsitz, "The Meaning of Memory: Family, Class, and Ethnicity in Early Television Networks" in *Time Passages*, pp. 39–75, for an analysis of how 1950s television shows were educating their viewers in the new consumerism and family norms. He argues that shows that featured working-class families capitalized on postwar anxieties about acquisitiveness and upward mobility in order to legitimate new consumerist social relations.

35. See Eisler, *Private Lives*, p. 109, and Carole L. Glickfield, *Useful Gifts* (Athens: University of Georgia Press, 1989), pp. 66, 55.

36. Sylvia Fraser, *My Father's House: A Memoir of Incest and Healing* (New York: Harper and Row, 1987), p. 75. The author of this memoir was an incest victim in whom feelings of marginality and separateness were often extreme, but whose perceptions were heightened versions of many teenage girls' feelings.

37. Eisler, *Private Lives*, p. 55.

38. See Mary Helen Washington, *Invented Lives: Narratives of Black Women, 1860–1960* (Garden City, N.Y.: Doubleday, 1987), pp. 398ff., for a discussion of postwar culture and black women. Also see Paula Giddings, *When and Where I Enter: The Impact of Black Women on Race and Sex in America* (New York: Bantam Books, 1984), pp. 241–56.

39. See Mary Wilson, *Dreamgirl: My Life as a Supreme* (New York: St. Martin's Press, 1986), and David Wallechinsky, *Class Reunion '65* (New York: Penguin Books, 1986), p. 74. I want to thank Elaine Scott for the point about experiences shared by both white and black girls.

40. Ann Moody, *Coming of Age in Mississippi* (New York: Dell, 1968),

p. 108; Alice Walker, "If the Present Looks Like the Past, What Does the Future Look Like?" *In Search of Our Mothers' Gardens* (New York: Harcourt Brace Jovanovich, 1984), p. 292; Assata Shakur, *Assata* (Chicago: Lawrence Hill Books, 1987), pp. 30–31. Thanks to George Lipsitz, private correspondence, March 29, 1990, for his point that black female sex symbols could have different shapes and features (bigger hips or lips or nappy hair) but were demeaned in the mass media. One way racism operated in the media was to imply that black men were not really men and that black women were not really women (on the basis of white norms).

41. See Susan Hartmann, *The Homefront and Beyond: American Women in the 1940s* (Boston: Twayne, 1982), pp. 199–205.

42. Marjorie Rosen, *Popcorn Venus*, p. 267.

43. Alfred Kinsey, *Sexual Behavior in the Human Female* (Philadelphia: W. B. Saunders, 1953), pp. 254–55; Horace Miner, "Body Ritual among the Nacerima," *American Anthropologist* 58 (1956): 506.

44. Mark Burns and Louis DiBonis, *Fifties Homestyle* (New York: Harper and Row, 1988), p. 57.

45. Bailey, *From Front Porch to Back Seat*, pp. 67, 74.

46. Caryl Rivers, *Aphrodite at Mid-Century* (Garden City, N.Y.: Doubleday, 1973), p. 194. Rivers echoes Lisa Alther's epigraph to this chapter. See also May, *Homeward Bound*, and Michael Paul Rogin, *Ronald Reagan: The Movie* (Berkeley: University of California Press, 1987), for academic treatments linking the decade's preoccupation with domesticity and powerful mothers with fears of communism.

47. Piercy, "Through the Cracks," p. 121; Susan Brownmiller, *Femininity* (New York: Simon and Schuster, 1984), p. 26.

48. Sara Davidson, Introduction to Dan Wakefield's *Going All the Way* (New York: Dutton, 1989), p. viii (the novel is about young male sexual frustration and obsession); Haskell, *From Reverence to Rape*, p. 235; Burns and DiBonis, *Fifties Homestyle*, pp. 58, 85.

49. Eisler, *Private Lives*, p. 64; Miller and Nowak, *The Fifties: The Way We Really Were* (Garden City, N.Y.: Doubleday, 1975), p. 329.

50. For studies that consider the narrowing of women's situation in the postwar period, especially in films, see Peter Biskind, *Seeing Is Believing: How Hollywood Taught Us to Stop Worrying and Love the Fifties* (New York: Pantheon Books, 1983); Brandon French, *On the Verge of Revolt: Women in American Films of the 1950s* (New York: Frederick Ungar, 1978); Haskell, *From Reverence to Rape*; Rosen, *Popcorn Venus*; Nora Sayre, *Running Time: Films of the Cold War* (New York: Dial Press, 1982).

51. Biskind, *Seeing Is Believing*, p. 272; Haskell, *From Reverence to Rape*, pp. 260, 255. See also Lois W. Banner, *American Beauty* (New York: Alfred A. Knopf, 1983), pp. 283–84, for a discussion of the power of film stars to define beauty ideals and for the characterization of a dichotomous model of beauty among movie stars in the 1950s, childlike and voluptuous. Marilyn Monroe, ac-

cording to Banner, combined both. For an interesting review of books on Marilyn Monroe, see Dean Maccannell, "Marilyn Monroe Was Not a Man," *Diacritics* 17 (1987): 114–26.

52. Biskind, *Seeing Is Believing*, p. 272.

53. Caryl Rivers, *Aphrodite at Mid-Century*, pp. 103–4; Eisler, *Private Lives*, p. 54. See also Rosen, *Popcorn Venus*, p. 269.

54. Wallechinsky, *Class Reunion '65*, p. 418.

55. Fraser, *In My Father's House*, p. 65. See also p. 78, where she describes wearing a dress like Marilyn Monroe should have worn in *How to Marry a Millionaire*.

56. Wilson, *Dreamgirl*, p. 14; Eisler, *Private Lives*, p. 56; Rivers, *Aphrodite at Mid-Century*, p. 232.

57. Eisler, *Private Lives*, pp. 56, 128; Burns and DiBonis, *Fifties Homestyle*, pp. 81–82. Also see Ewen, *Captains of Consciousness*, for the twentieth-century development of advertising techniques that consciously induced shame and loathing in Americans about their bodies and selves.

58. Rosen, *Popcorn Venus*, p. 261–62. For an interesting analysis of romance for girls, see Myra Connell et al., "Romance and Sexuality: Between the Devil and the Deep Blue Sea?" in *Feminism for Girls*, ed. Angela McRobbie and T. McCabe (London: Routledge and Kegan Paul, 1981), pp. 155–77.

59. Piercy, "Through the Cracks," p. 124.

60. Despite the fact that the study of popular song lyrics analyzes the music solely on the basis of the written text and thus outside the context of the culture, music, and audience, studies suggest that a very high percentage of fifties popular song lyrics were passive, based on wishing, dreaming, and longing. Lyrics celebrated ideal love and courtship, in contrast to sixties lyrics, which were less about love and which articulated an active physical desire and intention. See Donald Horton, "The Dialogue of Courtship in Popular Songs," *American Journal of Sociology* 62 (1957): 569–78; James Carey, "Changing Courtship Patterns in the Popular Song," *American Journal of Sociology* 74 (1969): 720–31; Richard A. Peterson and David G. Berger, "Three Eras in the Manufacture of Popular Song Lyrics," in *The Sounds of Social Change*, ed. Serge Denisoff and R. A. Peterson (Chicago: Rand McNally, 1972). See also Alice McDermott's novel *That Night* (New York: Harper and Row, 1987), p. 78, where she describes how the romanticism of the heroine is fed by "the love songs of the Shirelles and Shangri-las, the auto accident/undying love poems printed in odd spaces of her teen magazines."

61. Rivers, *Aphrodite at Mid-Century*, p. 229; Lynn Lauber, *White Girls* (New York: W. W. Norton, 1990), p. 38.

62. Bailey, *From Front Porch to Back Seat*, p. 59. In an essay about young Italian women in the 1950s, Simonetta Piccone Stella (manuscript, n.d.) suggests that "being seen" was important in their postwar modernization. Because of advertising and the availability of consumer goods, women were able to see themselves in new ways, to imagine themselves differently. For the first time, a

girl could self-consciously construct an image and imagine others looking at her. High school was a stage for looking.

63. Frederic Jameson, "Postmodernism and Consumer Society," in *Postmodernism and Its Discontents,* ed. E. Ann Kaplan (London: Verso, 1988).

64. See Christopher Lasch, *The Minimal Self* (New York: W. W. Norton, 1984), pp. 29–30. Not surprisingly, the 1950s and early 1960s generated the initial critical analyses by social theorists of the triumph of image, representation, and appearance in postwar capitalist society. For example, Daniel Boorstin's *The Image: A Guide to Pseudo-Events in America* (New York: Harper and Row, 1961); Herbert Marcuse's *One Dimensional Man* (Boston: Beacon Press, 1964); and Guy Debord's presentation of the French Situationists in *The Society of the Spectacle* (Detroit: Black and Red, 1970) all had their roots in the transformations of the 1950s. Such criticism is, in turn, linked to social movements of the 1960s and has found its most recent extension in the writings of Jean Baudrillard. See Jean Baudrillard, *Selected Writings,* ed. Mark Poster (Stanford: Stanford University Press, 1988).

65. Rosalind Coward, *Female Desires: How They Are Sought, Bought, and Packaged* (New York: Grove Press, 1985), p. 78. Also see Jane Root, *Pictures of Women* (London: Pandora Press, 1983), 51–68.

66. John Berger, *Ways of Seeing* (New York: Penguin Books, 1972), pp. 46–47. See Laura Mulvey, "Visual Pleasure and Narrative Cinema," in *Art after Modernism,* ed. B. Wallis (Boston: David Godine, 1984); E. Ann Kaplan, "Is the Gaze Male?" in *Powers of Desire,* ed. Ann Snitow, Christine Stansell, and Sharon Thompson (New York: Monthly Review Press, 1983); and Teresa DeLauretis, *Alice Doesn't: Feminism, Semiotics, Cinema* (Bloomington: Indiana University Press, 1984), for early contributions to a huge feminist literature on the representation of women as "other" by the male camera and gaze.

67. Elizabeth Douvan and Joseph Adelson, *The Adolescent Experience* (New York: John Wiley and Sons, 1966). Letters to Friedan: July 23, 1970, letter from Kansas City, Mo.; May 17, 1963, letter from Sioux Falls, North Dakota, Friedan Collection, Schlesinger Library, Radcliffe College.

68. For the preparation of girls for courtship and marriage in youth culture, see Frith, *Sound Effects,* pp. 225–34; Mike Brake, *The Sociology of Youth Culture and Youth Subcultures* (London: Routledge and Kegan Paul, 1980), ch. 5. Also see McRobbie and Garber, "Girls and Subcultures: An Exploration," in Hall and Jefferson's *Resistance through Rituals;* Savage, "The Enemy Within"; and Angela McRobbie, "Settling Accounts with Subcultures: A Feminist Critique," in *On Record: Rock, Pop, and the Written Word,* ed. Simon Frith and A. Goodwin (New York: Pantheon Books, 1990).

69. Letter to Friedan, November 18, 1963. Douvan and Adelson, *The Adolescent Experience,* pp. 24–26; see Shirley S. Angrist and Elizabeth M. Almquist, *Careers and Contingencies: How College Women Juggle with Gender* (New York: Dunellen, 1975), for a discussion of girls' "contingency orientation" with regard to marriage and work.

70. Douvan and Adelson, *The Adolescent Experience,* pp. 70, 40–46.

71. Eisler, *Private Lives,* p. 64; Miller and Nowak, *The Fifties,* p. 329. See May, *Homeward Bound,* pp. 140–41, for a discussion of how the ambitions of female film stars began to be presented in terms of fulfillment through motherhood.

72. Rosen, *Popcorn Venus,* p. 295.

73. *Photoplay,* February 1953, p. 37.

74. Ibid., March 1953, p. 39.

75. See Honey, "The 'Celebrity' Magazine"; also see David Sonenschein, "Love and Sex in Romance Magazines," in George H. Lewis, *Side-Saddle on the Golden Calf,* pp. 66–74.

76. Jane Gaines, "War, Women, and Lipstick: Fan Magazines in the Forties," *Heresies* 18–19 (1985): 45.

77. Kathy Peiss, *Cheap Amusements,* p. 6. "Double texts" is Brandon French's term. See Introduction, *On the Verge of Revolt,* p. xxi.

78. Gaines, "War, Women, and Lipstick," p. 44. See George Gerbner on the discrepancy between the confession magazine covers and their verbal messages, "The Social Role of the Confession Magazine," *Social Problems* 6 (1958): 29–40, and "The Social Anatomy of the Romance Conference Cover Girl," *Journalism Quarterly* 35 (1958): 299–306.

79. Charles Brown, "Self-Portrait: The Teen-Type Magazine," *Annals* 338 (1961): 20–21; Modell, *Into One's Own,* p. 224; Bailey, *From Front Porch to Back Seat,* on fifties advice books, pp. 20–21. See, for examples, *Photoplay* magazine, "What You Don't Know about Popularity," February 1958, p. 52, and "How Much Does a Boy Expect on a Date?" August 1958, p. 70.

80. Michael Zuckerman, "Dr. Spock: The Confidence Man," in *The Family in History,* ed. Charles Rosenberg (Philadelphia: University of Pennsylvania Press, 1975).

81. "What You Don't Know about Popularity," *Photoplay,* February 1958. See Brown, "Self-Portrait"; also see movie magazines for advice columns.

82. See Daniel Miller and Guy Swanson, *The Changing American Parent* (New York: John Wiley and Sons, 1958), pp. 202–3. Also Jules Henry, *Culture against Man* (New York: Vintage Press, 1963), p. 162. In an essay entitled "Personality and the Making of Twentieth-Century Culture," Warren Susman suggests the peculiarities of the American notion of personality consist of the quality of being "somebody" and distinguishing oneself from the crowd. This entails being different from others, standing out, being one's distinctive self. At the same time it requires being well-liked, one's success judged by attractiveness to the crowd. These qualities do not obviously mesh. The two kinds of advice found in personality manuals recommend that one should "be oneself" and follow one's own feelings but that one's personality would have to be acceptable to others in order to be successful or popular. Both injunctions were characteristic of teen and childrearing advice in the 1950s, which suggests the historical tradition out of which this advice grew, a notion of personality that depended

upon performance. See *Culture as History* (New York: Pantheon Books, 1984), pp. 271–84.

83. Rivers, *Aphrodite at Mid-Century,* p. 211; Eisler, *Private Lives,* p. 94. See also Brown, "Self-Portrait"; James Coleman, *The Adolescent Society: The Social Life of the Teenager and Its Impact on Education* (New York: Free Press, 1961); Henry, *Culture against Man.*

84. Henry, *Culture against Man,* p. 154; Bernard, "Teen-Age Culture," p. 5.

85. For discussion of the importance of social class, see Coleman, *The Adolescent Society,* pp. 47–57; Douvan and Adelson, *The Adolescent Experience,* p. 317; Graebner, *Coming of Age in Buffalo.*

86. Douvan and Adelson, *The Adolescent Experience,* p. 347; Ehrenreich et al., *Remaking Love,* p. 21. Martha Wolfenstein and Nathan Leites, *Movies: A Psychological Study* (Glencoe: Free Press, 1950), p. 31, suggest a similar configuration regarding 1940s movie heroines: "The attractiveness of the popular girl derives from her association with many men combined with the assurance that she had not gone too far with them."

87. Johnson, "Sex and the College Girl," p. 60.

88. Ibid., p. 59. Ira Reiss, "Sexual Codes in Teen-Age Culture," *Annals* 338 (1961): 57.

89. Ehrenreich et al., *Remaking Love,* p. 19; "The course of acceptable behavior had become almost impossibly narrow," writes Beth Bailey (*From Front Porch to Back Seat,* p. 94).

90. See, for example, Paul Landis, *Making the Most Out of Marriage* (New York: Appleton-Century Crofts, 1955), pp. 231, 198.

91. Jean Monroe, "From California Daughter/1950," in *I Never Told Anyone,* ed. E. Bass and L. Thornton (New York: Harper and Row, 1983), p. 96 (this is an incest memoir; see note 36 for reference to another incest memoir); Vivian Gornick, *Fierce Attachments* (New York: Simon and Schuster, 1987), p. 110.

92. Wakefield, *Going All the Way,* p. 90.

93. Barbara Raskin, *Hot Flashes* (New York: St. Martin's Press, 1987), p. 102; Michael Anania, *The Red Menace* (New York: Thunder's Mouth Press, 1984); Fraser, *My Father's House,* p. 94. See also Petchesky, *Abortion and Woman's Choice,* p. 219, where the author reports on a contemporary study of teenage girls' sexuality in which peer groups dictated rules for sexual behavior that set limits and restricted sexual activity. In many cases oral sex was taboo. See Joyce Canaan, "Why a 'Slut' is a 'Slut': Cautionary Tales of Middle-Class Teenage Girls' Morality," in Varenne's *Symbolizing America,* for an analysis of the discourse of romantic love and social control in contemporary girls' sexual behavior. Also see Frith, *Sound Effects,* p. 238, on peer groups setting sexual norms for teenagers.

94. Sylvia Fraser about Lulu, *My Father's House,* p. 103. For fiction about getting pregnant, see *Grown Up Fast: A True Story of Teenage Life in Suburban America,* by Betty Israel (New York: Poseidon Press, 1988), *White Girls* by Lynn Lauber, and *That Night* by Alice McDermott. Premarital intercourse among

teenagers increased dramatically after the 1950s, especially in the 1970s and 1980s. See Theodore Caplow, *Middletown's Families* (Minneapolis: University of Minnesota Press, 1982), pp. 168, 170, 378. For the incidence of premarital intercourse, see Kinsey, *Sexual Behavior in the Human Female*, pp. 286ff.; Roy J. Hopkins, "Sexual Behavior in Adolescence," *Journal of Social Issues* 33 (1977): 67-85; Ehrmann, *Premarital Dating Behavior*; Petchesky, *Abortion and Woman's Choice*, pp. 144, 211, 212. For an important consideration of how unwed, pregnant, white women and black women were perceived and treated in the postwar period, see Rickie Solinger, *Wake Up Little Susie: Single Pregnancy and Race in the Pre-Roe v. Wade Era, a Cultural Study* (New York: Routledge, 1992).

95. Modell, *Into One's Own*, pp. 189, 203, and "Dating Becomes the Way of American Youth," in *Essays on the Family and Historical Change*, ed. L. Moch and G. Stark (Arlington: Texas A and M University Press, 1983), p. 125.

96. Wallechinsky, *Class Reunion '65*, p. 281.

97. Modell, *Into One's Own*, p. 243.

98. Fraser, *In My Father's House*, p. 72.

99. Modell, *Into One's Own*, pp. 235-36. See also Johnson, "Sex and the College Girl," p. 57.

100. Modell, *Into One's Own*, p. 239; Bailey, *From Front Porch to Back Seat*, p. 49.

101. Eisler, *Private Lives*, p. 107.

102. Ann River Siddons, *Heartbreak Hotel* (New York: Ballantine Books, 1976), pp. 199-200; Wakefield, *Going All the Way*, p. 84.

103. Bell, *Premarital Sex in a Changing Society*, pp. 102-3; Ehrmann, *Premarital Dating Behavior*, p. 270; Kinsey, *Sexual Behavior in the Human Female*, p. 250; Margaret Mead, *Male and Female* (New York: Dell Publishing, 1949), p. 280; Reiss, "Sexual Codes in Teen-Age Culture," p. 58.

104. *Photoplay*, May 1958, p. 70: The question "How much does a boy expect on a date?" was answered by male stars who said, in effect, "Not much. Trust your own instincts." See Judson Landis and Mary Landis, authors of many best-selling text and advice books, *Building a Successful Marriage* ([1948; Englewood Cliffs: Prentice-Hall, 1953], pp. 70-71), where they discuss "learning to say no graciously," tactfully, and effectively and list fifteen techniques girls can utilize in order to control necking and petting.

105. Douvan and Adelson, *The Adolescent Experience*, p. 209; Modell, "Dating Becomes the Way of American Youth," p. 124.

106. Rivers, *Aphrodite at Mid-Century*, p. 255; Lazarre, *On Loving Men*, p. 45.

107. See Fass, *The Damned and the Beautiful*; Ellen K. Rothman, *Hands and Hearts: A History of Courtship in America* (New York: Basic Books, 1984); Bailey, *From Front Porch to Back Seat*. Ira Reiss argues that more egalitarian and permissive sexual codes led to an increase in petting but not intercourse among teenagers ("Sexual Codes in Teenage Culture," p. 59). Robert Bell also states there was more premarital petting (*Premarital Sex in a Changing Society*, p. 58).

See John Diepold, Jr., and Richard D. Young, "Empirical Studies of Adolescent Sexual Behavior," *Adolescence* 14 (1979): 45–64, for a review of the literature.

108. Bailey, *From Front Porch to Back Seat,* pp. 80–81; Kinsey, *Sexual Behavior in the Human Female,* pp. 286ff., 259. See also Rothman, *Hands and Hearts,* p. 300; E. E. LeMasters, *Modern Courtship and Marriage* (New York: MacMillan, 1957), pp. 199ff., where he also suggests that there was more petting in the middle class because they were taught to delay gratification.

109. See Ehrmann, *Premarital Dating Behavior,* p. 269; Kinsey, *Sexual Behavior in the Human Female,* p. 323; Mead, *Male and Female,* pp. 280–81; Reiss, "Sexual Codes in Teenage Culture," p. 57.

110. Lazarre, *On Loving Men,* p. 53.

111. See Ehrmann, *Premarital Dating Behavior,* for the survey, pp. 269–70, 187, 274; also see p. 181 where Ehrmann says for girls being in love meant a greater desire for sexual activities and willingness to flout the mores that limit them. See also Kinsey, *Sexual Behavior in the Human Female,* p. 286; Bell, *Premarital Sex in a Changing Society,* p. 82; LeMasters, *Modern Courtship and Marriage,* pp. 192, 204; Ira Reiss, *Premarital Sexual Standards in America* (Glencoe: Free Press, 1960), pp. 165–68. Some of the data suggests convergence as females and males got more involved, especially when they were engaged. Kinsey says, "The double standard is being resolved by the development of a single standard in which pre-marital coital activities have become extended among females to levels which are more nearly comparable to those in the male" (*Sexual Behavior in the Human Female,* p. 324).

112. Miller and Nowak, *The Fifties,* p. 159; Joe Dubbart, *A Man's Place: Masculinity in Transition* (Englewood Cliffs, N.J.: Prentice-Hall, 1979), p. 261. Robert Bell referred to the conflicts between young women and men as psychological warfare (*Premarital Sex in a Changing Society,* pp. 82, 78).

113. Mead, *Male and Female,* p. 280.

114. Russell Banks, *Success Stories* (New York: Harper and Row, 1986), p. 64.

115. Anania, *The Red Menace,* p. 136.

116. Banks, *Success Stories,* p. 93.

117. More explicit and crude talk about sex and body parts by males indicated a less romanticized and vague relationship to sex. For a discussion of gender in youth culture, see Brake, *Comparative Youth Culture,* pp. 178–83; Frith, *Sound Effects,* pp. 225–39; Root, *Pictures of Women,* pp. 24–35. Also see Sharon Thompson, "Search for Tomorrow: On Feminism and the Reconstruction of Teen Romance," and Julian Wood, "Groping toward Sexism: Boys' Sex Talk," in McRobbie and Nova's *Gender and Generation.* Both articles address boys' fears of sex in the contemporary period.

118. Plath, *The Bell Jar,* pp. 57, 66.

119. Elizabeth Ewen, private communication, February 2, 1986.

120. Bailey, *From Front Porch to Back Seat,* pp. 58, 55, 5.

121. Wolfenstein and Leites, *Movies,* p. 31.

122. Alther, *Kinflicks*, p. 46. See also Bailey, *From Front Porch to Back Seat*, pp. 50–51.

123. Siddons, *Heartbreak Hotel*, p. 87.

124. Wakefield, *Going All the Way*, pp. 143–44.

125. See Coward, *Female Desires*, for an extended discussion of this.

126. In *Premarital Sex in a Changing Society*, Robert Bell states that it is rare to find a society like America in which premarital sexual activity was prohibited and at the same time wide opportunity permitted for the privacy of youth (p. 60).

127. I want to thank Kay Trimberger for pointing out the popularity of the song "The Great Pretender."

128. Douvan and Adelson, *The Adolescent Experience*, p. 11. See also stories of pretense and dissimulation in the interviews in the Robert White study, *Lives in Progress*, White-Riggs Group, at the Murray Center for the Study of Lives, Radcliffe College. In another typical group of interviews, an interview subject stated she always thought of herself as an actress, disguising her feelings even from herself. Another remarked that she always did what she was supposed to do even while she experimented privately (D. M. Avery, "Critical Events in the Lives of College-Educated Minority and White Women," interviews 6 and 10, Murray Center). See also letters to Betty Friedan from this cohort in which natural inclinations of curiosity about life were hidden from others. Their mothers' conventional sexual values (as understood by the daughters) and the guilt instilled in the daughters as a result is a common theme in the daughters' understanding of differences between the two generations. See Modell, *Into One's Own*, p. 223, where he reports on a survey of high school girls, 26 percent of whom thought it was never right to pet or neck but 59 percent of whom thought their mothers believed this. Finally, see Marge Piercy's novel *Braided Lives*, where the heroine sees her college dormitory "as a minefield of sexual hypocrisy, all the women lying to each other about what they are doing or not doing with boys they also lie to, because the boys lie to and about them" (New York: Fawcett Crest, 1982), p. 123.

129. Eisler, *Private Lives*, p. 79.

130. Philip Roth, *Goodbye, Columbus* (New York: Bantam Books, 1959). Henry, *Culture against Man*, p. 274.

131. Leslie Johnson discusses girls in Australia in the 1950s. She argues that controlling their own images created in girls a sense of control over their own growing up, providing them with "a new social presence, a means of access to and legitimacy in public cultural life." Opportunities as consumers in postwar society gave them a stage and time in which to experiment that translated into activity on their own behalf ("The Modern Girl" [manuscript], p. 10).

CHAPTER 4   The Other Fifties

1. Paul Goodman, *Growing Up Absurd: The Problems of Youth in the Organized Society* (New York: Vintage Books, 1960), pp. 11, 13.

2. Caryl Rivers, *Virgins* (New York: Pocket Books, 1984), p. 65.

3. The formal interviews for this chapter were with Nancy Dannenberg, Cambridge, Massachusetts, March 3, 1990; and in New York City: Rosalyn Baxandall, December 26, 1988, October 7, 1989, May 6, 1989; Hettie Jones, May 5, 1989; Ann Lauterbach, May 6, 1989; Evan Morley, October 9, 1989; Carolee Schneeman, October 6, 1989; Alix Kates Shulman, December 26, 1988; Ellen Willis, May 4, 1989. As in chapters 2 and 3, informal interviews contributed to my interpretation.

4. See Sara Evans, *Personal Politics: The Roots of Women's Liberation in the Civil Rights Movement and the New Left* (New York: Alfred A. Knopf, 1979), pp. 60–61, and Doug McAdam, *Freedom Summer* (New York: Oxford University Press, 1988), pp. 20–21.

5. See, however, David Matza and Gresham Sykes, "Juvenile Delinquency and Subterranean Values," *American Sociological Review* 26 (1961): 712–19. Matza and Sykes argue that the values of juvenile delinquents were not different from the larger society's values, for example, leisure, aggression, conspicuous consumption. They suggest that juvenile delinquents acted out these values differently but that they were an extension of the adult world, not a rejection of it. Also see a critical review of *Growing Up Absurd* and other books on adolescence by Bennett Berger, "Adolescence and Beyond," *Social Problems* 10 (1963): 394–408; and F. Elkin and W. Westley, "The Myth of Adolescent Culture," *American Sociological Review* 20 (1955): 680–84, for similar points.

6. This was explicitly so in the study of juvenile delinquency. In a major study from the 1950s, for example, Albert K. Cohen says, "The subcultural delinquency we have been talking about is overwhelmingly male delinquency. In the first place, delinquency *in general* is mostly male delinquency" (*Delinquent Boys* [New York: Free Press, 1955], p. 44). See Mike Brake, *The Sociology of Youth Culture and Youth Subcultures* (London: Routledge and Kegan Paul, 1980), for a discussion of the masculine basis of the study of youth culture, especially chapter 7. Also see Berger, "Adolescence and Beyond."

7. A study of the popularity and reception of cowboy movies among this generation would yield interesting insights. There is evidence that girls watched and liked cowboy movies and identified with the cowboys (the good guys). In other words, they identified with men and with the racist project of wiping out the Indians. Alice Walker tells of being a tomboy and of playing cowboys, "rustling cattle, being outlaws, delivering damsels in distress" but of becoming an Indian when her brothers get BB guns. She, being a girl, doesn't get a gun. She

then becomes the hunted (and her eye is shot by one of her brothers). See *In Search of Our Mothers' Gardens* (New York: Harcourt Brace Jovanovich, 1984), p. 386. Stokely Carmichael recalls that he loved Westerns and cheered wildly for the cowboys until one day he realized *he* was an Indian and had been rooting for the wrong side. See Marion Meade, "The Degradation of Women," in *The Sounds of Social Change*, ed. Serge Denisoff and Richard Peterson (Chicago: Rand McNally, 1972), p. 174. Also see Carmichael on rooting for Tarzan as he attacked black natives until Carmichael realized that by yelling, " 'Kill the beasts, kill the savages, kill 'em.' I was saying: Kill *me*" (quoted in "What We Want," *The Sixties Papers*, ed. Judith Albert and Stewart Albert [New York: Praeger Publishers, 1984], p. 142). Anita Valerio, a Native American, writes, "Being an Indian . . . I didn't realize that's what I was—an Indian—in fact I jumped up and down in protest "I'm not an Indian—I'm not an Indian!" when my relatives would tell me I was. After all, Indians were the bad guys on T.V. and though we didn't have running water that year or even telephones—yes—we did have television" ("It's In My Blood, My Face—My Mother's Voice, The Way I Sweat," in *This Bridge Called My Back*, ed. Cherrie Moraga and Gloria Anzaldua [New York: Kitchen Table Press, 1981], p. 42). The social movements of the next decade, especially the civil rights movement, suggest that young people in the 1950s did not digest in intended ways the stories of the forces of good (cowboys) triumphing over the forces of evil (Indians) in Western movies, stories that duplicated similar struggles between whites and peoples of color in the United States and internationally.

8. Douglas Miller and Marion Nowak, *The Fifties: The Way We Really Were* (Garden City, N.Y.: Doubleday, 1975), p. 277.

9. William Heyen, *Vic Holyfield and the Class of '57* (New York: Ballantine Books, 1986), p. 20. See also Annie Dillard, *An American Childhood* (New York: Harper and Row, 1987); Caryl Rivers, *Aphrodite at Mid-Century: Growing Up Catholic and Female in Post-War America* (Garden City, N.Y.: Doubleday, 1973), and *Virgins* (New York: Pocket Books, 1984); Susan Toth, *Blooming: A Small Town Girlhood* (Boston: Little, Brown, 1978).

10. Michael Anania, *The Red Menace* (New York: Thunder's Mouth Press, 1984), p. 29.

11. Jessie Bernard, "Teen-Age Culture: An Overview," *Annals* 338 (1961): 10. Data from the first public opinion report on a fifteen-year youth survey called Purdue Opinion Poll, which polled 10,000–18,000 teenagers (Remmers and Radler, *The American Teenager* [1957], pp. 80–85). For other references to Radler and Remmer polls, see William Graebner, "Coming of Age in Buffalo: The Ideology of Maturity in Postwar America," *Radical History Review* 34 (1986): 59, and Charles H. Brown, "Self-Portrait: The Teen-Type Magazine," *Annals* 338 (1961): 18.

12. See Kenneth Keniston, *The Uncommitted: Alienated Youth in American Society* (New York: Dell Publishing, 1960), for a discussion of widespread alienation among white, upper-middle-class males. Also Richard Flacks, *Youth and So-*

cial Change (Chicago: Markham Publishing, 1971), quotations from pp. 56, 33.

13. Ibid., pp. 51, 52.

14. Referring to teenagers' confusion about what was permissible sexually, John Modell compares their uncertainty to that of their parents. See *Into One's Own* (Berkeley: University of California Press, 1989), p. 236.

15. Liz Heron, ed., Introduction to *Truth, Dare, or Promise: Girls Growing Up in the Fifties* (London: Virago, 1985), p. 6.

16. Elinor Langer, "Notes for Next Time," *Working Papers,* Fall 1973, p. 51.

17. Anne Snitow, "Pages from a Gender Diary: Basic Divisions in Feminism," *Dissent* 36 (1989): 219.

18. Rivers, *Virgins,* p. 23.

19. David Wallechinsky, "The Beatnik," *Class Reunion '65* (New York: Penguin Books, 1986), p. 398.

20. David Dalton, *Piece of My Heart: The Life, Times, and Legend of Janis Joplin* (New York: St. Martin's Press, 1985), p. 147.

21. Nora Sayre, *Running Time: Films of the Cold War* (New York: Dial Press, 1982), p. 102.

22. See Elizabeth Long, *The American Dream and the Popular Novel* (Boston: Routledge and Kegan Paul, 1985), and Miller and Nowak, *The Fifties,* ch. 14.

23. Hetty Jones, *How I Became Hetty Jones* (New York: E. P. Dutton, 1990), p. 26.

24. Joyce Johnson, *Minor Characters* (Boston: Houghton, Mifflin, 1983), p. 41.

25. Jan Clausen, *Sinking Stealing* (Trumansburg, N.Y.: Crossing Press, 1985), p. 146.

26. For Bonnie Raitt, *Boston Globe,* February 23, 1990, p. 53; Johnson, *Minor Characters,* p. 137. Marge Piercy wonders where she found the strength to "cling to [her] own flimsy reality" against official reality ("Through the Cracks: Growing Up in the Fifties," in *Parti-Colored Blocks for a Quilt* [Ann Arbor: University of Michigan Press, 1982], p. 119). See Tom Hayden's autobiography and memoir, *Reunion* (New York: Random House, 1988), about the 1960s for a new leftist who found inspiration in the Beats and other marginal characters: "There were several alternative cultural models beckoning to those of us who in a few years were to become activists: the fictional character Holden Caulfield, the actor James Dean, and the writer Jack Kerouac. The life crises they personified spawned not only political activism, but also the cultural revolution of rock and roll. Elvis Presley, it is said, watched James Dean in 'Rebel Without a Cause' a dozen times. These characters, in their different ways, were responding to the human absurdity and emptiness of the secure material life parents of the fifties had built" (p. 17). He says of Kerouac's inspiration in 1957, the year he graduated from high school and *On the Road* was published, "In the coming

three years, I too hitchhiked to every corner of America, sleeping in fields here, doorways there, cheap hotels everywhere, embracing a spirit of the open road without knowing where I wanted to go" (p. 18). The maleness of the models and options is hard to miss, and will be discussed below.

27. See Johnson, *Minor Characters*, pp. 29, 30; and Kathy Mulherin, "Memories of a Latter-Day Catholic Girlhood," in *The Movement toward a New America*, ed. Mitchell Goodman (Philadelphia: Pilgrim Press; New York: Alfred A. Knopf, 1970), p. 637 (reprinted from *Commonweal*, March 6, 1970).

28. Ellen Maslow, "Storybook Lives: Growing Up Middle Class," in *Liberation Now! Writings from the Women's Liberation Movement* (New York: Dell Publishing, 1971), p. 174. Describing Kate Millett, one of the older 1950s rebels, a former student, says, "Kate, like Joyce Glassman [Johnson], fell in love with the beat rebellion against orderliness, straightness, and ties based on friendship instead of blood" (Laurie Stone, "Memoirs Are Made of This," *Voice Literary Supplement* 16 [April 1983], p. 10).

29. Diane Di Prima, *Memoirs of a Beatnik* (1969; San Francisco: Last Gasp of San Francisco, 1988), p. 51. See also Alix Kates Shulman, *Burning Questions* (New York: Alfred A. Knopf, 1978).

30. Dalton, *Piece of My Heart*, p. 162.

31. Jack Kerouac, *On the Road* (New York: Signet Books, New American Library, 1957), p. 9.

32. Dillard, *An American Childhood*, p. 183.

33. Sheila Rowbotham, *Women's Consciousness, Man's World*, pp. 16, 14; *Truth, Dare, or Promise*, p. 208.

34. Jones, *How I Became Hetty Jones*, p. 71. See Di Prima, *Memoirs of a Beatnik*, and Johnson, *Minor Characters*, for similar points. Also see Wini Breines, *Community and Organization in the New Left: The Great Refusal* (New Brunswick: Rutgers University Press, 1989), for the importance of talk in the new left.

35. Shulman, *Burning Questions*, p. 64.

36. Di Prima, *Memoirs of a Beatnik*, p. 65; Johnson, *Minor Characters*, p. 208.

37. Ronald Sukenick, *Down and In: Life in the Underground* (New York: MacMillan, 1987), pp. 34, 27.

38. Di Prima, *Memoirs of a Beatnik*, p. 126.

39. Jones, *How I Became Hetty Jones*, p. 34.

40. Shulman, *Burning Questions*, p. 39.

41. See Andrew Ross, "Containing Culture in the Cold War," in *No Respect: Intellectuals and Popular Culture* (New York: Routledge, 1989), pp. 42–64, for a discussion of postwar and cold war intellectuals and their relationship to popular culture.

42. Al Young, *Things Ain't What They Used to Be* (Berkeley: Creative Arts Books, 1987), pp. 190, 194.

43. Di Prima, *Memoirs of a Beatnik*, p. 94.

44. Johnson, *Minor Characters*, p. 162. See also *How I Became Hetty Jones* for a description of Greenwich Village in the 1950s.

45. Young, *Things Ain't What They Used to Be*, p. 192.

46. Jones, *How I Became Hetty Jones*, p. 46.

47. For the Norman Podhoretz remark, see Todd Gitlin, *The Sixties: Years of Hope, Days of Rage* (New York: Bantam Books, 1987), p. 49. Also see Miller and Nowak, *The Fifties*, pp. 384–86, and Paul S. George and Jerold M. Starr, "Beat Politics: New Left and Hippie Beginnings in the Postwar Counterculture," in *Cultural Politics: Radical Movements in History*, ed. Jerold M. Starr (New York: Praeger Publishers, 1985), pp. 205–6. For material about postwar artistic ferment, see Young, *Things Ain't What They Used to Be*, pp. 189–233; Lewis A. Ehrenberg, "Things to Come: Swing Bands, Bebop, and the Rise of a Postwar Jazz Scene," in *Recasting America: Culture and Politics in the Age of the Cold War*, ed. Lary May (Chicago: University of Chicago Press, 1989); Charles Mingus, *Beneath the Underdog* (New York: Penguin Books, 1971); Serge Guilbaut, *How New York Stole the Idea of Modern Art: Abstract Expressionism, Freedom, and the Cold War* (Chicago: University of Chicago Press, 1983); Sukenick, *Down and In*.

48. Johnson, *Minor Characters*, pp. 261–62.

49. See Marjorie Rosen, *Popcorn Venus: Women, Movies, and the American Dream* (New York: Coward, McCann and Geoghegan, 1979), pp. 286–89. In *Sound Effects: Youth, Leisure, and the Politics of Rock and Roll* (New York: Pantheon Books, 1981), pp. 238–39, Simon Frith argues that music and dancing both expressed and released the sexual tensions implicit in girls' preparation for their domestic role. He suggests that the most important function of 1950s teenage culture was to articulate sexuality, "in a setting of love and marriage" where it reinforced peer-group sex conventions that emphasized marriage.

50. In a review of Joyce Johnson's *Minor Characters*, Laurie Stone says that the feminist Kate Millett, her teacher, was inspired by the Beats but understood they would never really see or hear her, that she would never be real to them ("Memoirs Are Made of This," pp. 8–11).

51. Jones, *How I Became Hetty Jones*, p. 81.

52. For the point about new left women, see Wini Breines, "A Review Essay: Sara Evans's *Personal Politics*," *Feminist Studies* 5 (1979): 496–506.

53. Miller and Nowak, *The Fifties*, p. 386.

54. Johnson, *Minor Characters*, p. 79.

55. Norman Mailer, "The White Negro," in *Advertisements for Myself* (London: Transworld Publishers, 1959), p. 242. Nelson George, *The Death of Rhythm and Blues* (New York: Pantheon Books, 1988), pp. 61–62. Also see Michael S. Harper's remarks in Young's *Things Ain't What They Used to Be*, especially p. 208 about Kerouac's racism, and Andrew Ross's discussion of the white hipster in "Hip, and the Long Front of Color," in *No Respect: Intellectuals and Popular Culture*, pp. 79ff.

56. Barbara Ehrenreich, *The Hearts of Men: American Dreams and the Flight from Commitment* (Garden City, N.Y.: Doubleday, 1983), p. 58.

57. Jon Savage, "The Enemy Within: Sex, Rock, and Identity," in *Facing the Music,* ed. Simon Frith (New York: Pantheon Books, 1989), pp. 143-44. It is undoubtedly true that for some white, middle-class girls a rejection of middle-class masculinity was also a rejection of heterosexuality. The role of lesbianism in some girls' rebelliousness is research waiting to be pursued.

58. Dillard, *An American Childhood,* p. 93.

59. Rowbotham, *Women's Consciousness, Man's World,* pp. 15-16; McDermott, *That Night.*

60. Ehrenreich, *The Hearts of Men,* p. 58. See Roland Marchand, "Visions of Classlessness, Quests for Dominion: American Popular Culture, 1945-1960," in *Reshaping America: Society and Institutions, 1945-1960,* ed. R. Bremmer and G. Richard (Columbus: Ohio University Press, 1982), pp. 163-82. Marchand says, "A mystique emerged that fused the elements of Marlon Brando's role in *The Wild One,* James Dean's portrayal in *Rebel Without a Cause,* J. D. Salinger's Holden Caulfield in *Catcher in the Rye,* and the rebels of *Blackboard Jungle,* and the driving energy and aggressive sexuality of the new heroes of rock 'n' roll into a single image. The mystique emphasized a hunger for authenticity and sensitivity . . . with nuances of sexuality, pain, and violence. Raucous, exhibitionist rock 'n' roll singers disdained the 'cool' of James Dean, but both expressed a contempt for hypocrisy and conventionality, and used body language to convey emotion" (p. 179).

61. Johnson, *Minor Characters,* p. 171.

62. John Tytell, Foreword to *Kerouac and the Beats,* ed. Arthur Knight and Kit Knight (New York: Paragon House, 1988), p. ix.

63. Catherine Stimpson, "The Beat Generation and the Trials of Homosexual Liberation," *Salmagundi* 58-59 (1982-83): 375. Stimpson argues that a sexist model of heterosexuality infected the Beats homosexual relations. Thus they mistreated the male identified as a fag, the submissive, passive, and degraded feminine partner, and in this way lessened the distinction between heterosexuality and homosexuality.

64. "The Beat Queens," *Voice Literary Supplement,* June 1989, pp. 18-23. Also interview and personal correspondence with Shulman, March 9, 1989. See Michael Davidson, *The San Francisco Renaissance: Poetics and Community at Mid-Century* (New York: Cambridge University Press, 1989), ch. 6. Also see less critical treatments of Beat and bohemian men in Johnson's *Minor Characters* and in *How I Became Hetty Jones.*

65. Frederika Randall, "Fifties Forever," *Working Papers,* May-June 1983, p. 50.

66. Rowbotham, *Woman's Consciousness, Man's World,* p. 16.

67. See "The Beatnik," in David Wallechinsky's *Class Reunion '65* (New York: Penguin Books, 1986), p. 397. She continues that she didn't participate in high school activities and never went to the cafeteria, "I used to spend that time each day writing poems on toilet paper in the stalls for privacy and inspiration, or else go to the library and read."

68. Shulman, *Burning Questions,* pp. 29, 15.

69. Dan Wakefield, *Going All the Way* (1970; New York: E. P. Dutton, 1989), pp. 219–20, 209.

70. Wallechinsky, "The Beatnik," p. 396.

71. Philip Roth, *Goodbye, Columbus* (New York: Bantam Books, 1959), p. 5. See Langer, "Notes for the Next Time," for a discussion of suburban Jews' painful efforts to assimilate in the postwar period.

72. Jones, *How I Became Hetty Jones*, p. 35.

73. In 1956, more money was spent on records than at any other time in history, with the most important share going to rock and roll (Thomas Doherty, *Teenagers and Teenpics* [Boston: Unwin Hyman, 1988], p. 57); Jessie Bernard states that teenagers spent $75,000,000 annually on popular records ("Teen-Age Culture," p. 4).

74. See Nelson George, *The Death of Rhythm and Blues* (New York: Pantheon Books, 1988); Charlie Gillett, *The Sound of the City* (New York: Pantheon Books, 1983); Steve Chapple and Reebee Garofalo, *Rock and Roll Is Here to Pay* (Chicago: Nelson Hall, 1977); George Lipsitz, "Cruising around the Historical Block: Postmodernism and Popular Music in East Los Angeles," in *Time Passages: Collective Memory and American Popular Culture* (Minneapolis: University of Minnesota Press, 1990), pp. 133–60; Alice Walker, "Nineteen Fifty-five," in *You Can't Keep a Good Woman Down* (New York: Harcourt Brace Jovanovich, 1981), pp. 3–20; Iain Chambers, "A Strategy for Living: Black Music and White Subcultures," in *Resistance through Rituals*, ed. Stuart Hall and Tony Jefferson (London: Hutchinson, 1976), pp. 157–66; Ross, "Hip and the Long Front of Color," pp. 65–101.

75. Eldridge Cleaver, *Soul on Ice* (New York: Dell Publishing, 1968), p. 38. Cleaver was writing in the sixties, but the trend he described began in the fifties. See Ross, "Hip and the Long Front of Color," where he discusses Cleaver and says that he was attempting, "however steeped in racial mythologies, to describe a symptomatic shift in official taste. His imagery, with its guided missiles and cold white asses, is clearly drawn from the Cold War verbal stockpile, enlisted here to describe a 'melting' of the national mood." Ross suggests that Cleaver's recognition of the "injection of Negritude" into mainstream culture through music was also a recognition of the uneven movement toward racial integration in this period (pp. 100–101).

76. See George Lipsitz, "Land of a Thousand Dances: Youth, Minorities, and the Rise of Rock and Roll," in May's *Recasting America,* and "Against the Wind: Dialogic Aspects of Rock and Roll" in *Time Passages*. See also Stuart Cosgrove, "The Zoot Suit and Style Warfare," in *Zoot Suits and Second-Hand Dresses*, ed. Angela McRobbie (Boston: Unwin Hyman, 1988), pp. 3–22, and Peter Guralnik, *Sweet Soul Music: Rhythm and Blues and the Southern Dream of Freedom* (New York: Harper and Row, 1986). Also see Charlie Gillett's *Sound of the City*. Thanks to Jeanne Laurel for her thoughts.

77. Gerald Early, "One Nation under a Groove," *New Republic,* July 15–22, 1991, p. 38.

78. George, *The Death of Rhythm and Blues*, p. 67.

79. Gillett, *Sound of the City*, p. viii; Graebner, *Coming of Age in Buffalo* (Philadelphia: Temple University Press, 1990), p. 41.

80. Lipsitz, "Land of a Thousand Dances," p. 280.

81. Dalton, *A Piece of My Heart*, p. 38. Joplin says she listened to a lot of jazz and one day found a record by Odetta and "really dug it." She listened to Billie Holiday too (p. 152). She tells the story of another white Southern female singer's formative experience as a little girl when she heard black gospel and was mesmerized (p. 231). The dramatic discovery and worship of gospel, rhythm and blues, blues, or jazz, was shared by many white teenagers, Southern and Northern. Bonnie Raitt, quoted in the *Boston Globe*, February 23, 1990, p. 53.

82. Rock and roll teen movies proliferated in the 1950s, featuring, except for the black performers, only white teenagers. It was as if no black teen audience existed. See Mary Wilson, *Dreamgirl: My Life as a Supreme* (New York: St. Martin's Press, 1986), for the importance of the music for northern urban black teens, not only as audience but as performers as well. Also see Charlotte Grieg, *Will You Still Love Me Tomorrow? Girl Groups from the Fifties On* (London: Virago Press, 1989). See Thomas Doherty's chapter "Rock 'n' Roll Teenpics" in *Teenagers and Teenpics*.

83. Eisler, *Private Lives*, pp. 69-72; Gerri Hirshey, *Nowhere to Run: The Story of Soul Music* (New York: Penguin Books, 1984), p. xii; Elinor Lerner, "Response to Robin Roberts," *NWSA Journal* 2 (1990): 331.

84. Gillett, *Sound of the City*, p. 19. James Brown's father quoted by Hershey, *Nowhere to Run*, p. xvi. Also see Simon Frith, *Sound Effects: Youth, Leisure, and the Politics of Rock and Roll* (New York: Pantheon Books, 1981), on the appeal of rock and roll for white youth (pp. 18-23, 263-64); Savage, "The Enemy Within"; Lipsitz, "Land of a Thousand Dances," and "Against the Wind." The film *Hairspray* amusingly portrays the racial and gendered aspects of white teenagers' attraction to and involvement with the extremely popular television show "American Bandstand." In documentaries or film footage from the period, the sense of teen culture is powerful indeed; it is impossible not to suspect a radical break by young people from the parent culture.

85. Wilson, *Dreamgirl*, p. 24.

86. For a more skeptical interpretation of the meaning of rock and roll and how it was managed in order to promote social control, including racial segregation, see William Graebner's *Coming of Age in Buffalo* and see Nelson George's *The Death of Rhythm and Blues* for a skeptical interpretation of rock and roll, from a black perspective. Also Richard Aquila, *That Old Time Rock and Roll: A Chronicle of an Era, 1954-1963* (New York: MacMillan, 1989), for the argument that rock and roll supported the status quo.

87. Jane Lazarre, *On Loving Men* (New York: Dial Press, 1980), p. 112.

88. Rowbotham, *Woman's Consciousness, Man's World*, p. 14; Elinor Lerner, "Response to Roberts," p. 332.

89. Anania, *The Red Menace*, p. 113.

90. Barbara Ehrenreich, Elizabeth Hess, and Gloria Jacobs, *Remaking Love:*

The Feminization of Love (Garden City, N.Y.: Doubleday, 1986), pp. 27, 32, 33; also see "Girls and Subcultures: An Exploration" by Angela McRobbie and Jenny Garber, in *Resistance through Rituals*, and Savage, "The Enemy Within," for discussions of girls and popular music. See too Angela McRobbie, "Settling Accounts with Subcultures: A Feminist Critique," in *On Record: Rock, Pop, and the Written Word*, ed. Simon Frith and Andrew Goodwin (New York: Pantheon Books, 1990), pp. 66–80.

91. George, *The Death of Rhythm and Blues*, pp. 62–63; Ross, "Hip and the Long Front of Color," p. 68, see also Savage, "The Enemy Within," p. 141.

92. See Linda Ray Pratt, "Elvis, or the Ironies of Southern Identity," in *Elvis: Images and Fancies*, ed. Jack L. Thorpe (Jackson: University Press of Mississippi, 1979); and Thomas Doherty, *Teenagers and Teenpics*, p. 89. Also see "Sexing Elvis" by Sue Wise, in *Women's Studies International Forum* 7 (1984): 13–17, where she points out that the only people who write about Elvis are men and they always interpret him sexually. She contends that their sexual interpretation flatters themselves, since they identify with Elvis. Male critics and male fans see in Elvis the expression of their sexual fantasies; in contrast, her infatuation was not sexual. See Ehrenreich et al., *Remaking Love*, for the remarks on the Beatles (pp. 34–35); also see Sheryl Garratt, "Teenage Dreams," in Frith and Goodwin's *On Record*, pp. 399–409, where she argues that androgyny in male stars is attractive to female fans.

93. Carolyn Heilbrun, *Reinventing Womanhood* (New York: W. W. Norton, 1979), p. 30; Jones, *How I Became Hetty Jones*, p. 13. See Bennett Berger, *Survival of a Counterculture* (Berkeley: University of California Press, 1981), pp. 198–200, where he discusses "why some people get free of the threats and promises, rewards and punishments that an established order uses to keep members from misbehaving" in order to reproduce the dominant order.

94. Caryl Rivers, *Aphrodite at Mid-Century* (Garden City, N.Y.: Doubleday, 1973), pp. 224–25.

95. Rowbotham, *Women's Consciousness, Man's World*, pp. 14–15.

96. Ellen Willis, "A Feminist Journal," *Conversations with the New Reality* (San Francisco: Canfield Press, 1971), p. 157.

97. Shulman, *Burning Questions*, pp. 13–14; Jones, *How I Became Hetty Jones*, p. 10.

98. Piercy, "Through the Cracks," p. 124.

99. Shulman, *Burning Questions*, pp. 36–37; Sylvia Fraser, *My Father's House: A Memoir of Incest and Healing* (New York: Harper and Row, 1987), p. 188. A theme of Kim Chernin's autobiography, *In My Mother's House* (New York: Harper and Row, 1983), is of high school years filled with duality and appearances.

100. Vivian Gornick, *Fierce Attachments* (New York: Simon and Schuster, 1987), p. 113.

101. Ursula Huws, "Hiraeth," in *Truth, Dare, or Promise*, p. 181. She says, "At the age of three, when asked what I wanted to be when I grew up I would

reply 'a witch,' presumably the only literary model I could find which seemed remotely likely to fit me" (p. 182). All the contributors to *Truth, Dare, or Promise* were girls who were identified as particularly bright and became feminists.

102. Shulman, *Burning Questions*, pp. 63, 95. The heroine of the bestselling 1950s novel *Marjorie Morningstar* expresses her restlessness by deciding to become an actress.

103. See Angela McRobbie, Introduction to *Feminism for Girls* (London: Routledge and Kegan Paul, 1981), pp. 19–20.

104. "To the more or less liberal youth of my generation, with no family tradition of activism to draw on, red-diaper babies were frequently our first contacts with the forbidden world of wholesale political criticism. They had grown up breathing a left-wing air; their sense of being different touched by nobility and consecrated by persecution, was magnetic; they had a perch from which to criticize" (in Gitlin, *The Sixties*, p. 67).

105. See Steven Mintz and Susan Kellogg, *Domestic Revolutions: A Social History of American Family Life* (New York: Free Press, 1988), p. 184; Gwendolyn Wright, *Building the Dream: A Social History of Housing in America* (New York: Pantheon Books, 1981), p. 256: "Only 9% of suburban women worked in 1950, compared to 27% for the population as a whole." The fertility rate in the suburbs was higher than in the cities.

106. I want to thank Ros Baxandall for suggesting this point to me.

CHAPTER 5 **Alone in the Fifties**

1. I want to thank Mrs. Helen Parsons for giving Anne Parsons's papers and their rights to Margaret Cerullo and myself and for her cooperation in this effort. This chapter is a condensed version of an essay that includes a more detailed analysis of her life and work: "Alone in the 1950s: Anne Parsons and the Feminine Mystique," *Theory and Society* 15 (1986): 805–43.

2. The main sources for her biography are her own writings. They are (1) her autobiography written in 1959 for entrance to the Boston Psychoanalytic Institute; (2) an eight-page single-spaced letter written in 1963 to Betty Friedan, whom she did not know and who did not reply; (3) her Progress Report to the Foundations' Fund for Research in Psychiatry, written in November 1963, two months after her admission as a patient to the Yale Psychiatric Institute; (4) letters and notes. Unless otherwise noted, the 1959 autobiography is the source. Charles Parsons, Anne's brother, kindly provided biographical corrections to the original essay version of this chapter.

3. Rose L. Coser and Renee C. Fox, "Anne Parsons," *Dissent* 11 (1964): 355.

4. After the war, the average marriage age for American women dropped to twenty years. By 1951 one woman in three was married at nineteen. In 1958 more women were married between the ages of fifteen and nineteen than any other comparable age span. The birth rate surged in the postwar period, reaching its peak in 1957. In that year the median age of mothers having their last

child was twenty-six years. More women were having more children at a younger age. The birth rate was not much lower for college-educated women than for the general female population. Thus Parsons's remark about children and suburbs, where much of the fertility took place, was not incorrect. See Nancy Woloch, *Women and the American Experience* (New York: Alfred A. Knopf, 1984), p. 496, and Carl Degler, "Revolution without Ideology: The Changing Place of Women in America," in *The Woman in America*, ed. R. J. Lifton (Boston: Beacon Press, 1964). Also see chapter 3 above for more discussion of the family in the 1950s.

5. Letter to Kenneth Burke, April 15, 1964. See a similar sentiment in John Osborne's play *Look Back in Anger* (New York: Penguin Books, 1957), in which Jimmy, a tormented Englishman of Parsons's generation, says, "I suppose people of our generation aren't able to die for good causes any longer. We had all that done for us, in the thirties and forties, when we were still kids . . . There aren't any good, brave causes left. If the big bang does come, and we all get killed off, it won't be in the aid of the old-fashioned grand design. It'll just be for the Brave, New nothing-very-much-thank-you. About as pointless and inglorious as stepping in front of a bus" (pp. 84–85). Note the reference to dying in an atom bomb blast, discussed in the Introduction as a potent source of anxiety in the postwar period.

6. Gurin, Veroff, and Feld observe in their survey of mental health in the 1950s, as they remark in the epigraph to this chapter, that single people were considered deviant in the 1950s. See G. Gurin, J. Veroff, and S. Feld *Americans View Their Mental Health* (New York: Basic Books, 1960), p. 231. See chapter 3 above for more on this mental health survey. Also see Barbara Ehrenreich, *The Hearts of Men* (Garden City, N.Y.: Doubleday), p. 17ff. where she talks of the significance of the highly touted concept of "maturity" in the 1950s. Among other indicators, marriage was proof of one's maturity.

7. In an interesting essay on Willa Cather, the role of Southern France is described: "France to Cather was the symbolic location of the Other, the sign for everything repressed or feared in commercial, puritanical northern climes: it was the decadent, liberated realm of the senses" (Sharon O'Brien, "The Thing Not Named: Willa Cather as a Lesbian Writer," *Signs* 9 [1984]: 588–99). Also see the story of Margaret Fuller, a New Englander like Parsons, and her relationship to Italy, *The Woman and the Myth: Margaret Fuller's Life and Writings*, by Bell Gale Chevigny (Old Westbury, N.Y.: Feminist Press, 1976).

8. Alfred Stanton figures prominently in her story since he was influential, in some ways her mentor, helped her to get the fellowship, and believed in integrating social scientific perspectives into psychiatry.

9. Rose Coser suggests that Parsons was never at home anywhere, always an outsider, and consistently in conflict about where she was and what she was doing. Personal correspondence with author, September 24, 1985.

10. In 1946 her father had entered the Boston Psychoanalytic Institute for psychoanalytic training as a nonmedical candidate.

11. It is tempting to categorize the Boston Psychoanalytic Institute as a male-dominated institution, which I did in an early draft, in an effort to analyze Parsons's situation. A number of readers pointed to the existence of strong female psychoanalytic leaders there, which complicates the issue but does not disprove the institute's inhospitability to women. Research on the social and political environment at the BPI would shed light on this.

12. Letter to her parents, November 15, 1959.

13. Letter to Dr. Jerome Frank, July 1, 1963.

14. A reviewer of the original essay on which this chapter is based suggested that it would have been obvious to anyone not suffering acute psychotic deterioration that by terminating her analysis she was in effect terminating her training and candidacy.

15. According to Parsons, unmarried people and homosexuals were usually rejected by the institute as inappropriate candidates.

16. Letter to her parents, April 15, 1964.

17. Letter from David Schneider to Talcott Parsons, September 18, 1963.

18. Letter to Stanley Diamond, April 16, 1964.

19. Letter to Talcott Parsons, November 24, 1963.

20. For example, see letters to Talcott Parsons, November 24, 1963, and December 8, 1963.

21. See letter to Talcott Parsons, November 24, 1963.

22. Letter to Rose Coser, November 6, 1963.

23. Letter to Talcott Parsons, November 24 1963.

24. Letter to Talcott Parsons, December 8, 1963.

25. Letter to her parents, January 1, 1964.

26. Letter to Charles Parsons, January 15, 1964.

27. Memorandum to Yale Psychiatric Institute, January 1964.

28. Letter to her parents, January 1, 1964.

29. Memorandum to Yale Psychiatric Institute, January 1964.

30. Letter to her parents, November 19, 1963.

31. Letter to Rose Coser, October 25, 1963.

32. Letter to her parents, November 19, 1963.

33. *Radcliffe Alumni Report, Class of 1952* (1977), pp. 7–8. See also Rona Jaffe, "A Real-life Class Reunion," *Ladies Home Journal,* June 1980, on the class of 1951 for similar points, quoted in Eugenia Kaledin, *Mothers and More: American Women in the 1950s* (Boston: Twayne Publishers, 1984), p. 43.

Conclusion

1. See Sara Evans, *Personal Politics: The Roots of Women's Liberation in the Civil Rights Movement and the New Left* (New York: Alfred A. Knopf, 1979).

2. Joan Morrison and Robert K. Morrison, *From Camelot to Kent State* (New York: Times Books, 1987), p. 176.

3. Sheila Rowbotham, "Revolt in Roundhay," in *Truth, Dare, or Promise,* ed. Liz Heron (London: Virago Press, 1985), p. 207.

4. See Ellen Kay Trimberger, "Women in the Old and New Left: The Evolution of a Politics of Personal Life," *Feminist Studies* 5 (1979): 432–50.

5. For one version of this point, see Susan Bordo, "Feminism, Postmodernism, and Gender-Skepticism," in *Feminism/Postmodernism,* ed. Linda Nicholson (New York: Routledge, 1990), pp. 133–56. Bordo discusses the tendency among postmodern feminist theorists to overlook women's commonalities.

Index